DAVID BUSCH'S CANON® POWERSHOT® G10/G11

GUIDE TO DIGITAL PHOTOGRAPHY

David D. Busch | Alexander S. White

D1378997

Course Technology PTR
A part of Cengage Learning

COURSE TECHNOLOGY
CENGAGE Learning™

Australia, Brazil, Japan, Korea, Mexico, Singapore, Spain, United Kingdom, United States

COURSE TECHNOLOGY
CENGAGE Learning™

David Busch's Canon® PowerShot®
G10/G11 Guide to Digital Photography
David D. Busch, Alexander S. White

Publisher and General Manager, Course Technology PTR:
Stacy L. Hiquet

Associate Director of Marketing:
Sarah Panella

Manager of Editorial Services:
Heather Talbot

Marketing Manager:
Jordan Castellani

Executive Editor:
Kevin Harreld

Project Editor:
Jenny Davidson

Technical Reviewer:
Michael D. Sullivan

Interior Layout Tech:
Bill Hartman

Cover Designer:
Mike Tanamachi

Indexer:
Katherine Stimson

Proofreader:
Sara Gullion

For product information and technology assistance, contact us at
Cengage Learning Customer & Sales Support, 1-800-354-9706.

For permission to use material from this text or product, submit all requests online at **cengage.com/permissions**. Further permissions questions can be e-mailed to **permissionrequest@cengage.com**.

Library of Congress Control Number: 2009934721

ISBN-13: 978-1-4354-5535-1

ISBN-10: 1-4354-5535-5

Course Technology, a part of Cengage Learning
20 Channel Center Street
Boston, MA 02210
USA

Cengage Learning is a leading provider of customized learning solutions with office locations around the globe, including Singapore, the United Kingdom, Australia, Mexico, Brazil, and Japan. Locate your local office at: **international.cengage.com/region**.

Cengage Learning products are represented in Canada by Nelson Education, Ltd.

For your lifelong learning solutions, visit **courseptr.com**.

Visit our corporate Web site at **cengage.com**.

Printed in the United States of America
1 2 3 4 5 6 7 12 11 10

For Cathy and Clenise

Acknowledgments

Once again thanks to the folks at Course Technology PTR, who have pioneered publishing digital imaging books in full color at a price anyone can afford. Special thanks to executive editor Kevin Harreld, who always gives me the freedom to let my imagination run free with a topic, as well as my veteran production team including project editor Jenny Davidson and technical reviewer Mike Sullivan. Also thanks to Bill Hartman, layout; Katherine Stimson, indexing; Sara Gullion, proofreading; Mike Tanamachi, cover design; and my agent, Carole Jelen, who has the amazing ability to keep both publishers and authors happy.

About the Authors

With more than a million books in print, **David D. Busch** is one of the best-selling authors of books on digital photography and imaging technology, and the originator of popular series like *David Busch's Pro Secrets* and *David Busch's Quick Snap Guides*. He has written eight hugely successful guidebooks for Canon digital camera models, including the all-time #1 best-sellers for several Canon EOS models, additional user guides for other camera models, as well as many popular books devoted to digital cameras, including *Mastering Digital SLR Photography, Second Edition* and *Digital SLR Pro Secrets*. As a roving photojournalist for more than 20 years, he illustrated his books, magazine articles, and newspaper reports with award-winning images. He's operated his own commercial studio, suffocated in formal dress while shooting weddings-for-hire, and shot sports for a daily newspaper and upstate New York college. His articles have appeared in *Popular Photography & Imaging, The Rangefinder, The Professional Photographer*, and hundreds of other publications. He's also reviewed dozens of digital cameras for CNet and *Computer Shopper*.

When About.com named its top five books on Beginning Digital Photography, debuting at the #1 and #2 slots were Busch's *Digital Photography All-In-One Desk Reference for Dummies* and *Mastering Digital SLR Photography*. During the past year, he's had as many as five of his books listed in the Top 20 of Amazon.com's Digital Photography Bestseller list—simultaneously! Busch's 100-plus other books published since 1983 include bestsellers like *David Busch's Quick Snap Guide to Using Digital SLR Lenses*.

Busch is a member of the Cleveland Photographic Society (www.clevelandphoto.org), which has operated continuously since 1887.

Visit his website at http://www.dslrguides.com./blog

Alexander S. White is an attorney, writer, and amateur photographer. He is the author of *Photographer's Guide to the Leica D-Lux 4: Getting the Most from Leica's Compact Digital Camera* and *Dauntless Marine: Joseph Sailer Jr., Dive-Bombing Ace of Guadalcanal*. He began his life-long interest in photography as a teenager, when he was fortunate enough to have his own darkroom in his parents' house in Philadelphia. He also discovered the magic of Super-8 cinematography, and coerced his friends into making numerous amateur productions. He later ventured into the production of sound films and went on to major in Communication at Stanford University, concentrating in Broadcasting and Film, before serving in the U.S. Army and later attending the University of Pennsylvania Law School. His other interests include genealogy; he maintains a family history website and continues to do research into his family's ancestry. He lives near Richmond, Virginia, with his wife, Clenise.

Contents

PART I: GETTING STARTED WITH YOUR CANON POWERSHOT G10/G11

Chapter 1
Your New Canon PowerShot G10/G11   5

Chapter 2
Taking Your First Canon PowerShot G10/G11 Photos   23

Chapter 3
Canon PowerShot G10/G11 Roadmap 41

Chapter 4
Setting Up Your Canon PowerShot G10/G11 69

PART II: GETTING THE MOST FROM YOUR CANON POWERSHOT G10/G11

Chapter 5
Fine Tuning Exposure   133

Chapter 6
Advanced Shooting and Movie-Making with Your Canon PowerShot G10/G11
169

Chapter 7
Getting the Most from Your Zoom
203

Chapter 8
Making Light Work for You   225

Chapter 9
Downloading and Editing Your Images   257

Preface

You don't want good pictures from your new Canon PowerShot G10/G11—you demand *outstanding photos*. After all, the PowerShot G10 and G11 are the most pocket-sized digital cameras that Canon has ever introduced. They boast 10 and 14 megapixels of resolution, blazing fast automatic focus, and a dozen and a half Special Scene modes that make it easy to take pictures under any type of conditions. But your gateway to pixel proficiency is dragged down by the slim little book included in the box as a manual. You know everything you need to know is in there, somewhere, but you don't know where to start. In addition, the camera manual doesn't offer much information on photography or digital photography. Nor are you interested in spending hours or days studying a comprehensive book on digital camera photography that doesn't necessarily apply directly to your G10/G11.

What you need is a guide that explains the purpose and function of the G10/G11's basic controls, how you should use them, and *why*. Ideally, there should be information about file formats, resolution, aperture/priority exposure, and special autofocus modes, but you'd prefer to read about those topics only after you've had the chance to go out and take a few hundred great pictures with your new camera. Why isn't there a book that summarizes the most important information in its first two or three chapters, with lots of illustrations showing what your results will look like when you use this setting or that?

Now there is such a book. If you want a quick introduction to the G10/G11's focus controls, flash, how to use the focal lengths available with the 5X zoom lens, or which exposure modes are best, this book is for you. If you can't decide on what basic settings to use with your camera because you can't figure out how changing ISO or white balance or focus defaults will affect your pictures, you need this guide.

Introduction

Canon has done it again! It's packaged up many of the most alluring features of its advanced digital SLR cameras and stuffed them into the tiny, pocket-sized confines of the Canon PowerShot G10 and G11 cameras. Your new camera is loaded with capabilities that few would have expected to find in a "point-and-shoot" digital camera. The G10 has 14 megapixels of resolution, while the G11 gets the most image quality out of its 10-megapixel sensor with astounding high-sensitivity performance that tops out at ISO 12,800!

Yet, the G10/G11 retains the ease of use that smoothes the transition for those new to digital photography. For those just dipping their toes into the digital pond, the experience is warm and inviting. The PowerShot G10/G11 isn't a snapshot camera—it's a point-and-shoot (if you want to use it in that mode) for the thinking photographer.

But once you've confirmed that you made a wise purchase decision, the question comes up, *how do I use this thing?* All those cool features can be mind numbing to learn, if all you have as a guide is the manual furnished with the camera. Help is on the way. I sincerely believe that this book is your best bet for learning how to use your new camera, and for learning how to use it well.

If you're a Canon PowerShot G10/G11 owner who's looking to learn more about how to use this great camera, you've probably already explored your options. There are DVDs and online tutorials—but who can learn how to use a camera by sitting in front of a television or computer screen? Do you want to watch a movie or click on HTML links, or do you want to go out and take photos with your camera? Videos are fun, but not the best answer.

There's always the manuals furnished with the G10/G11. They are compact and filled with information, but there's really very little about *why* you should use particular settings or features, and its organization may make it difficult to find what you need. Multiple cross-references may send you flipping back and forth between two or three sections of the book to find what you want to know. The basic manual is also hobbled by black-and-white line drawings and tiny monochrome pictures that aren't very good examples of what you can do.

Also available are third-party guides to the G10/G11, like this one. I haven't been happy with some of these guidebooks, which is why I wrote this one. The existing books range from skimpy and illustrated by black-and-white photos to lushly illustrated in full color but too generic to do much good. Photography instruction is useful, but it needs to be related directly to the Canon PowerShot G10/G11 as much as possible.

I've tried to make *David Busch's Canon PowerShot G10/G11 Guide to Digital Photography* different from your other G10/G11 learn-up options. The roadmap sections use larger, color pictures to show you where all the buttons and dials are, and the explanations of what they do are longer and more comprehensive. I've tried to avoid overly general advice, including the two-page checklists on how to take a "sports picture" or a "portrait picture" or a "travel picture." Instead, you'll find tips and techniques for using all the features of your Canon PowerShot G10/G11 to take *any kind of picture* you want. If you want to know where you should stand to take a picture of a quarterback dropping back to unleash a pass, there are plenty of books that will tell you that. This one concentrates on teaching you how to select the best autofocus mode, shutter speed, f/stop, or flash capability to take, say, a great sports picture under any conditions.

This book is not a lame rewriting of the manual that came with the camera. Some folks spend five minutes with a book like this one, spot some information that also appears in the original manual, and decide "Rehash!" without really understanding the differences. Yes, you'll find information here that is also in the owner's manual, such as the parameters you can enter when changing your G10/G11's operation in the various menus. Basic descriptions—before I dig in and start providing in-depth tips and information—may also be vaguely similar. There are only so many ways you can say, for example, "Hold the shutter release down halfway to lock in exposure." But not *everything* in the manual is included in this book. If you want a large table showing which settings are available in each of the various Image Zone and Creative Zone modes, you'd better have the Functions Available in Each Shooting Mode Table in the original manual (it's on page 300 in the Canon G10 manual, and page 180 of the G11 manual). But if you need advice on when and how to use the most important functions, you'll find the information here.

David Busch's Canon PowerShot G10/G11 Guide to Digital Photography is aimed at both Canon and digital camera veterans as well as newcomers to digital photography and digital cameras. Both groups can be overwhelmed by the options the G10/G11 offers, while underwhelmed by the explanations they receive in their user's manual. The manuals are great if you already know what you don't know, and you can find an answer somewhere in a booklet arranged by menu listings and written by a camera vendor employee who last threw together instructions on how to operate a camcorder.

Why the Canon PowerShot G10/G11 Needs Special Coverage

There are many general digital photography books on the market. Why do I concentrate on books about specific digital cameras like the PowerShot G10/G11? One reason is that I feel digital photographers deserve books tailored to their equipment.

When I started writing digital photography books in 1995, digital cameras cost $30,000 and few people other than certain professionals could justify them. Most of my readers a dozen years ago were stuck using the point-and-shoot low-resolution digital cameras of the time—even if they were advanced photographers. I took tons of digital pictures with an Epson digital camera with 1024×768 (less than 1 megapixel!) resolution, and which cost $500.

Today, that same $500 buys you a sophisticated model like the Canon PowerShot G10 or G11. The digital camera is no longer the exclusive bailiwick of the professional, the wealthy, or the serious photography addict willing to scrimp and save to acquire a dream camera. Digital cameras have become the favored camera for anyone who wants to go beyond point-and-shoot capabilities. And Canon cameras have enjoyed a dominating position among digital cameras because of Canon's innovation in introducing affordable cameras with interesting features and outstanding performance (particularly in the area of high ISO image quality).

You've selected your camera of choice, and you belong in the Canon camp if you fall into one of the following categories:

- Individuals who want to get better pictures, or perhaps transform their growing interest in photography into a full-fledged hobby or artistic outlet with a PowerShot G10/G11 and advanced techniques.

- Those who want to produce more professional-looking images for their personal or business website, and feel that the PowerShot G10/G11 will give them more control and capabilities than the typical fully automatic point and shoot camera.

- Small business owners with more advanced graphics capabilities who want to use the PowerShot G10/G11 to document or promote their business.

- Corporate workers who may or may not have photographic skills in their job descriptions, but who work regularly with graphics and need to learn how to use digital images taken with a Canon PowerShot G10/G11 for reports, presentations, or other applications.

- Professional webmasters with strong skills in programming (including Java, JavaScript, HTML, Perl, etc.) but little background in photography, but who realize that the G10/G11 can be used for sophisticated photography.

- Graphic artists and others who already may be adept in image editing with Photoshop or another program, and who may already be using a film camera (Canon or otherwise), but who need to learn more about digital photography and the special capabilities of the G10/G11 digital camera.

Who Are We?

After spending years as the world's most successful unknown author, I've become slightly less obscure in the past few years, thanks to a horde of camera guidebooks and other photographically oriented tomes. You may have seen my photography articles in *Popular Photography & Imaging* magazine. I've also written about 2,000 articles for magazines like *Petersen's PhotoGraphic* (which is now defunct through no fault of my own), plus *The Rangefinder*, *Professional Photographer*, and dozens of other photographic publications. You might have caught my advice on National Public Radio's *All Tech Considered*. But, first, and foremost, I'm a photojournalist and made my living in the field until I began devoting most of my time to writing books.

Although I love writing, I'm happiest when I'm out taking pictures, which is why I invariably spend several days each week photographing landscapes, people, close-up subjects, and other things. I spend a month or two each year traveling to events, such as Native American "powwows," Civil War re-enactments, county fairs, ballets, and sports (baseball, basketball, football, and soccer are favorites). A few months ago, I took 14 days for a solo visit to Europe, strictly to shoot photographs of the people, landscapes, and monuments that I've grown to love. And in the months prior to starting on this book, I spent time in Arizona, catching up on baseball Spring Training and natural wonders like the Sedona Red Rocks and the Grand Canyon. I can offer you my personal advice on how to take photos under a variety of conditions because I've had to meet those challenges myself on an ongoing basis.

Like all my digital photography books, this one was written by someone with an incurable photography bug. My first Canon camera was a Pellix back in the 1960s, and I've used a variety of newer models since then. I've worked as a sports photographer for an Ohio newspaper and for an upstate New York college. I've operated my own commercial studio and photo lab, cranking out product shots on demand and then printing a few hundred glossy 8 × 10s on a tight deadline for a press kit. I've served as a photo-posing instructor for a modeling agency. People have actually paid me to shoot their weddings and immortalize them with portraits. I even prepared press kits and articles on photography as a PR consultant for a large Rochester, N.Y., company, which shall remain nameless. My trials and travails with imaging and computer technology have made their way into print in book form an alarming number of times, including a few dozen on scanners and photography.

Like you, I love photography for its own merits, and I view technology as just another tool to help me get the images I see in my mind's eye. But, also like you, I had to master this technology before I could apply it to my work. This book is the result of what I've learned, and I hope it will help you master your PowerShot G10/G11 digital camera, too.

As I write this, I'm currently in the throes of upgrading my website and blog, which you can find at www.dslrguides.com/blog, adding tutorials and information about my other books. I'll be adding more tips and recommendations (including a list of equipment and accessories that I can't live without) in the next few months. I hope you'll stop by for a visit.

Meet My Co-Author, Alex

I am very happy and grateful to have, with this book, the opportunity to make my first foray into the "big leagues" of digital photography guidebooks. Like David, I have had a love affair with photography since the 1960s, when, as a teenager, my tolerant parents allowed me to set up a very smelly darkroom in the basement of their Philadelphia home. I was entranced by the process of rolling the exposed film onto a plastic spool, sealing it in a tank, and later placing the developed negatives into an enlarger to produce what to me seemed like great works of photographic art. For those who have long memories or a love of older movies, I must say that one strong influence that sparked my love of the darkroom was the terrific film *Blow-up* by Antonioni, which deepened the mystique of enlarging at leisure an image that was captured by the lens and film in an instant, and that may hold the key to an intriguing and disturbing mystery. I ventured into amateur cinematography and tried my best to emulate the great director, but I'm afraid my Super-8 productions fell a few light-years short.

Later, after studying broadcasting and film at Stanford, I got sidetracked by military service for a few years, and I guess it was my more practical side that guided me to law school, like several family members before me. But I have kept up with photography and filmmaking through the transitions to digital photography and video. I have used a wide array of equipment, and have been continually amazed at the increasing sophistication of the cameras that have become available in recent years. Finally, when I got a Leica D-Lux 4 in 2009, I was so impressed by the camera that I felt compelled to write a book about its use. No one asked me to write that book; I just wanted to do it. Because of that book, though, I was asked to help David write this one. I am immensely pleased to have this opportunity to share some of my love of photography and of modern digital cameras with a wider audience.

Part I

Getting Started with Your Canon PowerShot G10/G11

This Part consists of four chapters designed to help you get up and running with the Canon PowerShot G10 or G11. Of course, there's a distinct possibility that you've already *done* that prior to opening this book for the first time. You may have taken a few hundred or a few thousand photos with your PowerShot already. Indeed, this camera appeals directly to the sort of avid photographer who is likely to have jumped in and conducted some warmly rewarding experiments with the camera before deciding to buckle down with this book and learn all its features.

Why not? The PowerShot is incredibly easy to use. The initial steps, including charging the battery and inserting a Secure Digital memory card aren't exactly rocket science. Every control you need to begin snapping pictures is nestled on the top surface. There's a power button (cleverly labeled ON/OFF), the shutter release button, a large mode dial that includes an Auto position labeled with green text (plus other settings including one that looks suspiciously like an old-time movie camera), and a Zoom lever, located concentrically with the shutter release. The rawest neophyte can turn on the camera, spin the dial to one of those settings, and begin shooting. If you are an old hand with some experience with digital cameras, getting started with the G10 or G11 is even more of a no-brainer.

But, even if you didn't march out of a camera store with a G10 or G11 box under one arm, and my book in hand, you're probably ready to learn more. It's not a bad idea, once you've taken a few (hundred) orientation pictures with your camera, to go back and review the basic operations of the camera from the beginning, if only to see if you've missed something. This Part is my opportunity to review the setup procedures for the camera for those among you who are already veteran users, and to help ease the more timid (and those who have never worked with a digital camera before). For the uninitiated, as easy as it is to use initially, the PowerShot *does* have lots of dials and buttons and settings that might not make sense at first, but will surely become second nature after you've had a chance to review the instructions in this chapter and the next one.

Other camera guides I've seen throw you off the dock into deep water and expect you to learn how to swim before you go under for the third time. I've found that a more gentle approach works better. Depending on your experience level, you can either skim through the three chapters in this Part quickly, or pore over them attentively, soaking up the information you need to hit the ground running. (Don't worry: the PowerShot includes a feature called *image stabilization* that will help you avoid blurry images if you try to shoot while hitting the ground and/or running. Your Canon is more than a match for any metaphor!)

Start with any of these four chapters:

- **If you need help in setting up your camera, read:** *Chapter 1: Your New Canon PowerShot G10/G11.* This chapter introduces you to the Canon PowerShot, and will help sort out the array of things found in the compact box your camera came in as you prep the camera for your first shots. I'll explain what each and every item is, how'll you'll be using it, and provide a list of must-have items you'll want to check out as soon as possible. You'll find a summary of a few nice-to-have accessories to consider, too. By the time you finish this brief chapter, you'll have your camera's battery charged and inserted, your digital "film" ready to capture photos, and a basic understanding of the camera and its key accessories.

- **If you want a quick start to snapping great shots right away, begin with:** *Chapter 2: Taking Your First PowerShot G10/G11 Photos.* Here, I'll guide you through a pre-flight checklist of actually taking your first pictures. Rather than bog you down with excessive detail, I'll leave discussions of the more advanced features for the other Parts of the book. Indeed, I'm going to tell you just what you absolutely *must* understand, accompanied by some interesting tidbits that will help you become acclimated. I'll go into more depth and even repeat some of what I explain here in later chapters, so you don't have to memorize everything you see. Just relax, follow a few easy steps, and then go out and begin taking your best shots—ever.

- **If you know the basics and want a quick introduction to the controls, go to:** *Chapter 3: Canon PowerShot G10/G11 Roadmap.* There are lots of buttons and dials on your PowerShot camera. That may be intimidating but, actually, this is a *good* thing, because your G10/G11 provides direct control over many functions, such as shooting mode, sensor sensitivity, and exposure adjustments. Many lesser cameras (including most point-and-shoot models) send you off to a command buried in a menu each time you want to change some of these functions. This chapter provides a street-level roadmap of all those controls.

- **If you want to jump ahead and begin customizing the camera's settings, start with:** *Chapter 4: Setting Up Your Canon PowerShot G10/G11.* The PowerShot G10 or G11 has so many cool features that you will need to access its well-designed menu system to use some of them. This chapter explains all the shooting menu settings (which you'll adjust from time to time as you take pictures), the setup menu settings (which you can often set and forget, until you need to change how your camera behaves), and even ways to design your own custom menu of the commands that you use most often.

1

Your New Canon PowerShot G10/G11

The PowerShot G10 and G11 represent the latest technology in the Canon PowerShot G series, and judging by the reception afforded by serious photographers, they are easily the most popular cameras in the PowerShot line yet. That's because they combine the small size, portability, and ease of use of point-and-shoot digital cameras with the high image quality and control that avid photographers—both professional and amateur—demand. Indeed, the G10 and G11 are the first cameras in a long time that are a serious contender as a "second" or "walk-around" camera for those who use a more advanced digital SLR, too.

That's why I purchased my G10, and, a few months later, the G11. I wanted a smaller camera to carry around all the time, but I wasn't willing to give up image quality or creative control. Many other happy PowerShot G-series owners are photographers who are stepping up from a less-capable point-and-shoot-type camera, because they need the options and extra capabilities, including the 10 to 14.7 megapixel (MP) resolution these cameras offer. No other cameras I've seen are as popular among serious shooters of all types as the G10 and G11. In fact, I decided to write this book after overhearing a "pro" photographer at a camera club explaining why he loved this camera to several dedicated amateur photographers—who also had selected the PowerShot G10 or G11 as their no-compromise "pocket" camera.

TECHIE ALERT

I'll explain about megapixels, LCD displays, telephoto/wide-angle zoom ranges, and movie making as we continue with this book. I included technical gobbledygook in this introduction as a summary for the photo-techie types the PowerShot G10/G11 seems to attract. If you're not of that ilk, you can learn these terms later, as you don't need to understand them to continue with this chapter.

Of course, neither Canon PowerShot really fits in a pocket, unless you're sporting a photo vest or are of the marsupial persuasion. Both cameras, to a certain extent, follow in the tradition of the 35mm *rangefinder* film camera, including the pioneering Leica models, which were solid, well-made compact cameras prized for their image quality, quietness, precision construction, and versatility. The G10 and G11 both depart from that model considerably. For example, they have a 28-140mm non-interchangeable automatic focus zoom lens instead of a complement of Leica-style fixed focal length manual focus non-zoom lenses. Nor is there a rangefinder focus viewfinder, although they do retain a vestigial optical window for framing pictures. Instead, most viewing of images prior to exposure is done using a 3-inch LCD (on the G10) or swiveling 2.8-inch LCD (on the G11), which do triple duty as the display for pictures *after* they've been taken (something not possible with a film camera at all) and for showing menus used to select camera features.

In truth, the G10 and G11 are both evolutionary descendants of the PowerShot G6, G7, and G9 (which they most closely resemble in many dimensional and feature respects). The 12 MP G9 (there was no G8) had a very similar body and also had a 3-inch LCD, although the 14.7 MP G10 and 10 MP G11 both have double the number of pixels in their backlit displays. The newer cameras also boast a more powerful, longer-lasting battery, a wider field of view (equivalent to a 28mm true wide angle), compared to the 35mm (equivalent) mild wide-angle perspective of the G9. But the 5X zoom on the G10/G11 loses some of the G9's 6X telephoto range—it zooms in to only a 140mm medium telephoto setting compared to the G9's 210mm maximum (both equivalents). The G10/G11 also lacks the previous model's $1024 \times 768/15$ frames per second movie mode, topping out at $640 \times 480/30$ frames per second. Canon giveth, and Canon taketh away—but on balance there is more adding than subtracting.

Contents of the Table

You probably spread out on a table or desk the contents of the handsome box that transported the Canon PowerShot from its birthplace in Japan. The box is filled with stuff, including connecting cords, booklets, a CD, and lots of paperwork. The first thing you should do (or the *next* thing you should do, if you've already been taking pictures with your camera), is to double-check the contents of the box to make sure nothing was left out, or accidentally removed by the retailer. Someone might have checked out the camera for you as a quality assurance method, or a curious store employee might have rooted through the box to see what this cool new camera actually looks like. In either case, it's entirely possible that something went astray, and it's good to know that *now,* when you can easily bring any missing pieces to the attention of the store that sold you the camera. Otherwise, a month down the road, you're going to decide to see what the output of your PowerShot looks like on your TV screen, and discover that the video cable you *thought* you had has gone AWOL at some unknown time.

So, check the box at your earliest convenience, and make sure you have (at least) the following:

- **Canon PowerShot G10 or G11 camera.** This is hard to miss. The camera is the main reason you laid out the big bucks, and it is tucked away inside a soft envelope you should save for protection in case the G10/G11 needs to be sent in for repair.

- **Battery pack NB-7L (with terminal cover).** The power source for your PowerShot G10 is packaged separately. You'll need to charge this 7.4V, 1050mAh (milliampere hour) battery before using it. It should be charged as soon as possible (as described next) and inserted in the camera. Save the protective cover. If you transport a battery outside the camera, it's a good idea to re-attach the cover to prevent the electrical contacts from shorting out.

- **Battery charger CB-2LZ or CB-2LZE.** One of these two battery chargers will be included. They are similar, except that the CB-2LZ plugs directly into the wall, while the CB-2LZE uses a cord.

- **Neck strap NS-DC9.** Canon provides you with a suitable neck strap, emblazoned with discreet Canon advertising proclaiming the model name. Unlike the straps provided with some other cameras, the Canon strap is low-key enough that it doesn't attract unwanted attention from potential thieves. It's entirely acceptable as a "starter" strap. However, if you want a strap that won't easily slip off your shoulder, I recommend the UPstrap RF/DC, which is made especially for smaller cameras like the Leica M series and Canon PowerShot G-series. It has a patented non-slip pad and 3/8-inch webbed strap, and can be found at www.upstrap.com. (See Figure 1.1.) The strap offers reassuring traction and eliminates the contortions we sometimes go through to keep the camera from slipping off. I know several photographers who refuse to use anything else. If you do purchase an UPstrap, be sure you mention to photographer-inventor Al Stegmeyer that I sent you hence. You won't get a discount, but Al will get yet another confirmation of how much I like his marvelous neck straps.

Figure 1.1
You'll probably like a non-slip premium strap like the UPStrap better than the one Canon furnishes with the G10 or G11.

■ **Interface Cable IFC-400PCU.** You can use this USB cable to transfer photos from the camera to your computer, although I don't recommend using that mode extensively, because direct transfer uses a lot of battery power. It is a standard cable, so you may be able to use it with other cameras you own, or keep it as a spare.

■ **AV Cable AVC-DC300 (G10)/AVC-DC400 (G11).** Use this cable to view your camera's LCD output on a larger television screen, monitor, or other device with a yellow RCA composite input jack.

■ **Canon Digital Solution Disk CD.** The disk contains useful software that will be discussed in more detail in Chapter 9.

- **Printed instruction manuals.** These include the Canon PowerShot G10 (or G11) Camera User Guide, and the Software Starter Guide. Even if you have this book, you'll probably want to check the printed user's guide that Canon provides, if only to check the actual nomenclature for some obscure accessory, or to double-check an error code. Both books contain a mind-numbing six-page matrix that shows each of the functions available/not available in more than two dozen of the G10 or G11's shooting/scene/movie modes. Google "Canon G10 (or G11) manual PDF" to find a downloadable version that you can store on your laptop, a CD-ROM, or other media in case you want to access this reference when the paper version isn't handy. If you have an old SD card that's too small to be usable on a modern camera (I still have some 128MB and 256MB cards), you can store the PDF on that. But an even better choice is to put the manual on a low-capacity USB "thumb" drive, which you can buy for less than $10. You'll then be able to access the reference anywhere you are, because you can always find someone with a computer that has a USB port and Adobe Acrobat Reader available. You might not be lucky enough to locate a computer with an SD card reader.

- **Warranty and Canon Customer Support leaflet.** Don't lose these! You can register your Canon G-series camera by mail or online, although you don't really need to in order to keep your warranty in force, but you may need the information in this paperwork (plus the purchase receipt/invoice from your retailer) should you require Canon service support.

Don't bother rooting around in the box for anything beyond what I've listed previously. There are a few things Canon classifies as optional accessories, even though you (and I) might consider some of them essential. Here's a list of what you *don't* get in the box, but might want to think about as an impending purchase. I'll list them roughly in the order of importance:

- **Secure Digital (SD) card.** First-time digital camera buyers are sometimes shocked that their new tool doesn't come with a memory card. Why should it? The manufacturer doesn't have the slightest idea of how much storage you require, or whether you want a slow/inexpensive card or one that's faster/more expensive, so why should they pack one in the box and charge you for it? Plan on buying one right away if you already don't own one. For a camera like the PowerShot G10, with a whopping 14.7 MP of resolution, or the 10MP G11, you shouldn't consider any card smaller than 4GB. A larger 8GB or 16GB card is an even better idea, especially if you travel on vacation or business and won't be able to transfer your photos from the camera to a computer on a daily basis.

- **Software manual PDF files.** In an alarming trend that I expect to continue, Canon has eschewed a second CD with instructions for the Digital Photo Professional and ZoomBrowser EX (PC)/ImageBrowser (Mac) software you may opt to use with your images. You can download the manuals as Adobe Portable Document Format

(PDF) files, which may be viewed with Adobe Acrobat Reader or similar software, from http://web.canon.jp/imaging/information-e.html.

- **Extra Battery pack NB-7L.** Even though you might get 400 or more shots from a single battery, it's easy to exceed that figure. Batteries can unexpectedly fail, too, or simply lose their charge from sitting around unused for a week or two. Buy an extra, keep it charged, and free your mind from worry.

- **Add-on speedlight.** Your Canon PowerShot's built-in electronic flash is fine for snapshots or as fill for inky shadows when shooting in daylight. But it can produce the dreaded "red-eye" effect (or yellow/green eyes in some animals) when subjects are looking directly at the camera lens, especially in a darkened environment. And, the built-in flash only illuminates a scene out to about 15 feet (at best). You may want an add-on electronic flash, such as the small High-Power Flash HF-DC1 that was designed especially for small cameras like the Canon PowerShot G10. This unit, which is furnished with a bracket that allows you to mount it side-by-side with the camera (see Figure 1.2), needs no connecting cord, as its firing is triggered by the main flash. You can also opt for even more powerful flash units, such as the top-of-the-line Canon 580EX II or the less expensive 270EX and 430EX II. I'll explain your options and how they affect your pictures in more detail in Chapter 8.

Figure 1.2 The High-Power Flash HF-DC1 boosts the range of the PowerShot's built-in speedlight.

- **AC Adapter Kit ACK-DC50.** This includes the Compact Power Adapter CA-PS700 and DC Coupler DR-50, which are used with a supplied cord to power the G10/G11 independently of the batteries. There are several typical situations where this capability can come in handy: when indoors shooting tabletop photos, portraits, class pictures, and so forth for hours on end; when using your G10 for remote shooting as well as time-lapse photography (using external timer/remotes that are readily available from third parties); for extensive review of images on your television; or for file transfer to your computer. These all use prodigious amounts of power, which can be provided by this AC adapter.

- **Remote switch RS60-E3.** This "cable release"-style control (for you old-timers) electronically triggers the camera's shutter when its button is pressed, allowing taking an exposure without actually touching the camera and creating blur-causing vibrations.

- **Conversion Lens Adapter LA-DC58K/Tele-converter TC-DC58D.** Although they are sold separately, you need both. The Teleconverter lens boosts the PowerShot's focal length to a range of 39mm-196mm, which is roughly the same range offered by the earlier PowerShot G9. You'd use this accessory when you wanted a little extra telephoto reach, and didn't care about narrowing your field-of-view at the wide-angle end. The Conversion Lens Adapter bayonets around the G-series camera's fixed lens, and the tele-converter screws into that. As Canon doesn't offer any other accessories for the lens adapter, they really should have been bundled together. While the adapter has a 58mm thread, it can produce darkened corners (*vignetting*) at many zoom settings. In Chapter 7, I'll describe alternative adapters from LensMate (www.lensmateonline.com) that are more versatile.

- **Other stuff.** There are other accessories you might find useful, including brackets, off-camera shoe cords for flash units, printers, and waterproof cases for underwater shooting, but I'll describe these as appropriate in other chapters as we go along.

MMC CARDS WORK, TOO

Your Canon PowerShot also accepts MultiMediaCard (MMC) memory cards, which look very similar to SD cards (but are slightly less thick), and which have been used in cell phones, digital audio players, and other devices. They have largely been supplanted by other media, which may be smaller and/or faster, but if you own some older MMC cards, you can use them with your G10 or G11. If your new cell phone requires a microSD card, you now have a use for the MMC card your old phone included.

Initial Setup

The initial setup of your Canon PowerShot G10 or G11 is fast and easy. Basically, you just need to charge the battery, attach the strap, and insert a memory card. I'll address each of these steps separately, but if you already feel you can manage these setup tasks without further instructions, feel free to skip this section entirely. You should at least skim its contents, however, because I'm going to list a few options that you might not be aware of.

Battery Included

Your Canon PowerShot is a sophisticated hunk of machinery and electronics, but it needs a charged battery to function, so rejuvenating the NB-7L lithium-ion battery pack furnished with the camera should be your first step. A fully charged power source should be good for approximately 400 shots under normal temperature conditions, or up to 1,000 shots if the LCD is switched off. (In that case, you'd be using the optical viewfinder to frame your images, and not be reviewing them after they are taken.) If you use the built-in flash, expect to achieve fewer shots per charge. Remember that things like picture review, playing with menus, and using the image stabilization features of your lens can use up more power than you might expect. If your pictures are important to you, always take along one spare, fully charged battery.

And remember that all rechargeable batteries undergo some degree of self-discharge just sitting idle in the camera or in the original packaging. Lithium-ion power packs of this type typically lose a few percent of their charge every few days, even when the camera isn't turned on. So, it's very likely that the battery purchased with your camera, even if charged at the factory, has begun to poop out after the long sea voyage on a banana boat (or, more likely, a trip by jet plane followed by a sojourn in a warehouse), so you'll want to revive it before going out for some serious shooting.

There are many situations in which you'll be glad you have that spare battery:

■ **Remote locales.** If you like to backpack and will often be far from a source of electricity, rechargeable cells won't be convenient. They tend to lose some charge over time, even if not used, and will quickly become depleted as you use them. You'll have no way to recharge the cells, lacking a solar-powered charger that might not be a top priority for your backpacking kit.

■ **Unexpected needs.** Perhaps you planned to shoot landscapes one weekend, and then are given free front row tickets to a Major League Soccer game. Instead of a few dozen pictures of trees and lakes, you find yourself shooting hundreds of images of David Beckham and company, which may be beyond the capacity of the single battery you own. If you have a spare battery, you're in good shape.

- **Unexpected failures.** I've charged up batteries and then discovered that they didn't work when called upon, usually because the rechargeable cells had passed their useful life, the charger didn't work, or because of human error. (I *thought* I'd charged them!) That's one reason why I always carry three times as many batteries as I think I will need.

- **Long shooting session.** Perhaps your niece is getting married, and you want to photograph the ceremony, receiving line, and reception. Several extra batteries will see you through the longest shooting session.

Power Options

Several battery chargers and power sources are available for the Canon PowerShot G10 or G11. The compact CB-2LZ, shown in Figure 1.3, plugs directly into a wall socket and is commonly furnished with the camera. Canon also provides the CB-2LZE, which is similar, but has a cord. Purchasing one of the optional charging devices offers more than some additional features: You gain a spare that can keep your camera running until you can replace your primary power rejuvenator. Here's a list of your power options:

- **CB-2LZ.** The standard charger for the G10 and G11, this one is the most convenient, because of its compact size and built-in wall plug prongs that connect directly into your power strip or wall socket and require no cord. This charger, as well as the CB-2LZE, has a switching power module that is fully compatible with 100V to 240V 50/60 Hz AC power, so you can use it outside the US with no problems. When I travel to Europe, for example, I take my charger and an adapter to convert the plug shape for the European sockets. No voltage converter is needed.

Figure 1.3
The NB-7L battery fits only one way into the charger.

■ **CB-2LZE.** This is similar to the CB-2LZ, and also charges a single battery, but requires a cord. That can be advantageous in certain situations. For example, if your power outlet is behind a desk or in some other semi-inaccessible location, the cord can be plugged in and routed so the charger itself sits on your desk or another more convenient spot. The cord itself is a standard one that works with many different chargers and devices (including the power supply for my laptop), so I purchased several of them and leave them plugged into the wall in various locations. I can connect my charger, my laptop computer's charger, and several other electronic components to one of these cords without needing to crawl around behind the furniture. The cord itself draws no power when it's not plugged into a charger.

■ **AC Adapter Kit ACK-DC50.** This device consists of a Compact Power Adapter CA-PS700 and DC Coupler DR-50, and allows you to operate your PowerShot directly from AC power, with no battery required. Studio photographers need this capability because they often snap off hundreds of pictures for hours on end and want constant, reliable power. The camera is probably plugged into a flash sync cord (or radio device), and the studio flash are plugged into power packs or AC power, so the extra tether to this adapter is no big deal in that environment. You also might want to use the AC adapter when viewing images on a TV connected to your camera, or when shooting remote or time-lapse photos.

Charging the Battery

To charge your battery, just follow these steps:

1. **Remove battery.** If the battery is already in the camera, remove it by sliding open the battery cover door (move it towards the nearest outer edge of the camera) and pressing the red/brown lever inside towards that same edge of the camera. The battery will pop out. (See Figure 1.4.)

2. **Insert in charger.** Tilt the battery downward so that the gray triangle on the battery is aligned with the matching white triangle on the socket in the battery charger. (You can't insert the battery if you try to stuff the aft end in first.) The battery will click when in place.

3. **Connect to power.** Flip out the plug on the back of the CB-2LZ charger or, if you're using the CB-2LZE, attach the supplied cord. Plug the charger into a power outlet.

4. **Charge battery.** The upper LED, labeled CHARGE, will begin to glow red/orange, and will continue to illuminate while the charging process continues. When charging is complete, the CHARGE LED will turn off, and the lower, FULL LED will glow green. The process will take about 2 hours and 20 minutes.

5. **Remove battery.** Extract the battery from the charger by lifting up on the back end, using the semi-circle cutout area for access.

6. **Insert in camera.** Unfortunately, Canon neglected to "key" the NB-7L battery, so there are four different ways you can insert it into the bottom of the PowerShot. Three of them are wrong, and won't let you seat the battery fully. The end with the gold contacts goes into the battery cavity first, and the side with the large Canon logo faces the back of the camera; the "fine print" information faces the front. (See Figure 1.5.)

7. **Close door.** When the battery is seated fully, flip the door shut, and slide it towards the center of the camera to lock it.

Figure 1.4 Press the red-brown lever towards the back of the camera to remove the battery.

Figure 1.5 Insert the battery into the camera with the Canon logo facing the back.

Final Steps

Your Canon PowerShot G10/G11 is almost ready to fire up and shoot. You'll need to adjust the viewfinder for your vision, and insert a memory card. Each of these steps is easy, and if you've used any Canon camera (or most other brands) in the past, you already know exactly what to do. I'm going to provide a little extra detail for those of you who are new to the Canon or digital camera worlds.

Adjusting Diopter Correction

Those of us with less than perfect eyesight can often benefit from a little correction in the optical viewfinder (which is rather tiny and difficult to view through in any case). Your contact lenses or glasses may provide all the correction you need, but if you are a glasses wearer and want to use the optical viewfinder of the PowerShot without your glasses, or use your glasses with your camera's optical window and can benefit from some additional correction, you can take advantage of the camera's built-in diopter adjustment. It can be varied from −3 to +1 correction. Press the shutter release halfway then rotate the adjacent diopter adjustment wheel (see Figure 1.6) while looking through the window until the image appears sharp. If more than one person uses your camera, and each requires a different diopter setting, you can save a little time by noting the number of clicks and direction (clockwise to increase the diopter power; counterclockwise to decrease the diopter value) required to change from one user to the other. There are 10 detents in all.

Figure 1.6
Viewfinder diopter correction from −3 to +1 can be dialed in.

Diopter correction dial

Inserting a Memory Card

You can't take photos without a memory card inserted in your PowerShot. The LCD will scold you with a No Memory Card warning if you try. So, your final step will be to insert a memory card, which fits in the same compartment as the battery. Slide the door on the underside of the body toward the near outer edge of the camera to release the cover, and then open it. You should only remove the memory card when the camera is switched off. If you open the compartment door when not actively shooting, the camera switches off automatically; if you try that while actually taking pictures, the G10 or G11 will beep a warning before turning off. (The beep is your cue to expect that you might have just lost the most recent shot you took.) In practice, we rarely try to replace a battery or memory card while in the midst of shooting, so in most cases your images will be safe.

To remove a memory card that's already in the camera, press down on the edge of the card. It will pop right out. Insert a memory card with the label facing the front of the camera (towards the battery), as shown in Figure 1.7, oriented so the edge with the gold contacts goes into the slot first.

Figure 1.7
The memory card is inserted with the label facing the front of the camera.

WRITE PROTECT?

Some (but by no means all) SD and SDHC cards have a notch on the long side opposite the one with the diagonal cutout. If the notch is exposed (that is, the write-protect slide is in the upper position, or not present), the card cannot be used by the camera to store photographs. A Card is Locked message appears on the LCD screen. Not all devices recognize the write protect notch (which is an optional feature for SD/SDHC cards), but the PowerShot G10 and G11 are two of them.

Formatting a Memory Card

There are four ways to create a blank SD card for your G10 or G11, and three of them are at least partially wrong. Here are your options, both correct and incorrect:

- **Erase images in the camera.** The Playback menu (discussed in Chapter 4 of this book) allows you to select individual images to delete, or to choose them by range, date, or folder. You can create a blank memory card by selecting All Images. This method won't give you a truly blank card, however, as it doesn't affect files you've labeled as Protected (using the Protect Images function in the Playback menu). Nor does it identify and lock out parts of your memory card that have become corrupted or unusable since the last time you formatted the card.

- **Transfer (move) files to your computer.** When you transfer (rather than copy) all the image files to your computer from the SD card (either using a direct cable transfer or with a card reader, as described later in this chapter), the old image files are erased from the card, leaving the card blank. Theoretically. As with the Erase Images function, this method does *not* remove files that you've labeled as Protected, nor does it "freshen" your card as the Format command (found in the Setup menu) does. The main reason for erasing or transferring images is when you *want* to leave the protected/unerased images on the card for a while longer, say, to share with friends, family, and colleagues.

- **(Don't) Format in your computer.** With the SD card inserted in a card reader or card slot in your computer, you can use Windows or Mac OS to reformat the memory card. Don't! The operating system won't necessarily arrange the structure of the card the way the camera likes to see it (in computer terms, an incorrect *file system* may be installed). The only way to ensure that the card has been properly formatted for your camera is to perform the format in the camera itself. The only exception to this rule is when you have a seriously corrupted memory card that your camera refuses to format. Sometimes it is possible to revive such a corrupted card by allowing the operating system to reformat it first, then trying again in the camera.

- **Setup menu format.** The best way to create a blank card is to use the recommended method to format a memory card, using the Setup menu.

To format a memory card, just follow these steps:

1. **Turn on the camera.** Since you won't necessarily be taking a photo at the moment, the fastest way to switch the camera on is to press the Playback button on the back of the camera (with the blue right-pointing triangle), next to the optical viewfinder. You can also turn on the camera by pressing the ON/OFF button, because the Setup menu you'll be using is available in either Playback or Shooting mode.

MODES FOR MENUS

When you turn the camera on using the Playback button, the lens remains retracted behind its protective cover, and the Playback, Print, Setup, and (with the G10) Theme menus become available when you press the Menu button. If you turn on the camera using the ON/OFF button on the top panel, the lens pops out so you can take a picture, and the available menus that pop up when you press the Menu button are the Shooting, Setup, Theme (on the G10 only), and My Menu options. In that mode, you can also press the Playback button to switch to the second complement of menus. Just remember that to access the Shooting and My Menu options, the camera must be in *Shooting* mode; to access the Playback and Print menus, the camera must be in *Playback* mode. The Setup and (with the G10) Theme menus are always available in either mode.

---

2. **Press the Menu button.** The button is located in the lower-right corner of the back of the camera. The main menu appears. Press the right cross key (which has a lightning bolt on it, because it is also used for other things, including Flash functions). Press the cursor key until the Setup menu (with wrench and mallet icons) is highlighted. Figure 1.8 shows the Setup menu as it appears in the G10 at the left and the G11 version at the right when accessed from playback mode; the menu is located one tab to the left when you access it from shooting mode.

3. **Rotate the control dial.** It's located concentric with the cursor pad. Continue scrolling down with the control dial until the Format command is highlighted. Then press the center FUNC./SET button. You'll see a screen like the one in Figure 1.9, which presents the G10 version. (The G11 version differs only in color scheme.)

4. **Choose OK.** Cancel will be highlighted, so you'll need to press the right cursor button to highlight OK. Then press Set to begin the formatting step. There is no final confirmation screen (which is found in some other cameras, including Canon models), so make sure you really want to format the card before you press the button!

Figure 1.8 Navigate to the Format command in the Setup menu.

Figure 1.9
Choose your
Format options
and press the
Set button to
begin.

LOW LEVEL FORMAT

When the Format screen appears, you can also use the up or down cross keys to navigate to the Low level format box. Press the left or right cross keys to mark or unmark this box. Activating this option tells the G10 or G11 to perform an additional, more thorough, formatting of the card after the initial format is finished. The low level format serves to remove data from all writable portions of your memory card while locking out "bad" sectors, and can be used to restore a memory card that is slowing down as it "trips" over those bad sectors. This extra step takes a bit longer than a standard reformat, and need not be used every time you format your card.

Powering Up/Setting Date and Time

Tap the On/Off switch on top of the camera to switch the camera on, if you intend to take a picture. Or, if you just want to review shots already on your memory card, or need to access a menu, press the blue right-pointing triangle that marks the Playback button on the back of the camera to the right of the optical viewfinder. As I mentioned, this powers up the camera, but doesn't cause the lens to pop out.

The first time you use the PowerShot, it may ask you to enter the time and date. (This information may have been set by someone checking out your camera on your behalf prior to sale.) Just follow these steps:

1. **Press the Menu button.** The button is located in the lower-right corner of the back of the camera. The main menu appears. Press the right cross key until the yellow Setup menu is highlighted.

2. **Rotate the control dial.** Continue scrolling down with the control dial until the Date/Time command is highlighted. Then press the center FUNC./SET button. The screen shown in Figure 1.10 appears. The time zone you've currently selected will be indicated by an icon next to the Set Date/Time entry. Either the House icon (Home) or Airplane icon (World Time) will appear. The sidebar that follows explains a little more about this option.

3. **Select the values for your currently selected time zone.** There are seven values you can change: Month, Day, Year, Hour, Minutes, Date Format, and Daylight Savings Time (On or Off). Use the left/right cursor keys to select the value you want to change. When the gold box highlights the value you want to modify, press the Set button to activate that value. A pair of up/down pointing triangles appears above the value.

4. **Modify the values.** Press the up/down keys to adjust the value up or down.

Figure 1.10
Choose the
Date/Time
options from
the Setup
menu.

5. **Change other values.** Repeat steps 3 and 4 for each of the other values you want to change. The date format can be switched from the default mm/dd/yy to yy/mm/dd or dd/mm/yy.

6. **Confirm your settings.** When finished, press the Set button to confirm, or the Menu button to cancel your changes and return to the Setup menu.

HOME AND WORLD TIME ZONES

You can set the correct Time Zone for your Canon PowerShot G10 or G11 using the Time Zone entry in the Setup menu. Two settings appear: Home and World zones. Use the cursor key to choose either the Home (House icon) or World (Airplane icon) option, then select the city from a scrolling map. Then, you can switch back and forth between them at any time. Perhaps you spend most of your time on the East Coast of the United States, but frequently visit another exotic location, like Cairo or Los Angeles, on business. Specify one location for your Home zone, and the second for your World (travel) zone, and switch between them easily. If you hop around a lot, you can change your World setting as many times as you want. I'll give you step-by-step instructions on how to make—and use—this useful adjustment in Chapter 4.

2

Taking Your First Canon PowerShot G10/G11 Photos

If you've read Chapter 1, or have decided to begin with this chapter because your camera is all set up and ready to go, you'll find all the basic information you need to take your first photos with your PowerShot G10 or G11. In the first part of this chapter, I'm going to give you the 52 Second No-Option Quick Tour that will have you taking great pictures in less than a minute. Then, in the second part of this chapter, you'll find the Ten Minute Introduction, which allows you to make a few choices that will have you taking even better photos with only a few minutes' prep.

This chapter is strictly an introduction to some basic features. You'll learn how to make simple settings, and, later in the chapter, select the easiest exposure, metering, and autofocus modes. After you've finished either of this chapter's crash courses and taken a few pictures, you can return to this book with Chapters 3 and 4 to learn more about how your Canon PowerShot G10/G11 operates, as you work your way towards Part II, which *really* looks at the camera's great features in depth. But first, let's get snapping.

52-Second No-Option Quick Tour for Still Photos

To begin taking still photos immediately, just follow these easy steps:

1. **Press the ON/OFF switch on top of the camera.** The lens will pop out of the camera body, a green LED illuminates in the center of the power button, the start-up sound plays through the speaker on the left side of the camera body, and the start-up image displays on the LCD monitor on the back of the camera. I'll show you how to change the start-up sound and image (or to disable them) in Chapter 4.

2. **Set the fully automatic shooting mode.** Rotate the mode dial (the tallest dial on the right top of the camera) to the green Auto setting. (See Figure 2.1.) The PowerShot makes all the exposure settings for you at this setting.

Microphone   Mode dial   Zoom lever

Figure 2.1
These are the shooting controls located on the top of the camera that you'll use to take your first pictures and movies.

Shutter release

Power switch

3. **Frame your image.** View the image on the LCD on the back of the camera. (If you have the G11, make sure you've rotated the LCD into viewing position!) It will look something like Figure 2.2 (some of the information overlaid on the image may differ, depending on how your camera is set up). Reframe, as desired, by rotating the Zoom lever located concentric with the shutter release button: a clockwise push zooms in; counterclockwise zooms out.

4. **Focus.** When the image is composed the way you want, press the shutter release button halfway to set the focus. The upper LED to the immediate right of the optical viewfinder window will flash green, and you'll hear a beep (unless the camera has been set to Mute) when focus is achieved. If the light is dim and the electronic flash will fire, the LED will flash orange instead.

Figure 2.2
Frame your
photo using the
color LCD.

5. **Take your best shot.** Press the shutter release down the rest of the way to take the picture. The same green LED that indicated focus will flash as the picture is being stored on your memory card. The admonition Busy will appear on the LCD at the same time.

6. **Review your result.** Continue to hold down the shutter release button after you've taken a picture and your shot will display on the LCD until you release the button. If you release the button immediately, the picture will be displayed for review for about 2 seconds. (I'll show you how to increase this display time in Chapter 4.)

52-Second No-Option Quick Tour for Movies

To begin taking movies immediately, just follow these easy steps:

1. **Press the ON/OFF switch on top of the camera.** The lens will pop out of the camera body, a green LED illuminates in the center of the power button, the start-up sound plays through the speaker on the left side of the camera body, and the start-up image displays on the LCD monitor on the back of the camera. I'll show you how to change the start-up sound and image (or to disable them) in Chapter 4.

2. **Set the movie shooting mode.** Rotate the mode dial (the tallest dial on the right top of the camera) to the Movie setting. (It's three clicks clockwise past the green Auto setting on the G10, four clicks on the G11.)

3. **Choose Standard movies.** Rotate the control dial (located to the right of the LCD) until Standard is selected, as shown in Figure 2.3.

Control dial

Figure 2.3

4. **Frame your image.** View the image on the LCD on the back of the camera. Reframe, as desired, by rotating the zoom lever located concentric with the shutter release button: a clockwise push zooms in; counterclockwise zooms out.

5. **Focus.** When the image is composed the way you want, press the shutter release button halfway to set the focus. The upper LED to the immediate right of the optical viewfinder window will flash green, and you'll hear a beep (unless the camera has been set to Mute) when focus is achieved.

6. **Begin shooting a movie clip.** Press the shutter release down the rest of the way to begin shooting video. A • Rec indicator displays in the upper-right corner of the LCD monitor while recording is underway, and an elapsed time indicator counts off the recording time in the lower-right corner. (See Figure 2.4.)

7. **Finish shooting.** When finished recording, press the shutter release a second time. The green LED at the optical window will blink green while the remaining portion of your clip is stored on the memory card. If your card fills, or you reach the maximum clip size of one hour duration or 4GB in size, recording will stop automatically.

Figure 2.4

Indicators on the LCD show that you're shooting a video clip, and display the elapsed time.

Your Ten-Minute Introduction

If you have more than 52 seconds to spare, read or skim through this section to begin shooting, and apply a few options that will make your images even better. You'll learn how to choose a shooting mode, metering mode, focusing mode, and make other simple settings.

That's a lot of modes! Here's what each of the main types of settings do for you:

■ **Shooting mode.** These are set using the large raised dial on the top-right side of the G10/G11. They include automatic exposure modes like the Special Scene (SCN) and Auto settings; the semi-automatic Av (Aperture Priority), Tv (Time/ Shutter Priority), P (Program Auto Exposure/AE); and M (Manual) modes. Also on this dial are the Movie setting and, with the G10, Stitch Assist (which merges multiple images together to form a panorama). The G11 replaces the Stitch Assist choice with Low Light mode (which allows you to shoot under dim illumination) and Quick Shot mode (which continuously adjusts settings automatically to help you capture impromptu grab shots). Both cameras also have two Custom Setting modes that store and retrieve personalized options in slot positions labeled C1 and C2.

- **Metering mode.** Three metering modes are available that allow you to choose what areas of the image the PowerShot G10 or G11 uses to calculate correct exposure. They include Evaluative (which combines information from several different zones within the image); Center Weighted Averaging (which meters the entire image but places the emphasis on the subject matter in the center); and Spot AE (which calculates exposure based on a small area, either the center of the frame or current point being used to calculate autofocus).

- **Focusing modes.** The PowerShot G10 and G11 have two different types of AF (autofocus) options. AF mode determines *when* the camera locks in focus. You can choose Continuous AF, which adjusts focus for whatever subject is in the frame at all times; or Single AF (G10)/Continuous Autofocus Off (G11), which focuses only when the shutter release is pressed (which saves battery power). AF Frame mode determines *where*: what areas of the image are used to calculate focus.

I'll introduce each of the shooting, metering, and focus modes separately in the sections that follow.

Selecting a Shooting Mode

You can choose a shooting method from the mode dial located on the top right of the Canon PowerShot G10/G11. (See Figure 2.5.) The camera has two different types of shooting modes. There are three or four Image Zone shooting settings encompassing a total of 19 different automated modes, in which the camera makes virtually all the decisions for you (except when to press the shutter), and six Creative Zone modes, which allow you to provide input over the exposure and settings the camera uses. The Auto mode is considered neither an Image Zone nor Creative Zone mode.

If you're very new to digital photography, you might want to set the camera to Auto (highlighted in green on the mode dial) or P (Program AE mode) and start snapping away. Either mode will make all the appropriate settings for you for many shooting situations. If you have a specific type of picture you want to shoot, you can try out one of the SCN or Special Scene modes indicated on the mode dial with appropriate icons (see Figure 2.6 which shows the modes available with the G10). (The G11's Low Light mode substitutes for the ISO 3200 mode available with the G10.) Here, I'll provide a quick introduction to each.

Tip

If you want a more complete discussion of both Image Zone and Creative Zone modes, and the differences between them, jump to Chapter 5.

Figure 2.5
The mode dial includes both Image Zone and Creative Zone settings.

Creative Zone

Image Zone

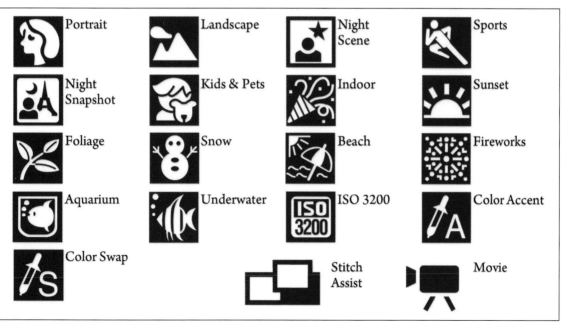

Portrait

Landscape

Night Scene

Sports

Night Snapshot

Kids & Pets

Indoor

Sunset

Foliage

Snow

Beach

Fireworks

Aquarium

Underwater

ISO 3200

Color Accent

Color Swap

Stitch Assist

Movie

Figure 2.6 The icons for the Image Zone modes indicate what type of pictures each is suited for.

First, the Image Zone modes. Select Auto and Movie modes (plus Stitch Assist on the G10) by turning the mode dial to their icons. When the mode dial is set to the SCN position, you can rotate the control dial (the knurled ring to the right of the LCD) until the Special Scene mode you want is shown in the upper-right corner of the LCD. The Image Zone modes are as follows.

- **Auto.** With the mode dial set to this position, the G10/G11 makes all the exposure decisions for you, and will fire the flash if necessary under low light conditions.

- **Portrait.** This Special Scene mode, and the 16 that follow, are set by rotating the mode dial to the SCN position and turning the control dial to choose a specific mode. Use this option when you're taking a portrait of a subject standing relatively close to the camera and want to de-emphasize the background, maximize sharpness, and produce flattering skin tones.

- **Landscape.** Select this mode when you want extra sharpness and rich colors of scenes.

- **Night Scene.** Correctly exposes people in the foreground, using electronic flash, while allowing a slow shutter speed so the background can be properly exposed, too. (You may need a tripod to avoid blurring the background during the longer exposures.)

- **Sports.** Use this mode to freeze fast-moving subjects.

- **Night Snapshot.** Applies the G10/G11's anti-shake feature to allow slower shutter speeds when photographing people against night backgrounds without a tripod or flash.

- **Kids & Pets.** An "action" scene mode for capturing fast-moving pets and children without subject blur.

- **Indoor.** Uses the G10/G11's anti-shake feature for shooting inside at slow shutter speeds, while adjusting the color for fluorescent or tungsten lighting.

- **Sunset.** Offers rich colors for photos at dusk (and dawn).

- **Foliage.** Another saturation-rich setting for shooting trees and leaves, with emphasis on bright and vivid greens.

- **Snow.** Properly exposes people and other subjects, despite glaring ice and snow, while removing the blue tinge often caused by snow backgrounds.

- **Beach.** This also provides properly exposed human subjects against a bright background of water, sand, and reflected sunlight.

- **Fireworks.** Offers vivid photos of fireworks with a longer exposure to capture an entire burst.

- **Aquarium.** Chooses a higher sensitivity setting for the camera for exposures at indoor aquariums, with white balance set for underwater photos.

- **Underwater.** This setting is intended specifically for use under the surface with the optional Canon Waterproof Case WP-DC-28. It removes bluish color casts, and reduces the flash.

- **ISO 3200 (G10 only).** On the PowerShot G10, this "emergency" setting reduces the resolution of the camera to 2MP (1600 × 1200 pixels), and changes the ISO sensitivity setting to ISO 3200. Shutter speed is increased to reduce blurring from subject and camera motion. Use this mode to take pictures under very dim conditions; the image quality won't be top-notch, but you'll be able to get photos you could not take otherwise, except with flash.

- **Low Light mode (G11 only).** The G11 has a native ISO 3200 setting for full resolution images. However the Low Light mode position on the mode dial has a similar "boosting" function for shooting under very poor lighting conditions. When you choose the Low Light mode on the mode dial, the G11 will select an ISO setting from ISO 3200 to ISO 12,800 and reduce resolution to 2.5 megapixels (1824 × 1368 pixels). If you need to use higher ISO settings, the G11 obviously has an advantage over the G10, both in terms of ISO range and resolution.

- **Color Accent.** Creates a special effect: Choose one color on the LCD, and all the other colors in an image are converted to black-and-white.

- **Color Swap.** Changes one color to another. If you want to see Kentucky bluegrass that's *really* blue, this is the mode for you.

- **Stitch Assist.** Rotate the mode dial to this position (with the G10), or select it from the Special Scene choices (with the G11) and a display appears that helps you expose two or more overlapping images (up to 26 in total) that are merged to create a panorama on your computer with the supplied PhotoStitch program. I'll give you step-by-step instructions on how to use this feature later in the book.

- **Movie.** Rotate the mode dial to this position when you want to shoot videos, as described earlier in this chapter, and in Chapter 6.

If you have more photographic experience, you might want to opt for one of the Creative Zone modes. These, too, are described in more detail in Chapter 5. These modes let you apply a little more creativity to your camera's settings. These modes are indicated on the mode dial by letters M, Av, Tv, and P. There are also two Custom Setting positions on the dial, labeled C1 and C2, which can be used to store any of the

Creative Zone modes and its settings, plus additional parameters, like the current zoom and manual focus settings at the time you load the settings into C1 or C2, and My Menu settings.

- **M (Manual).** Select when you want full control over the shutter speed and lens opening, either for creative effects or because you are using a studio flash or other flash unit not compatible with the PowerShot's automatic flash metering.

- **Av (Aperture Priority).** Choose when you want to use a particular lens opening, especially to control sharpness or how much of your image is in focus. The G10/G11 will select the appropriate shutter speed for you. Av stands for *aperture value*.

- **Tv (Shutter Priority).** This mode (Tv stands for *time value*) is useful when you want to use a particular shutter speed to stop action or produce creative blur effects. The camera will select the appropriate f/stop for you.

- **P (Program).** This mode allows the G10/G11 to select the basic exposure settings, but you can still override the camera's choices to fine-tune your image.

Choosing a Metering Mode

Metering mode determines what areas of the frame are used when calculating exposure. You might want to select a particular metering mode for your first shots, although the default Evaluative metering (which is set automatically when you choose an Image Zone mode) is probably the best choice as you get to know your camera. I recommend staying with Evaluative metering as you begin shooting with your PowerShot.

Tip

If you want to learn more about how to select and use the Evaluative, Center Weighted Averaging, or Spot AE Point metering modes, jump to Chapter 5.

To change metering modes, switch to any Creative Zone mode and press the Metering mode button, located on the back of the camera just northeast of the control dial. A screen pops up on the LCD offering three choices. Rotate the control dial until the choice you want is highlighted. Then press the Metering mode button again to confirm your choice. The options are shown in Figure 2.7:

- **Evaluative metering.** The standard metering mode; the G10/G11 attempts to intelligently classify your image and choose the best exposure based on readings from several different zones in the frame. (Canon doesn't specify how many there are, or where the zones are located.) Use this mode for most scenes, especially when the most important areas are located outside the center of the frame.

- **Center Weighted Averaging metering.** The G10/G11 meters the entire scene, but gives the most emphasis to the central area of the frame. This mode is most useful when the most important subject matter is in the middle of the frame.

- **Spot AE Point metering.** Exposure is calculated from a smaller spot. The metering frame is either the center of the LCD monitor, or, when you're using FlexiZone autofocus mode, the same position as the AF frame you've chosen. I'll show you how to set the autofocus mode and zone in Chapter 5. This metering mode is useful when there is a large difference between the brightness of your main subject and other areas of the photo, and you want to be able to zero in on a specific area.

Figure 2.7
Metering modes (left to right) Evaluative, Center Weighted, Spot AE Point.

Choosing a Focus Mode

The Canon PowerShot G10 and G11 offer both manual focus and automatic focus, and, when using autofocus (AF), you can choose *when* and *where* focus is calculated. *When*, in this case, means whether the camera continuously refocuses when your subject moves within the frame, or whether focus is locked down when you press the shutter release halfway. *Where*, on the other hand, determines what part of the frame is considered your main subject when the camera decides to lock in focus. You can select from four different types of "focus frames," including automatic detection of human faces; auto switching among nine possible areas within the frame; focus locked on the center area of the image; and FlexiZone, which allows you to choose what part of the image to focus on.

Tip

For more detail on selecting each of these focusing modes, and their advantages, jump to Chapter 5.

Manual Focus

You can manually focus the G10 or G11, either entirely by yourself if you want to set the focus point precisely, or by using the Safety MF, which allows you to set the focus point manually, at which point the camera uses its autofocus features to fine-tune the focus for you. See Figure 2.8, which shows manual focus with the G10. The screen looks the same with the G11, except that the MF indicator is at the top of the screen instead of the bottom. I'll explain all the manual focus options in Chapter 5. In this quick start,

Magnified area   Manual focus scale   Control dial   Safety MF   MF button

Figure 2.8 Press the MF button to initiate manual focus.

all you need to know is to initiate manual focus, press the up cross key, and rotate the control dial to adjust the focus point. A scale at the right side of the LCD shows you the approximate focus point as a guideline, and a magnified area in the center (it can be turned off as described later) shows an enlarged view of the center of the frame as you focus. To turn off manual focus, press the MF (Up) button a second time.

Tip

To use Safety MF, press the AF Frame Selector/Single Frame Erase (Trash) button. The G10/G11 will fine-tune your exposure and beep.

Other Settings

There are a few other settings you can make if you're feeling ambitious, but don't feel ashamed if you postpone using these features until you've racked up a little more experience with your PowerShot G10 and G11.

Adjusting White Balance and ISO

If you like, you can custom tailor your white balance (color balance) and ISO sensitivity settings when you're using Creative Zone settings. To start out, it's best to set white balance (WB) to Auto, and ISO to ISO 100 or ISO 200 for daylight photos, and ISO 400 for pictures in dimmer light.

To set the white balance quickly, press the FUNC./SET button in the center of the control dial (the directional pad) and use the up/down cross keys to navigate to the White Balance entry at the top of the left-side menu. Then use the left/right cross keys or rotate the control dial to select from among Auto, Daylight, Cloudy, Tungsten, Fluorescent, Fluorescent H, Flash, Underwater, or Custom white balance. (See Figure 2.9.) I'll show you how to use each of these in Chapter 4, where you'll also learn how to tweak settings slightly by pressing the DISP. button to produce an adjustments screen (G11 only).

ISO sensitivity is even easier to adjust. Just rotate the ISO dial (which is concentric to the mode dial) to the setting you want to use, from ISO 80 to 1600 (or 3200 on the G11), or to the Auto position to allow the camera to choose an appropriate ISO setting for you.

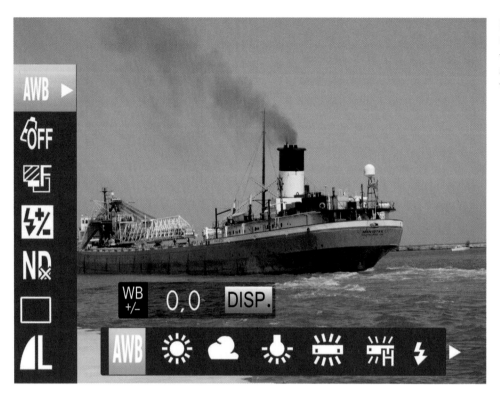

Figure 2.9
Choose the white balance setting you want.

Using the Self-Timer

If you want a short delay before taking a picture—say, to allow the camera to steady itself, or to allow you to get in the shot, the built-in self-timer is at your beck and call. The self-timer is accessed by pressing the down cross key on both the G10 and G11, but the functions available from that point on differ. I'll explain them in more detail in Chapter 4. But here's a quick introduction:

PowerShot G10 Self-Timer

With the G10, the down cross key functions both as a self-timer control, and to select various Drive mode settings, such as Single Image (take one picture with each press of the shutter release), and three different Continuous shooting variations: Continuous (1.3 frames per second with fixed focus); Continuous AF (0.7 frames per second with automatic focus for each shot); Continuous Live View (0.7 frames per second using manual focus and the image being recorded displayed on the LCD during shooting).

The self-timer function offers four variations. Select Self-Timer (with timer icon) and press the Menu button to be given a selection of the four different types of timer available:

■ **10 sec. Self-Timer.** A picture is taken 10 seconds after the shutter release is pressed, with the self-timer lamp on the front of the camera and a beep repeating slowly until the last two seconds, when they speed up to indicate that the picture is about to be taken.

■ **2 sec. Self-Timer.** A picture is taken 2 seconds after the shutter release is pressed, with the self-timer lamp on the front of the camera and a beep repeating quickly during that span.

■ **Custom Timer.** You can choose a delay time of 0 to 10 seconds (in one second increments) or 15, 20, or 30 seconds; and select the number of shots (from 1 to 10) to be taken after the timer elapses. If a delay time of more than 2 seconds has been selected, the beeper sounds quickly 2 seconds before the shutter releases for the first (or only) shot.

■ **Face Self-Timer.** After the shutter release is pressed, the camera takes a picture two seconds after a face is detected in the frame (with a 2-second beeper warning). You can select from 1-10 shots to be taken after the delay has elapsed, with a 2-second interval between shots. If a face is not detected, the shutter will release after 30 seconds.

PowerShot G11 Self-Timer

With the G11, the down cross key functions only as the self-timer control. Once the countdown is started by pressing the shutter release, it can be cancelled by pressing the down cross key again. Press the down cross key, then use the down cross key or control dial to select:

■ **Off.** The self-timer is not activated.

■ **10 sec. Self-Timer.** A picture is taken 10 seconds after the shutter release is pressed, with the self-timer lamp on the front of the camera and a beep repeating slowly until the last two seconds, when they speed up to indicate that the picture is about to be taken.

■ **2 sec. Self-Timer.** A picture is taken 2 seconds after the shutter release is pressed, with the self-timer lamp on the front of the camera and a beep repeating quickly during that span.

- **Face Self-Timer.** After selecting this option, press the Menu button and the left/right cross keys to select 1-10 shots taken when the timer elapses. After the shutter release is pressed, the camera takes a picture two seconds after a face is detected in the frame (with a 2-second fast beeper/blinking light warning). You can select from 1-10 shots to be taken after the delay has elapsed, with a 2-second interval between shots. If a face is not detected, the shutter will release after 30 seconds.

- **Custom Timer.** Choose this option and you can select a delay time of 0 to 10 seconds (in one second increments) or 15, 20, or 30 seconds; and select the number of shots (from 1 to 10) to be taken after the timer elapses. If a delay time of more than 2 seconds has been selected, the beeper sounds quickly 2 seconds before the shutter releases for the first (or only) shot. Press the FUNC./SET button to confirm your choice.

Using the Built-in Flash

Working with the G10/G11's built-in flash (as well as external flash units like the Canon 270EX) deserves a chapter of its own, and I'm providing one. (See Chapter 8.) But the built-in flash is easy enough to work with that you can begin using it right away, either to provide the main lighting of a scene, or as supplementary illumination to fill in the shadows. The G10/G11 will automatically balance the amount of light emitted from the flash so that it illuminates the shadows nicely, without overwhelming the highlights and producing a glaring "flash" look. (Think *Baywatch* when they're using too many reflectors on the lifeguards!)

For now, all you need to do is learn how to turn the flash on and off. Just press the right cross key, and choose either Flash Off (to disable the flash) or On (to enable it). The third choice, Slow Synchro (available with the G11 only), can be used to provide a balance between the ambient light and the flash, avoiding dark backgrounds. I'll explain the use of that mode, as well as the other flash options that appear when you press the Menu button while using this Flash menu, in Chapter 8.

Reviewing the Images You've Taken

The Canon PowerShot G10 has a broad range of playback and image review options, including the ability to jump ahead by 10 or 100 images at a time, or to jump using other parameters, such as date. I'll cover the other options, including filtering and viewing images in the form of slide shows, in Chapter 3. For now, you'll want to learn just the basics.

- **View an image.** Press the Playback button (marked with a blue right-pointing triangle) to the right of the optical viewfinder to display the most recent image on the LCD.

- **Scroll among images.** Press the left cross key to view a previous image. Press the right cross key to view the next image.

- **Zoom in and out.** Press the zoom lever towards the right to zoom in on an image. Press towards the left to zoom out. While zoomed in, you can use the cross keys to move the zoomed area around within the frame.

- **View index thumbnails.** From full-frame view, keep pressing the zoom lever towards the left to view four or nine thumbnails (with the G10), or continue (with the G11) to view 36 and 100 increasingly smaller thumbnail images. Use the cross keys to maneuver around the index images, and press the FUNC./SET button to view a highlighted thumbnail as a full frame image.

Transferring Photos to Your Computer

The final step in your picture taking session will be to transfer the photos you've taken to your computer for printing, further review, or image editing. Your G10/G11 allows you to print directly to PictBridge-compatible printers and to create print orders right in the camera, plus you can select which images to transfer to your computer. I'll outline those options in Chapter 3.

For now, you'll probably want to transfer your images either by using a cable transfer from the camera to the computer or by removing the memory card from the G10/G11 and transferring the images with a card reader. The latter option is usually the best, because it's usually much faster and doesn't deplete the battery of your camera. However, you can use a cable transfer when you have the cable and a computer, but no card reader (perhaps you're using the computer of a friend or colleague, or at an Internet café).

To transfer images from the camera to a Mac or PC computer using the USB cable:

1. Turn off the camera.

2. Pull up the cover that protects the PowerShot's USB port on the right side of the camera (as you hold it in the shooting position), and plug the USB cable furnished with the camera into the USB port. (See Figure 2.10.)

3. Connect the other end of the USB cable to a USB port on your computer.

4. Turn on the camera. Your installed software usually detects the camera and offers to transfer the pictures, or the camera appears on your desktop as a mass storage device, enabling you to drag and drop the files to your computer.

To transfer images from a memory card to the computer using a card reader, as shown in Figure 2.11:

1. Turn off the camera.

2. Slide open the memory card/battery door on the bottom of the camera, and press on the card, which causes it to pop up so it can be removed from the slot.

3. Insert the memory card into your memory card reader. Your installed software detects the files on the card and offers to transfer them. The card can also appear as a mass storage device on your desktop, which you can open, and then drag and drop the files to your computer.

Figure 2.10 Images can be transferred to your computer using a USB cable.

Figure 2.11 A card reader is the fastest way to transfer photos.

3

Canon PowerShot G10/G11 Roadmap

One of the reasons that the Canon PowerShot lineup of cameras has been popular with beginning snapshooters, avid photo hobbyists, and advanced photographers—including both amateurs and pros—is their easy access to features. The latest models, the G10 and G11, continue this combination of a rich set of functions that is quickly available from a well-designed array of controls and menus. Whether you're just learning to work with your PowerShot G10/G11 as your first advanced digital camera, or you're a seasoned photographer looking for the kind of tools you expect from a sophisticated compact camera, you'll easily find what you need.

Whenever a camera manufacturer develops a new camera, there have to be tradeoffs among several design goals: easy access to controls, clarity of control functions, and simplicity. There's no perfect approach to the physical layout of the camera. If it bristles with dozens of buttons and wheels, the photographer can immediately get access to many functions, but may not intuitively understand which one to use for a particular purpose. On the other hand, a camera may be sleek and streamlined with few physical controls, but that design may require the user to master an obscure and deeply buried array of menu commands to carry out even the simplest of functions.

With the PowerShot G10/G11, Canon has done a good job of providing ready access to the tools you need. Easily accessible dials and buttons simplify tasks like setting the ISO sensitivity of the sensor, modifying the brightness/lightness of the image through exposure compensation, and switching among available shooting modes. However, as is the case with any camera as capable and sophisticated as these, the average user needs a clear guide to explain what each control does, and how to achieve the desired results using the various switches and dials.

Traditionally, there have been two ways of providing a roadmap to guide you through this maze of features. The most common approach, taken by Canon in the pocket-sized user's guide that ships with the PowerShot G10 and G11, uses a few 2 × 3-inch black-and-white line drawings or photos that are peppered with dozens of labels or callouts keyed to the numbers of the pages in the book that tell you what these components do. (See, for example, pages 40-42 of the G10 Camera User Guide and pages 42-43 of the G11 Camera User Guide.) Even if you can decipher these illustrations without a magnifying glass, getting the information you need from a miniature camera diagram is a lot like being presented with a world globe when what you really want to know is how to find the capital of Belgium.

I originated a more useful approach in my field guides, providing you with, instead of a long-range satellite view, a street-level map that includes close-up full-color photos of the camera from several angles (see Figure 3.1, for example), with a smaller number of labels clearly pointing to each individual feature. And, I don't force you to flip back and

Figure 3.1

forth among dozens of pages to find out what a particular component does. Each photo is accompanied by a brief description that summarizes the controls available in that view, so you can begin using the features right away. Only when a particular function deserves a lengthy explanation do I direct you to a more detailed write-up later in the book.

So, if you're wondering what the DISP. button does, I'll tell you up front, rather than have you flip to Page 45 of the camera's user guide, where there isn't much information anyway. This book is not a scavenger hunt. But after I explain how to use the ISO dial to change the sensitivity of the G10/G11, I *will* provide a cross reference to a longer explanation later in the book that clarifies noise reduction, ISO, and its effects on exposure.

It's really not possible to explain *everything* about *every* feature the first time that capability is mentioned. Many features of the PowerShot cameras are interdependent. To really understand ISO sensitivity, you also need to understand how exposure works. So, to avoid having humongous 150-page chapters, I'll provide the key information you can use immediately up front, and use limited cross references to direct you to the in-depth discussions you need to really understand a feature, and all its options. I think this kind of organization works best for cameras as sophisticated as the PowerShot G10/G11.

By the time you finish this chapter, you'll have a basic understanding of every control and what it does. I'm not going to delve into menu functions here—you'll find a discussion of your Setup, Shooting, and Playback menu options in Chapter 4. Everything here is devoted to the button pusher and dial twirler in you.

Front View

When we picture a given camera, we usually imagine the front view. That's the view that your subjects see as you snap away, and the aspect that's shown in product publicity and on the box. The frontal angle is, for all intents and purposes, the "face" of a camera like the PowerShot G10/G11. But, not surprisingly, most of the "business" of operating the camera happens *behind* it, where the photographer resides. The front of the G10/G11 actually has very few controls and features to worry about. Seven front-located features are readily visible in Figures 3.2 and 3.3 (These views show the G11, but there is no meaningful difference in the same views for the G10):

- **Hand grip.** This gently raised area has a lightly textured leather-like coating that provides a comfortable handhold, so the camera does not slip readily out of your grip.

- **Red-eye reduction/Self-timer/Autofocus assist lamp.** This LED provides a blip of light shortly before a flash exposure to cause the subjects' pupils to close down, reducing the effect of red-eye reflections off their retinas. When using the self-timer,

Figure 3.2

Built-in flash

Viewfinder window

Red-eye reduction/ Self-timer/ Autofocus assist lamp

AV-Out/ Compartment door

Hand grip

Figure 3.3

Neck strap mount

Speaker

Ring release button

this lamp also flashes to mark the countdown until the photo is taken. For its third trick, this versatile light beams into poorly illuminated areas in front of the camera to help the PowerShot's autofocus apparatus see what it's doing.

■ **Viewfinder window.** This is the "eye" of the photographer when he or she is looking through the viewfinder, as opposed to using the LCD screen to compose a shot.

■ **Built-in flash.** The PowerShot G10/G11 sports this very handy little built-in flash tube that is always ready to fire at your command, unlike the units on some cameras that need to be manually popped up in order to be ready. Of course, this flash is not nearly as powerful as the external units that can be connected to the camera's accessory shoe, but it serves a very useful purpose for general snapshooting and as a fill-in flash for some outdoor shots.

■ **AV-Out/compartment door.** This little door on the right side of the camera (as you hold it to shoot) conceals the location of the ports or jacks that are used to connect your camera to a computer, TV set, or remote switch. These ports are set up a bit differently on the two cameras. On the G10, the top jack is for the standard audio-video (AV) cable that comes with the camera and connects it to a standard TV set. The middle jack is for the optional RS60-E3 remote switch. The bottom port is for the mini-USB cable that connects the camera to a computer. On the G11, the top port is for an optional HTC-100 HDMI cable to connect the camera's video output to a high-definition TV set (but without high-definition quality, which the camera lacks); the middle jack is for the optional remote switch; and the bottom one is a mini-USB port that accepts two cables that come with the camera: one for normal audio-video output to a standard TV set, and the other for connecting to a computer.

■ **Speaker.** When you're playing back movies or (with the G10) audio memos, the sound will emanate from the tiny speaker built into the side of the camera. If the sound is muted, move your hand!

■ **Ring release button.** This inconspicuous little button is reminiscent of the lens release buttons found on dSLRs and other cameras that take interchangeable lenses. The difference is that this button does not release the lens; it just releases the ring around the lens, so you can install an adapter that is required when you are attaching certain accessories, such as a tele-converter lens or macro ring flash. And, if you're a somewhat wild and sporty type, there's good news—you have the option of changing the ring color by purchasing a different colored ring from Canon!

■ **Neck strap mounts.** On both sides of the camera there are mounting brackets for the neck strap that's included with the camera. It's a good idea to install that strap as one of your first steps after taking the camera out of the box, to give you some protection against dropping your new acquisition while getting acquainted with its features.

The LCD Screen: To Swivel, or Not to Swivel

At this point in our tour of the PowerShot G10/G11's real estate, before we embark on our perusal of the back yard, we need to pause for a close examination of one of the main features of the camera, and one of the features that most clearly highlights the distinctions between these two closely related models. I'm talking about the LCD screen—that marvelously informative rectangular expanse on the back of each camera that, depending on the context, shows you the shot you're composing, displays the scenes you've already captured, or provides you with detailed information about those images, as well as the camera's menus and settings.

The two cameras both have highly useful LCD displays, but they represent markedly different design strategies. As you can see in Figure 3.4, the PowerShot G10's screen is a fixed 3-inch LCD (at top), while the screen of the PowerShot G11 is a swiveling display (bottom), reduced to a 2.8-inch LCD, with the same 461,000 pixel resolution as that of the G10, but with the added feature of its ability to rotate on both vertical and horizontal axes.

The swiveling capability of the PowerShot G11's LCD screen is no small matter, and it is worth taking a few moments to discuss the benefits (and tradeoffs) that this enhancement brings to the camera.

Let's start with the tradeoffs, or disadvantages, which are not major. First, in order to be able to swivel, the G11's screen needs to have a swiveling mechanism, which adds some weight and complexity to the camera, and introduces the possibility of failure or breakage of that mechanism. However, the Canon design is rugged, and your swivel screen pivot is likely to last as long as the rest of the camera. Second, the addition of that mechanism necessarily reduces the diagonal size of the actual display area, but only slightly, from 3 inches to 2.8 inches. The G11's swiveling screen has 87 percent of the area of the G10's fixed LCD, but exactly the same resolution and sharpness.

Now let's discuss how the swiveling screen works, and what advantages that capability provides. When you first take the camera out of its box, you will find that the LCD screen is in its "closed" position (see Figure 3.5). In this position, the screen is folded in against the back of the camera, with its display surface hidden from view.

Why is this a useful configuration? For several reasons. First, it's a great way to protect the screen from damage, dirt, or the elements. Other cameras, including the G10, have their screens exposed to possible harm whenever they're out of their cases. The ability to fold the screen in provides a built-in screen protection system. In addition, in some situations you may want to take your pictures in as discreet a way as possible, such as at concerts or religious ceremonies, and you may not want to distract persons near you by having the LCD display showing. Of course, you can turn off the display of other digital cameras—at least those that have optical viewfinders like the PowerShot G10,

Figure 3.4

so you won't be shooting blind. But it may be easier and more effective to just fold it in against the camera.

Flip open the LCD on the PowerShot G11 and take a look at what it has to offer in the way of photographic versatility. First, check out Figure 3.6. In this position, the LCD screen is swiveled out to the left at various angles, allowing you to view your subject from one side, or even turn the display so you're looking around a corner. From here, you can swivel the screen vertically so it is aiming up at the sky, down towards the ground, or even turned all the way around to face in the same direction as the lens. These positions give you several options. With the screen swiveled out to the left and then flipped upwards, you can easily hold the camera down at waist level and compose your image without bending over. In this way, you can compose a photograph that looks better when taken from a low angle, and you don't have to get down on your belly or crouch in a squat. On the other hand, if you flip the screen downwards, you can hold the camera above your head to peer over the tops of crowds or physical obstructions, and compose the image in the LCD, sort of like submarine commanders with their raised periscopes. I appreciate this mode at concerts, because I can raise the camera up over the heads of the multitude milling around in front of me. Finally, swivel the screen around to face the front, and you can indulge your narcissistic side by pointing the camera at yourself and taking a self-portrait that is nicely framed in the versatile LCD. (See Figure 3.7.)

Figure 3.5

Figure 3.6

Figure 3.7

The Canon PowerShot G10/G11's Business End

The back panels of the PowerShot G10 and G11 are dominated by the nonswiveling/ swiveling LCD screen, but the designers also managed to find room for about a dozen different controls in the form of buttons and dials. That might seem like a lot of controls to learn, but I think you'll find, as I noted earlier, that it's usually a good deal easier to press a dedicated button or spin a dial than to navigate through a menu system every time you want to change a setting.

You can see the controls that populate the backs of the G10 and G11 in Figure 3.8, which shows the G11, but which applies also for the G10, except for the different functions of the bottom cross key, as noted below. Because there are so many different controls, I've divided them into two illustrations. First, the controls on the upper half of the camera, as shown in Figure 3.9. The key controls and components and their functions are as follows:

- **Viewfinder eyepiece.** You can frame your composition by peering into the viewfinder. On the PowerShot G10/G11, there is no luxurious rubber eyecup or other frills; all you get is a small window to peer into. And, unlike the situation with the typical dSLR camera, you get absolutely no information in the viewfinder other than an image of what the camera is pointing at.

  But you should be fairly happy with that view; there are quite a few cameras in this class that have no optical viewfinder at all, leaving you holding the unsteady camera out at arm's length, even in low-light situations where steadying the camera against your forehead might provide a more stable view. Or, without recourse to an optical viewfinder, you might be forced to squint at an LCD screen that can be washed out in bright sunlight. The viewfinder on the G10/G11 is not fancy, but it provides a very useful capability.

Figure 3.8

Shortcut/ Print Share button   *Diopter adjustment dial*   *Viewfinder eyepiece*   *Upper indicator LED*   *Lower indicator LED*   *Playback button*   *AE lock/FE lock/ Microphone button*

Figure 3.9

■ **Diopter adjustment dial.** The little wheel just to the left of the viewfinder lets you adjust the viewfinder to correct for your eyesight, as described in Chapter 1.

■ ***AE/FE (Auto exposure/Flash exposure) lock/(Microphone).** This button, which has a * label, has several functions, which differ depending on the AF point and metering mode. You can find more about these variations in Chapter 4.

In Shooting mode, pressing this button locks the exposure or flash exposure that the camera sets when you partially depress the shutter button. The exposure lock will be released if you press another button after releasing the AE/FE lock button.

When using flash, pressing the * button fires an extra preflash that allows the unit to calculate and lock exposure prior to taking the picture with the flash.

On the G10, press this button during Playback mode to bring up the controls for recording an audio memo of up to 60 seconds to attach to the image being displayed. A musical note icon will be displayed on the image after the memo has been recorded. (The G11 does not have any such audio-only recording capability; it records audio only with movies.)

■ **Upper Indicator Light.** The G10/G11 is equipped with a set of two indicator lights just to the right of the viewfinder window. Because you can see them out of the corner of your eye, the information is available to you even when you're using the optical viewfinder. The upper indicator light provides these signals:

■ **Green.** Ready to shoot.

■ **Blinking green.** Image recording/reading/erasing/transfer underway. While that is happening, be careful not to turn off the camera, open the memory card door, or otherwise disturb the process. If you do, data could be lost or corrupted.

■ **Orange.** Ready to shoot (flash on).

■ **Blinking orange.** Ready to shoot (camera shake warning).

- **Lower Indicator Light.** This is a yellow LED signal for focus conditions.

  - **Yellow.** Indicates you're using macro or manual focus modes, or AF lock mode.

  - **Blinking yellow.** Accompanied by a single beep, indicates that the camera is having trouble focusing.

- **Set shortcut/Direct print button.** This button, sitting away from its peers way up on the left side of the camera, is like a wildcard or programmable function button, giving you the chance to take one favorite action and assign it to this button for one-press access. To take advantage of this capability on either camera model, go to the Shooting menu and select the Set Shortcut Button option, scroll to the function you want to assign to the button, and press FUNC./SET to confirm your selection. I'll explain the use of the Shooting menu in more detail in Chapter 4.

  On the G10 your choices are ND filter, White Balance, Custom White Balance 1, Custom White Balance 2, Red-Eye Correction, Tele-Converter, i-Contrast, AF Lock, and Display Off. On the G11, the possible selections are the same, with the addition of Servo AF.

  What you do with this button depends on your own working habits. If you often attach and detach the tele-converter lens, having that setting at your fingertips could be a bonus; or, if you want to save battery power by turning the display off when you don't need it, you might assign that function to the shortcut button.

  Finally, this button, like many of the others, has a second, completely unrelated function as the Direct Print button. If you connect the G10 or G11 to a PictBridge-compatible printer, you can use this button to send images directly to the printer. I'll also describe this function in Chapter 4.

- **Playback button.** Displays the last picture taken (unless you use the menu system to change to showing the last picture viewed). Thereafter, you can move back and forth among the available images by pressing the left/right cross keys to advance or reverse one image at a time, or the control dial to move forward or back, either image by image or using a jump method you've selected. (See the section below for more on jumping.) To quit playback, press this button again. The G10/G11 also exits Playback mode automatically when you press the shutter button (so you'll never be prevented from taking a picture on the spur of the moment because you happened to be viewing an image).

PLAYBACK PAYBACK

There's one other convenient feature of the G10/G11: when the camera is turned off, you can turn it back on with the Playback button, so you are immediately in Playback mode. Press the Playback button again to turn it off. However, once you're in Recording mode, pressing the Playback button toggles back and forth between Recording and Playback. You'll need to use the Power button to turn the camera off. The Playback on/Playback off trick works only if you remain in Playback mode the whole time the camera is on, for example, simply to review images.

The right half of the PowerShot G10 and G11 is dominated by a set of buttons that includes the cross keys, which serve as your directional controls for navigating around the screen and menus, and which do double duty with other direct-access functions. The key controls shown in Figure 3.10 are as follows:

■ **Menu button.** Summons/exits the menu displayed on the rear LCD of the G10/G11. When you're working with submenus, this button also serves to exit a submenu and return to the main menu.

Figure 3.10

AF Frame selector/
Single Image Erase button

Metering mode/Jump button

Cross keys

Manual focus button

Flash button

Macro button

Self-timer button

Continuous shooting button (G10)

Display button

Menu button

- **DISP. button.** When pressed repeatedly, changes the amount of picture information displayed. In Playback mode, pressing the DISP. button cycles among basic display of the image; a display with limited information, including battery life, image number, date, and time; a detailed display with a thumbnail of the image, shooting parameters, and a brightness histogram; and a display with two views of the image for checking focus. (I'll discuss that function later in this chapter.) The DISP. button also serves a variety of other purposes, such as selecting various options in connection with particular camera functions. These uses will be discussed in their respective sections.

- **LCD.** This is the 3-inch (G10) or 2.8-inch (G11) display that shows the image that is being composed; image review after the picture is taken; information display before the photo is snapped; and all of the menus used by the PowerShot G10/G11.

- **Cross keys.** This array of four directional keys provides left/right/up/down movement to navigate menus, and is used to cycle among various options (usually with the left/right cross keys) and to choose amounts (with the up/down cross keys). The four cross keys also have secondary functions to select macro shooting, manual focus, flash options, and self-timer (and, for the G10, Drive mode) settings. (I'll describe these separately next.)

- **Left cross key/Macro button.** Press this button to engage Macro mode. In Macro mode, the camera's focusing system is limited to close-up focusing. The distance range in Macro mode is about 0.4 in (1 cm) to 1.6 ft (50 cm) from the subject to the end of the lens, when the camera is zoomed out to the wide-angle setting. At the telephoto end of the zoom range, the distance range for macro shooting is about 1 ft (30 cm) to 1.6 ft (50 cm).

- **Top cross key/MF button.** One push of this button and the camera enters Manual focus mode, in which you adjust the focus using the control dial on the back of the camera. I'll supply more information about this procedure in Chapter 6.

- **Right cross key/Flash button.** This button gives you access to various functions associated with the built-in flash unit. If you press it lightly, each press moves to one of several options (depending on the shooting mode) for the flash setting: Automatic; Always on, slow synchro; and Always off. If you hold the button down firmly, the camera displays the Flash Control menu, giving you access to additional flash settings. All of this is discussed more fully in Chapter 8.

- **Bottom cross key/Self-timer/(Drive mode) button.** On both the G10 and the G11, this button gives you instant access to the camera's versatile self-timer capability. On the G10, the button does double duty as the drive mode selector, so the operation is a bit different on the two cameras.

■ **FUNC./SET button.** Push this button in to confirm a selection or activate a feature. It also provides direct access to the Function menu, described in detail in Chapter 4. The Function menu allows you to quickly access frequently changed settings, such as white balance and image size. As you'll see in Chapter 4, making those settings can be accomplished much faster, and you'll also find that less-used parameters are tucked away in the main menus.

■ **AF Frame Selector/Single Image Erase button.** This button's primary function is to let you perform certain functions in connection with the autofocus system. It acts differently on the two camera models, as described in the autofocus section in Chapter 4. On both cameras, this button's secondary function is to erase individual images. Press the button once when an image is displayed in Playback mode, and the image will be erased if you confirm the operation with the navigation buttons and the FUNC./SET button.

■ **Metering Mode/Jump Target button.** The primary job of this button is to let you select the exposure metering mode to be used by the camera, as described in Chapter 5.

  ■ In Shooting mode, press the button, then turn the control dial directly below the button to choose Evaluative (to base exposure on several different areas within the frame); Center Weighted Averaging (to emphasize the center area when calculating exposure); or Spot (to meter from a small area in the frame).

  ■ In Manual mode, press this button to cycle back and forth between setting aperture, shutter speed, or choosing the (backup) metering method with the control dial.

  ■ When reviewing images, the button's third function is to let you specify the way the camera "jumps" between images when rotating the control dial. I'll talk more about this capability a little later in this chapter.

Self-Timer/Drive Mode

The PowerShot G10/G11, like virtually all modern digital cameras, has a self-timer mechanism that adds considerably to the camera's usefulness in more than one situation. The obvious application of the self-timer is when you are taking a group photograph, of a family or school group, say, and you, the photographer, need to be in the picture as part of the group. Following the standard drill, you set the camera firmly on a tripod, and compose the group photo nicely using the viewfinder or LCD screen, leaving a gap in the assembled group that you can slip into quickly. Then you activate the self-timer, setting it for ten seconds; the self-timer starts to beep or flash, and you race around the tripod to insert yourself into the group. You manage to plant your feet firmly in place and smile just before the beeping and flashing speed up before the final shutter sound and flash.

Both the PowerShot G10 and G11 are quite capable of handling this scenario, with a bit of extra sophistication thrown in. Here is the basic method for taking a picture using the self-timer on either model of the PowerShot G10/G11:

- **Select a shooting mode.** Turn the camera on, and set it to an appropriate shooting mode. For a group photo using the self-timer, I suggest using the Auto mode, since you won't be behind the camera to tweak any settings; you may as well let the camera's automation earn its keep. But choose another mode if it's called for, such as Aperture Priority if the group is several rows deep and you need a small aperture to maintain a large depth of field. If you choose a mode other than Auto, the steps to follow below will be slightly different, because a few more options for setting the self-timer are available in other shooting modes.

- **Press the Self-timer button.** Press the button once to summon a submenu on the right side of the screen. On the G10, unlike the G11, this button also controls the camera's drive mode (for rapid-fire shooting) as well as the self-timer. (The G10's Self-Timer/Drive mode screen is shown in Figure 3.11; Figure 3.12 shows the G11 Self-Timer-only version.) To bypass the icons for the options you don't want, keep pressing the down cross key one or more times as needed, taking you to the icon for the standard self-timer with the number 10 beside it, meaning it will be set for a 10-second delay. Press FUNC./SET to accept that setting, or just do nothing, and that setting will take effect. A little self-timer icon will show up on the LCD screen, and will remain there if the display is set to show detailed information.

- **Press the shutter button.** Take one last look at the LCD screen or through the viewfinder, then get a bead on the space you're going to occupy in the group photo, press the shutter button, and run like the dickens to get into place! Just as you get settled, the flashing and beeping on the camera will speed up, then the shutter will fire, the flash will go off (if needed), and the historical record of your membership in that group will be a bit more complete.

Tip

On both the G10 and the G11 there are several variations to the self-timer settings that you can explore as needed. You can set the delay to shorter periods, including a preset 2-second delay or a custom delay between 1 and 30 seconds, and you can set the camera to take from 1 to 10 shots when the self-timer triggers the shutter. You also can select the Face Self-timer, which won't fire the camera until it detects that a face is in the picture. (If you're shooting a group, have everyone look away from the camera until you're ready to take a picture.)

The available settings vary with the current shooting mode; they can be selected by pressing the Self-timer button or by pressing the Menu button when you're already viewing the self-timer's screen.

Figure 3.11

Figure 3.12

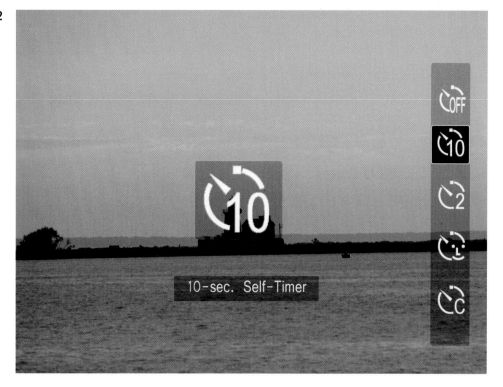

Other Uses for the Self-Timer

Although the group photo described above is probably the most common scenario for using the self-timer, there are a couple of other situations when you might want to consider it. One is candid photography. There may be occasions when you want to catch your subject(s) off-guard, and you might be able to accomplish that in some cases by leaving the camera sitting off to the side of an elementary school classroom, say, or hold it casually down beside your hip and leave it set to take 10 shots when the self-timer triggers it. You might snag some good shots of kids who were not aware they were going to be photographed.

Another possible use for the self-timer is when you need to make sure the camera is not moved or jiggled, as it can be when you press the shutter, even if it's on a tripod. This can be important when you're taking long exposures of the night sky, for example. If you don't have a remote release switch available, the self-timer can be a workable substitute, because you won't be touching the camera when the shutter is pressed, so the risk of camera shake is greatly reduced.

Using Drive Mode on the G10

Although the PowerShot G10 and G11 models have similar sets of controls, they are not identical, and the Self-timer button is one example of a clear difference. On the G11, that button is dedicated to the self-timer alone (apart from its other role as the bottom cross key). On the G10, though, this button also serves to choose your Drive mode—that is, either single shots, or continuous, rapid-fire shooting. (On the G11, continuous shooting is selected through the FUNC. menu, which is discussed in Chapter 4.)

To activate continuous shooting on the G10, here are the basic steps:

1. **Choose a compatible shooting mode.** If you want the ability to fire off a continuous stream of shutter clicks, you will have to sacrifice the convenience of Auto shooting mode. Continuous shooting is not available when the camera is set to Auto shooting. Select Program, Aperture Priority, Shutter Priority, Manual, or almost any of the SCN shooting varieties, such as Portrait, Night Snapshot, Kids & Pets, etc.

2. **Press the Self-timer/Drive mode button.** A submenu will pop up on the LCD screen, as in Figure 3.11 shown earlier, displaying icons for the available Drive mode and self-timer options.

3. **Select continuous or continuous AF.** Scroll to the icon showing plain stacked frames (for Continuous mode) or the one showing stacked frames with the letters AF (for Continuous AF). Press FUNC./SET to make your selection.

4. **Press and hold down the shutter button.** There is no preset limit on the number of continuous shots you can take with the PowerShot G10/G11—even if you're shooting in RAW quality with autofocus working. There may be a second or two between shots in conditions like that, but the camera will keep cranking them out like a real trouper until the battery or memory card is filled up. (Or, maybe the more likely scenario, you get tired of holding down the shutter button.)

Going Topside

The top surface of the Canon PowerShot G10/G11 has a few frequently accessed controls of its own. The key controls, shown in Figure 3.13, are as follows:

■ **Exposure compensation dial.** One of the very attractive features of the G10/G11 is the existence of this dial, which gives you instant access to adjust the exposure compensation, without having to immerse yourself in the menu system or embark on a series of button pushes. One quick twist of this knob, and you can dial in the amount of compensation you need, to account for backlighting or other challenging exposure conditions. We'll discuss exposure in more depth in Chapter 5.

■ **Flash hot shoe.** Slide an electronic flash into this mount when you need a more powerful speedlight. A dedicated flash unit, like those from Canon, can use the multiple contact points shown to communicate exposure, zoom setting, white balance information, and other data between the flash and the camera. There's more on using electronic flash in Chapter 8.

■ **ISO dial.** As with the exposure compensation dial, this dial is a very welcome feature of the G10/G11. ISO (sensitivity to light) is a very important concept for getting exposure right, and we will delve into it in some detail in Chapter 5. It's great to be able to dial in your desired ISO setting without the fanfare or fuss required on cameras that bury this function in menus or behind obscure buttons.

ISO DIFFERENCES

There is a slight difference between the ISO dials of the two cameras: the G10 has two Auto settings on the ISO dial: a regular Auto setting, which emphasizes picture quality over obtaining a fast shutter speed, and a second, HI setting, which causes the camera to raise the ISO as much as necessary to achieve a shutter speed that will reduce camera shake. The highest direct setting on the G10's ISO dial is 1600, although the camera has a SCN mode setting for ISO 3200.

The G11, on the other hand, has only one Auto setting on the ISO dial, and has settings that go up to 3200. In addition, the G11 has an additional dedicated "Low Light" shooting mode, in which the ISO setting can go as high as 12800, depending on conditions.

ISO
speed
lamp

Hot
shoe

Exposure
compensation
dial

Microphone

Mode
dial

ISO
speed
dial

Zoom
lever

Shutter
button

On/Off
button

Figure 3.13

- **Mode dial.** This dial is used to select among the various shooting modes offered by the G10/G11. We'll discuss the shooting modes in Chapter 4.

- **Shutter release button.** Partially depress this button to lock in exposure and focus. Press all the way to take the picture. You can partially depress the shutter button to switch from Playback mode to Recording mode, also.

- **Zoom lever.** This control has quite a few functions. Its primary purpose is to change the focal length of the PowerShot G10/G11's lens between its 28mm wide-angle setting and its full optical zoom length of 140mm. It also will magnify the image beyond the optical zoom length, using the digital zoom feature, discussed in Chapter 4. In Playback mode, discussed later, it changes views of your images, and when viewing menus, you can use this lever to switch from one menu system (Shooting, Playback, Setup) to another.

- **On/Off switch.** Press down to turn the PowerShot G10/G11 on, and back to turn it off again. The green power light in the center of the button will illuminate while the power is on.

Port-Side Terminals

When you're holding the PowerShot G10 or G11 in your hands, the starboard (right) side of the camera is, oddly enough, the "port" side, where, underneath the terminal cover you'll find three ports that let you connect the G10/G11 to the outside world. These connectors, shown in Figure 3.14, are:

- **Audio/Video OUT terminal.** On the G11, this upper terminal accepts the optional Canon HDMI cable, model number HTC-100. With that cable, you can connect the camera to a high-definition (HD) television set or monitor, although the camera does not record or output video in HD. On the G10, the terminal in this location is a composite video-out jack that connects the camera to a standard TV using the AV cable that comes with the camera.

- **Remote terminal.** This terminal, the same on both the G10 and G11, accepts a wired remote switch, the Canon RS60-E3 that you can use to control the camera from a distance in the same way as the cable releases used on film cameras. There also are wireless remote switches available that are compatible with this connection.

- **USB/Digital terminal.** Although this terminal is very similar on the G10 and the G11, it is not identical, as a close inspection will reveal; the shape is slightly more expansive on the G11. On the G10, this connector has a single purpose—to connect the camera to a computer or a PictBridge printer to transfer or print images. On the G11, this one connector has two purposes—to connect the camera to a computer or printer, and also to connect it to a standard TV set, using the supplied AV cable.

Figure 3.14

Audio/Video Out terminal

Remote terminal

USB/Digital terminal

LCD Panel Readouts

The PowerShot G10/G11 does not have a monochrome status LCD, like the one found on the top panel of the digital SLR cameras. Lacking this auxiliary information display, the G10/G11 uses the color LCD to show you everything you need to see, from images to a collection of informational data displays. Here's an overview of these displays, and how to access them.

Image Playback Displays

When the G10/G11 shows you a picture for review, you can select from among four different information overlays. To switch among them, press the DISP. button while the image is on the screen. The LCD will cycle among:

- **Single image display.** This display shows just the image that is on the memory card; no other information is displayed (Figure 3.15).

- **Single image display with recording quality**, which also shows the image number, date, and time the image was taken (Figure 3.16).

- **Histogram display**, which shows basic shooting information such as shutter speed and aperture as well as a brightness histogram at bottom left (Figure 3.17). (I'll explain how to work with histograms in Chapter 4.)

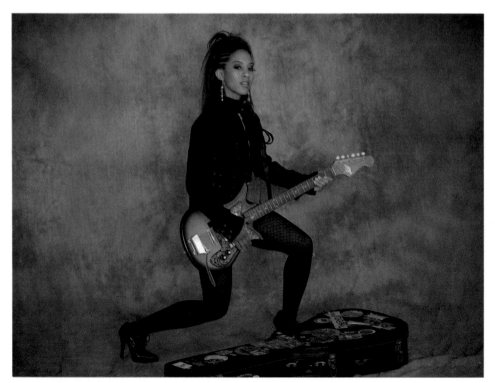

Figure 3.15
Single image display.

Figure 3.16
Single image
display with
recording
quality.

Figure 3.17
Histogram
display.

■ **Focus checking display.** A special screen designed to let you make a detailed assessment of the image's focus. This screen (shown in Figure 3.18) shows one view, on the left, of about normal size, with an orange frame showing where the camera's focus was set when the picture was taken. On the right is a smaller frame, enlarged. Move the zoom lever to the right to switch to the enlarged view, which then becomes highlighted. You can then change the magnification of this view with the zoom lever and scroll around it with the cross keys, to check the focus.

Figure 3.18
Focus checking display.

Jumping/Zooming Around

When you're ready to view the pictures you've taken, either on the camera's own LCD display or on a connected TV set, the PowerShot G10/G11 offers plenty of options for viewing them. You'll find more details about some of these functions later in this chapter or in other chapters that I point you to. Here is the must-know information.

■ **Start review.** To begin reviewing your pictures, press the Playback button located above the LCD screen to the right of the viewfinder window. The image that shows up on the screen will be either the most recently viewed one or the most recently taken one, depending on your settings in the Playback menu. If the next item is a movie, press the FUNC./SET key to call up a VCR-like set of controls on the screen. Use the FUNC./SET key to operate those controls.

- **Cycle through information displays.** To view more or less information on the screen, press the DISP. button to move through the four different levels of items that show up on the screen. These displays can be invaluable in helping you to check composition, exposure, and focus, using tools such as the histogram and the focus check display.

- **View thumbnail images.** To change the view from a single image to 9, 36, or 100 thumbnails, or to use the Jump button to move among shots by categories, dates, and other criteria, see the "Viewing Thumbnails" and "Jumping Around" sections that follow.

- **Zoom in and out.** To zoom in or out, press the zoom lever, following the instructions on "Zooming Around" in the next section.

- **Move back and forth.** To advance to the next image, press the right cross key; to go back to a previous shot, press the left cross key. When you reach the first or last photo in your memory card's folder, the display "wraps around" to the next shot in the sequence.

- **Move back and forth rapidly.** To advance through the images rapidly using the single image display, turn the control dial on the back of the camera quickly, and the images will scroll in a way similar to the "cover flow" scrolling on an iPod. On the G11, a pair of up and down arrows will appear on the screen, inviting you to select images by date; choose a date by moving these arrows up or down with the up/down cross keys.

- **Erase images.** To delete an image that's currently on the screen, press the Trash button, then move the highlight from Cancel to Erase on the screen, and press the FUNC./SET key to confirm the operation.

- **Cancel playback.** To cancel image review, press the Playback button again, or simply tap the shutter release button.

Zooming Around

When an image is displayed in Playback mode, press the zoom lever to the right (in the direction for zooming the lens) to fill the screen with a slightly magnified version of the image. You can keep pressing the zoom lever to magnify images up to about 10 times the normal size. Press the lever in the other direction as many times as needed to reduce the size to normal, or press the Menu button to reduce it to normal immediately. While the image is zoomed, you can scroll through the zoomed image with the four cross keys. You can move to other images with the control dial while the images are zoomed.

Viewing Thumbnails

The PowerShot G10/G11 provides other options for reviewing images in addition to zooming in and out. On the G10, you can switch between single image view and an index screen with nine thumbnail images by moving the zoom lever to the left, toward the wide-angle view. One of the thumbnail images will be highlighted by a frame, and you can move to the other images on the screen with the cross keys or control dial. Move the zoom lever to the left once more and the whole screen of nine images is bordered by a green box; you can now move through screens of nine images with the same controls.

On the G11, moving the zoom lever to the left multiple times takes you to successive index screens with 4, 9, 36, and 100 thumbnail images, assuming you have that many images stored on your memory card. Move the zoom lever back to the right to highlight an individual image on any given screen, or to move back to screens with fewer thumbnails.

With either the G10 or the G11, when an individual image is highlighted on an index screen, you can erase it by pressing the Trash button and then confirming the action when prompted by the camera.

Jumping Around

The PowerShot G10/G11 has one more image viewing trick up its sleeve, and a pretty powerful one at that. Some previous Canon models (not to mention models from other brands) have a Calendar function that lets you view images taken on a particular date. The G10 and G11 can perform a similar feat, but with added punch—they will let you "jump" to other images not just by date, but also by category, first image in the folder, movies versus stills, 10-image jumps, and 100-image jumps. So, for example, if, like me, you use 16GB SD cards (which can hold thousands of images each) this is a welcome way to narrow down your search for images on a given card. Here's how this works:

1. **Press the Playback button.** The camera enters Playback mode.

2. **Press the Jump button.** That's the button above the right side of the control dial, directly below the * button. This action brings up a submenu on the left of the screen showing a line of icons. From top to bottom, these icons represent date; category; first image in folder; movie; 10 images; and 100 images.

3. **Scroll to the search type you choose.** Scroll down to highlight one of the above criteria you want to use to base your search on. If you're basing your search on the categories of images, see the discussion of the available categories in Chapter 4.

4. **Select the filter data.** If there is more than one possibility for the search, such as with dates, folders, or categories, use the left/right cross keys to select the details of the search you want. For example, select the particular date you're searching for. If

there's only one possibility for the search, such as jumping to movies, go directly to the next step below.

5. **Turn the control dial.** This is the step that actually takes you to the first image that meets the search factors you have chosen. Turn the dial to the right to select that first image of the search set, then keep turning it to continue displaying those images.

6. **Press the Jump button again.** Pressing the Jump button again will exit from search mode.

Underneath Your PowerShot G10/G11

There's not a lot going on with the bottom panel of your PowerShot G10/G11. Besides the door to the battery and memory card compartment, you'll find a tripod socket, which secures the camera to a tripod, or to certain optional accessories, such as the BKT-DC1 bracket, which is used to mount a macro ring flash unit and other external flash units. Figure 3.19 shows the underside view of the camera.

Figure 3.19

4

Setting Up Your Canon PowerShot G10/G11

For a highly portable "point-and-shoot" camera, the PowerShot G10/G11 provides you with an impressive selection of options and settings that let you customize the way your camera operates. Not only can you change shooting settings used at the time the picture is taken, but you can adjust the way your camera behaves. Indeed, if your G10/G11 doesn't operate in exactly the way you'd like, chances are you can make an adjustment in the Shooting menu, the Playback menu, or the Setup menu to tweak the camera's behavior to your liking. If you don't like the organization of the menus themselves, you can create a customized mini-menu system of your own by gathering your favorite functions into one using the My Menu feature. In addition, you can get virtually instant access to several of the most important choices for setting up your shots through the FUNC. menu, which is summoned with one press of your finger.

This chapter will help you sort out the settings for all the G10/G11's menus. These include the aforementioned Shooting, FUNC., and Playback menus, which determine how the G10/G11 uses many of its shooting features to take a photo and how it displays images on review. In addition, I'll show you how to use the Setup menu to adjust items such as power-saving timers, screen brightness, and others.

As I've mentioned before, this book isn't intended to replace the manual you received with your G10/G11, nor have I any interest in rehashing its contents. The owner's manual is useful as a standby reference that lists every possible option in exhaustive (if excruciating) detail—without really telling you how to use those options to take better pictures. There is, however, some unavoidable duplication between the Canon manual and this chapter, because I'm going to explain all the key menu choices and the options you may have in using them. You should find, though, that I will give you the information you need in a much more helpful format, with plenty of detail on why you should make some settings that are particularly difficult to understand.

I'm not going to waste a lot of space on some of the more obvious menu choices in these chapters. For example, you can probably figure out, even without my help, that the Sound Options item on the PowerShot G11's Setup menu deals with the solid-state sound chip in your camera that produces electronic chirps and beeps during various activities (such as the self-timer countdown). In this chapter, I'll devote no more than a sentence or two to the blatantly obvious settings and concentrate on the more confusing aspects of G10/G11 setup, such as autofocus. I'll start with an overview of using the G10/G11's menus themselves.

Anatomy of the PowerShot G10/G11's Menus

The main menu system of the PowerShot G10/G11 should seem quite familiar to anyone who has used a similar-sized digital camera, especially another PowerShot, within the past few years. After all, given the profusion of features found on modern cameras, there are only so many ways that engineers can organize menu items for all of those features in a logical and user-friendly manner.

The designers of the PowerShot G10/G11 menu system have succeeded quite well in the user-friendliness arena. To make use of the system, just press the Menu button, located in the lower-right corner of the back of the camera, and use either the left/right cross keys or the zoom lever (next to the shutter button) to highlight the menu tab you want to access—Shooting or Playback, depending on the mode the camera is in, or Setup, which is accessible from either Shooting or Playback mode. (There's also a printing menu, for functions relating to printing images directly from the camera.) Then, scroll up and down within a menu with the up/down cross keys or by spinning the control dial.

Here's one shortcut: If you happen to get stuck one or more screens down in the options of one of the menus, you can quickly switch back to either of the other menus by moving the zoom lever to the right or left. That way, you don't have to scroll all the way back up to the top of one menu system before switching to another one, as you otherwise would. One more tip: when you get to the bottom (or top) of a menu, you can wrap around by continuing in that direction. For example, if you're on the top item of a long menu and want to get to the bottom item, your quickest route will be to scroll up beyond the top item, which will take you straight to the last item. This technique can save lots of time when you need to navigate the menus in a hurry.

On the PowerShot G11, pressing the Menu button brings up a typical menu like the one shown in Figure 4.1. (If the camera goes to "sleep" while you're reviewing a menu, you may need to wake it up again by tapping the shutter release button or the Menu button.) There are three menu tabs visible while the camera is set to Shooting mode: Shooting, Setup, and My Menu. (When the camera is in Playback mode, the three menu choices are Playback, Printing, and Setup. We'll discuss those later.)

The tabs are labeled with icons: a camera for the Shooting menu, a wrench and hammer for the Setup menu, and a star for the My Menu tab. (The Playback menu is represented by a right-pointing triangle, and the Printing menu by a printer icon. Neither is shown in the view presented in Figure 4.1; you'll work with them later in this chapter.)

As you can see in Figure 4.2, the menu setup on the G10 is slightly different from the G11; the G10 has another menu called My Camera with a few settings such as start-up image and operation sounds, which are found on the Setup menu for the G11. The currently selected menu's icon is highlighted by appearing brighter than other choices on the G10, and is highlighted in orange on the G11. Here are the things to watch for as you navigate the menus:

■ **Menu tabs.** In the top row of the menu screen, the menu that is currently active will be highlighted as described earlier. Just remember that the camera icon stands for shooting options; the right-pointing triangle represents playback options; the wrench/hammer icon stands for set-up options; and the star stands for personalized menu options.

■ **Selected menu item.** The currently selected menu item will be highlighted by a colored bar.

Figures 4.1 and 4.2 The PowerShot G11 (left) and G10's (right) menus are arranged in a series of tabs.

- **Other menu choices.** The other menu items visible on the screen will have a dark gray background. With the PowerShot G11, you won't always see "grayed-out" menu lines for items that are not available in a particular mode. Instead, in some cases, those items just will not appear on the menu if they are not available. For example, when the camera's shooting mode is set to Auto, several Shooting menu options, such as AF Frame, Servo AF, and certain Flash Control options are not available, and simply do not show up—they are left out of the menu list. (See Figure 4.3.) However, there are other situations in which the camera *does* use the "grayed out" approach. If you remain in a particular shooting mode but select an option that renders some menu selections unusable, those selections will be "grayed out." For example, if you are in Program mode, most of the menu options are available. But if you then select manual focus by pressing the MF button on the back of the camera, Presto! No more AF options are available on the menu, and they are "grayed out." (The G10, similarly, sometimes uses the "disappearing menu item" trick and sometimes the "grayed out" approach for menu items that are not currently available.)

- **Current setting.** The current settings for visible menu items are shown in the right-hand column. Unlike some other cameras' menu systems, in most cases, the full screen of the G10/G11 menu stays visible on the camera's display while you select the value for a particular menu item. (With some other cameras, when you select a menu item, it takes up the whole screen, and all other menu items disappear until that item's value has been selected.)

Figure 4.3 When the PowerShot G11 is set to Auto shooting mode, some menu options simply don't appear, such as AF Frame (left). When the camera is set to Program shooting mode, that option reappears (right).

When you've used the up/down cross keys (or the control dial) to move the menu highlight bar to the menu item you want to work with, press the left/right cross key to select the desired value for the item. Many of the items can be set only to on or off, but others can have one of several values. For example, the Review function, which determines how long a new image stays on the screen for review, can be set to a time from 2 to 10 seconds, to hold indefinitely, or to be off altogether—a total of 11 separate choices, any of which can be selected by moving the left and right cross keys.

In a few cases, such as Flash Control, once you've highlighted the menu item, you need to press the FUNC./SET key to get access to a submenu with further options (see Figure 4.4). In most cases, though, you can make all your selections for the various menu items without leaving the main menu screen. This system makes it clean and easy to make your settings without having to go through a lot of extra button pushes or to go into and out of a series of submenus.

In order to select your desired menu option, you ordinarily only have to highlight it; you don't have to press the FUNC./SET key to select it. Once your selection is highlighted, just press the Menu key to exit the menu system, and you're ready to shoot with the newly selected option activated.

Figure 4.4
The Flash Control item on the Shooting menu includes numerous options, in some shooting modes.

Shooting Menu Options

The various direct setting buttons on the top and back panels of the camera, including those for ISO sensitivity, metering mode, exposure compensation (EV) adjustments, and flash, are likely to be the most common settings changes you make, with changes during a particular session fairly common. You'll probably find that the Shooting menu options, along with the FUNC. menu options, which I'll discuss later, are those that you access second-most frequently when you're using your PowerShot G10/G11. You might make such adjustments as you begin a shooting session, or when you move from one type of subject to another. Canon makes accessing these changes very easy.

This section explains the options of the Shooting menu and how to use them. As noted earlier, both of these PowerShot models sometimes change their lists of visible menu options according to the current context, such as whether the camera is set to Auto shooting mode. This system is good in that it eliminates the need to scroll through a series of options that you can't select, but it has the negative aspect of making it somewhat confusing to discuss the options that are available, because some of them will be invisible to you if the camera is set to a mode in which you can't make certain selections. (If you would like to go through the Shooting menu and see almost all of the available options, on the G11, set the camera to Shutter Priority mode by turning the mode dial to the Tv setting; that mode leaves more Shooting menu options available than any other mode, as you can see from the chart at pages 182-183 of the camera's User Guide. On the G10, choose Shutter Priority mode or Program mode; see the chart at page 300 of that camera's User Guide.)

With that caveat, then, the options you'll find in the Shooting menu, at least in some shooting modes, are the following:

- AF Frame
- Digital Zoom
- AF-Point Zoom
- Servo AF
- Continuous AF (AF Mode on G10)
- AF-assist Beam
- MF-point Zoom
- Safety MF
- Flash Control
- i-Contrast

- Spot AE Point

- Safety Shift

- Wind Filter (On Setup menu under Audio on PowerShot G10)

- Review

- Review Info

- Blink Detection

- Custom Display

- Reverse Display (PowerShot G11 only)

- IS Mode

- Converter

- Date Stamp (PowerShot G11 only)

- Record RAW + L

- Set Shortcut button

- Save Settings

- Auto ISO Shift (PowerShot G10 only)

- Drive Settings (PowerShot G10 only)

- Auto Category (PowerShot G10 only)

AF Frame

The first choice presented to you in the Shooting menu is AF Frame, which gives you two options for the behavior of the autofocus frame. The first choice on the PowerShot G11 is Face AiAF, which I am going to venture to translate as "artificial intelligence autofocus." With this option, the camera attempts to find a human face in the scene before the camera. When it has found one or more likely candidates, it puts a white frame on what seems to be the main subject, as shown in Figure 4.5, and places gray frames on other faces. The camera sets itself to use evaluative exposure metering and auto white balance. If it finds no apparent faces, or no apparent main face, the camera will set up to nine green frames to show the points it will use for autofocus. (The AF Frame options are slightly different with the G10; more about that in Chapter 6.)

Your other option here is FlexiZone, which I personally find preferable to Face AiAF. With FlexiZone, you work with a single AF frame, whose size and position you can change, so you can focus on a particular area of the scene in question to achieve a fairly precise level of control over your composition. Once you have selected this AF method,

Figure 4.5
Face AiAF can locate faces in a frame, and lock in focus.

press the AF Frame/Trash button, and the AF frame will turn green (on the G10, orange on the G11). The frame then becomes movable. Move it around the screen with the control dial or the cross keys. If you press the DISP. button, you can then change the size of the frame between normal and small. Also, if the camera has detected faces, you can move the AF frame from face to face with presses of the Menu button.

If you do a lot of photography involving groups of people and the face-detection works for you, that's great. For me, though, the FlexiZone system offers an excellent approach to achieving sharp focus. Of course, with a camera like the PowerShot G10/G11, with its small sensor and large depth-of-field, focus often will not be a major issue, particularly when the lens is zoomed back to its wide-angle position. For those shots when focus is more of a concern, though, FlexiZone can help. Decide what part of the image you want to be in the sharpest focus, select FlexiZone, and place a small-sized AF frame over that area while the lens is zoomed in. (If focus is sharp when the lens is zoomed in, it's sure to be sharp when zoomed back also.) Then zoom the lens back out if that's the view you want, and take the picture. Your focus should be right on the mark.

We'll discuss your focus options in more detail in Chapter 6.

Digital Zoom

Digital zoom, quite frankly, is not a feature to get particularly excited about. The PowerShot G10/G11, like most compact digital cameras, has a nice "optical zoom" capability, going from 28mm (wide angle) to 140mm (telephoto), using the standard 35mm-equivalent ratings of focal length. That means that the camera's lens zooms in to a focal length that makes objects look five times larger than at the shortest focal length. That capability can be called a "real" zoom capability, because the image is magnified as with binoculars or a telescope; in other words, you actually get more information through the viewfinder and in your final image than without the zoom.

With the "digital zoom," on the other hand, you really don't get any more picture information for your final image. What happens is that the camera electronically magnifies a portion of the image that the lens sees, in the same way that you can blow up the image on your computer to enlarge a small part of it. Just as on a computer, the enlarged part becomes blocky, or pixelated, and you don't really see any more information than without the enlargement. That's not to say that digital zoom has no useful purpose at all. When the camera magnifies your view like this, then the exposure metering can be limited to a small part of the image, and you may be able to compose your shot better by zooming in digitally. But don't expect to get the benefit of a real enlargement of the image, as with optical zoom.

There's not much more to say about this feature. Your choices are to leave it off, turn it on at a zoom factor of 1.7 or 2.2 (1.4 or 2.3 on the G11), or set it to Standard, which provides the full digital zoom range of 28mm to 560 mm. I recommend leaving it off, unless you're faced with a situation in which it may be of some advantage to have your image electronically enlarged for purposes of exposure or composition.

AF-Point Zoom

This is a handy little feature that gives you the option of having a magnified autofocus frame. The only option is to turn it on or off. When it's on, if the AF Frame is set to FlexiZone, the AF frame will be magnified when you press the shutter button down halfway to check the focus. This system lets you check to make sure the autofocus has locked on and focused properly. If you find the magnified frame distracting, turn it off, but I find it quite useful and reassuring to be able to see the focus point more clearly. Note that the feature does not function in all situations, such as when the AF Frame is set to Face AiAF and no faces are detected. It also cannot function if Servo AF is activated or Digital Zoom is set to 1.4X or 2.3X (a Standard setting is fine). (So, if you find that AF-Point Zoom is grayed out on the menu, check to see if Digital Zoom or Servo AF are interfering; if so, deactivate the offending setting and AF-Point Zoom will become available again.)

Servo AF

Ordinarily, when you press the shutter button down halfway, the focus and exposure are locked in. If you keep the shutter halfway down and move the camera, you will keep the same settings until you press the shutter all the way in. If you have a digital SLR, that function is often called *Single Servo AF,* or AF-S. With the G10/G11, Servo AF is the equivalent of *Continuous Servo AF* (AF-C) on a digital SLR. In Servo AF mode, the G10/G11 readjusts focus as required. So, when you press the shutter halfway, the focus and exposure will continuously adjust as the subject or camera moves, or as lighting conditions change. You will hear the camera make a continuous whirring or clicking sound as the focus mechanism keeps adjusting. This feature is great if you are tracking a moving subject and want to have the focus and exposure ready for the instant when you snap the picture. As you might guess, the downside is that you may run through batteries faster than you would like. I'll discuss the uses of this feature in more detail in Chapter 6.

Continuous AF

This feature, which has a name that's similar to the continuous servo found in digital SLRs, is similar to Servo AF, but in a different context. Normally, when this feature is off, the camera autofocuses on your subject only when you press the shutter button halfway. If you turn this feature on, then the camera constantly alters its focus as you move the focus frame over different subjects, *without the need to partially depress the shutter release.* In other words, this feature controls whether the camera constantly focuses *before* you press the shutter halfway, and the Servo AF feature controls whether the camera constantly focuses *after* you have pressed the shutter halfway. Of course, this feature, like the previous one, has a good side and a bad side: it can help you achieve sharp focus quickly, but it also can drain your battery quite rapidly. More about this feature in Chapter 6.

AF-assist Beam

The autofocus mechanism sometimes needs some extra light in order to figure out whether the scene before the camera is in sharp focus. Without that light, the shape in question might be too indistinct for the camera to find the straight lines that can help it determine focus. If you're shooting at a religious ceremony or in another environment in which you don't want to send out beams of light, and you believe your focus will be adequate without that help, go ahead and set this feature to Off in the menu system. Be warned, though, that you may still see the same beam of light, because the camera also sends out a similar beam to reduce the red-eye effect. So, unless you have Red-eye reduction *and* AF-assist Beam turned off, beware the Light Beams!

MF-Point Zoom

When you set the camera to manual focus using the MF button, ordinarily the focus area in the center of the LCD screen is magnified so you can fine-tune the focusing by turning the control dial. If for some reason you prefer not to have that enlarged area appear (maybe you find it distracting from the composition), you can turn off the enlarging effect with this menu option.

Safety MF

This is another feature that works in conjunction with manual focus. Ordinarily, even when you are using manual focus, you have the option of fine-tuning the focus to full sharpness, after first focusing roughly with the control dial, by pressing the shutter button halfway, or pressing the AF Frame/trash button. This feature is called "Safety MF." If you want to disable this feature, you can do so with this menu option. You might want to disable it if you have a tricky manual focusing situation, and you don't want the camera to change your manual focus when you press the shutter button down to take the picture.

Flash Control

This menu item is one of those that leads to several other options; it's not just an on-or-off feature. I'll be talking about the use of flash in more detail in Chapter 8, but I'll discuss the main options of the Flash Control menu here for reference.

Flash Exposure Compensation

This entry is a way to set flash exposure compensation (that is, raising or lowering the normal flash output) as an alternative to doing so through the FUNC. menu. To set this value using the Shooting menu, highlight this option, then dial in the amount of flash EV compensation you want using the left/right cross keys. Press the Menu button to exit.

Flash Mode

This option, available only in the Shutter Priority and Aperture Priority shooting modes, can be set to either Auto or Manual. It lets you control the flash output in those modes. When this option is set to Manual, the Flash Output option becomes available so you can control the intensity of the flash. When it is set to Auto, the Flash Exposure Compensation option is available instead of Flash Output.

Flash Output

As discussed in connection with Flash Mode, above, this option becomes available when the camera is set to Shutter Priority or Aperture Priority shooting mode and the Flash Mode is set to Manual. In those circumstances, you can set the intensity of the flash manually using this feature. You can also use this feature when the shooting mode is set to Manual.

Shutter Sync.

You can choose 1st Curtain sync, which fires the flash as soon as the shutter is completely open (this is the default mode). Alternatively, you can select 2nd Curtain sync, which fires a preflash used to measure exposure as soon as the shutter release is pressed down all the way, but before the shutter opens, and then triggers a second flash at the end of the exposure, just before the shutter starts to close. This action allows photographing a blurred trail of light of moving objects with sharp flash exposures at the beginning and the end of the exposure. I'll explain how it works in Chapter 8.

Slow Synchro (PowerShot G10 Menu Only)

Use this setting when you're taking an indoor picture with flash, but you want the background to show up also. This setting causes the camera to use a slower shutter speed than it normally would, allowing time for the background to be adequately exposed by ambient light so it's not just a dark blot. I'll talk more about this and other flash topics in Chapter 8. On the PowerShot G11, this item does not appear on the Flash Control menu, but is available in certain shooting modes by pressing the Flash button and selecting Slow Synchro from the group of options that appears.

Red-Eye Correction

You're probably familiar with the red-eye effect that populates snapshots at parties with people looking as if they wandered off the set of a cheap vampire movie. The problem is that electronic flash (or, rarely, illumination from other sources) bounces off the retinas of the subjects, with the red from retinal blood vessels adding the unwanted coloration to the eyes. The PowerShot G10/G11 attacks this problem with two distinct approaches, which are very different even though they both are housed on the Flash Control menu. The camera uses both *correction* and *reduction*. Reduction involves shining a light at the subject's eyes to narrow the pupils, thereby reducing the chance of reflections from the retinas. We'll return to that approach in a moment; it's the next menu choice. For now, the topic is red-eye correction.

The first arrow in the G10/11's quiver of anti-red-eye measures is digital correction. Put simply, this means that the camera's circuitry looks for unnaturally red areas in or near people's eyes, and attempts to de-redden them digitally. This system is not perfect; this correction technique may take effect when someone has red makeup applied near the eyes, so don't rely on it too heavily to fix red-eye. This feature can be turned either on or off.

Red-Eye Lamp

This is the second way the G10/G11 combats the scourge of red-eyed photos. If this feature is turned on, the camera lets loose a beam of light toward the subject before the flash fires for taking the picture, in order to narrow his or her pupils, as discussed above. (You may have to ask your subject to look straight at the lamp to gain maximum effect.) Actually, the best way to truly eliminate red-eye is to raise the flash up off the camera so its illumination approaches the eye from an angle that won't reflect directly back to the retina and into the lens. That alone is a good reason for using an external flash. If you're working with your G10/G11's built-in flash, your only recourse may be to use the two red-eye-reduction strategies discussed here. Figure 4.6 shows the effects of wider pupils (left) and those that have been contracted using the G10/G11's Red-Eye Lamp feature.

Figure 4.6
Red-eye is blatant (left), but tamed (right) thanks to the PowerShot G10/G11's Red-eye reduction lamp.

Safety FE

This final option on the Flash Control menu is a safety mechanism programmed into the camera. When this feature is activated (as it is by default), the camera automatically adjusts the aperture and shutter speed when the flash fires, to prevent a situation in which the shot is overexposed by an overly powerful flash discharge. If you turn this feature off, the camera will let the chips fall where they may, and your highlights may be blown if the flash turns out to be too bright for the conditions.

i-Contrast

This is a feature that is available both while shooting and for adjustment of images that were previously recorded. When it is activated during shooting, the camera will attempt to balance the highlights and shadows and retain shadow detail in a scene so that no area is either excessively bright or excessively dark. It also will try to add contrast to a scene that is lacking in that regard. As you can expect, your mileage may vary with this feature; it's a good one to experiment with in a variety of situations to see if it can improve some of your images.

Drive Settings (PowerShot G10 Menu Only)

On the PowerShot G10, options for continuous shooting (Drive mode) and the self-timer are located on the Shooting menu under this heading. On the G11, those settings are accessed through the FUNC. menu instead. For information about using continuous shooting, see Chapter 3.

Spot AE Point

This feature has one very specific purpose—to link the exposure frame to the focus frame when you have the camera set for both FlexiZone autofocus and Spot metering. Here are the steps to follow:

1. Using the Metering mode button and the control dial, select Spot as the metering method.

2. Set the AF Frame option on the Shooting menu to FlexiZone.

3. Select Spot AE Point on the Shooting menu, and set the option to AF Point (as opposed to Center).

4. In the center of the LCD screen you will see a double set of brackets enclosed within a rectangle, indicating that both the focus and the exposure are being determined by this small area in the middle of the screen (see Figure 4.7).

Now, since the camera is set to the FlexiZone focusing mode, you can press the AF Frame button and then move or resize the focus frame as you wish. You may notice dramatic changes in exposure of the scene as you move the small exposure and focus area to different parts of the scene before you, because of the effect of the spot metering. You won't want to use this technique without a good reason, but if you know your exposure and focus should both be determined by the same small area of the scene, it's a good item for your photographic toolkit.

Figure 4.7
The FlexiZone
focus frame is
linked to the
Spot metering
frame using the
Spot AE Point
feature.

Safety Shift

This feature is another one with a very limited purpose. When you activate Safety Shift and have the shooting mode set to either Aperture Priority or Shutter Priority with the flash turned off, the camera will automatically shift the setting you made (for aperture or shutter speed) if proper exposure cannot be obtained using that setting. For example, let's say you're using Shutter Priority mode and have set the aperture at 1/2000th of a second in a dimly lit room with the flash turned off. With Safety Shift off, if you take the picture at these settings, you can enter the result into a contest for photos of coal-bin interiors with a good chance of victory. With Safety Shift turned on, the camera is quite likely to switch your shutter speed to something like 1/6th of a second, and you will now have a reasonably visible representation of your dimly lit room.

Auto ISO Shift (PowerShot G10 Only)

This feature, found on the G10 only, has a very specific purpose. It comes into play only when you are shooting without flash in the Aperture Priority, Program, or Auto shooting mode, and the lighting is such that there may be a problem with camera shake because of a slow shutter speed. If this feature has been turned on through the Shooting menu, in such a situation the Set shortcut button will glow with a blue light when you press the shutter button to evaluate the exposure. (That's one reason this feature can only be on the G10; the G11's Set shortcut button doesn't have a light built into it.) When you see the blue light, then you have the option of pressing the Set shortcut button, which will increase the ISO setting in an effort to prevent camera shake. Maybe it's just me, but this feature seems a bit clunky, involving too many steps and buttons. It seems to me you would be better off just setting the ISO as high as necessary yourself, or using the flash.

Wind Filter (PowerShot G11 Menu Only)

I'm discussing this feature here in the interest of covering all items on the Shooting menu, even though this one applies only to movies, and not to stills, and doesn't appear on the menu unless the PowerShot G11 is set to Movie mode. With this feature activated, the camera will attempt to suppress wind noise coming into its tiny microphone. It may or may not help, so experiment and see if it's useful in your particular situation. On the PowerShot G10, this option is not found on the Shooting menu; rather, it's tucked away under the Audio option on the Setup menu.

Review

This menu option controls how long an image displays on the LCD screen after it has just been recorded. You can set the review time to any value from 2 to 10 seconds; to hold on the screen until the shutter button is pressed; or not to display at all (see Figure 4.8).

Figure 4.8

The Review function determines how long an image displays on the screen after the picture is taken.

Review Info

This menu option works in conjunction with the Review function, discussed above, to set how images display on the screen right after they've been shot. The choices are Off, Detailed, and Focus Check. With Off, there's no information displayed; just the image. With Detailed, the screen provides details about the exposure as well as a histogram showing the brightness values graphically. With Focus Check, you are presented with two small images, with an ability to check the focus of the image in fine detail. I discuss histograms in Chapter 5, and Focus Check in Chapter 3.

Blink Detection (PowerShot G11 Only)

With this setting turned on, the camera will display a frame with a little blinky eyed face if it detects that an image you have taken has a person with his or her eyes shut. This option may seem at first blush to be a bit Big Brotherish, but it actually could be useful, because it can be pretty hard for the photographer to check your subject's eyes.

Custom Display

This menu option lets you customize the information that is shown on the LCD screen when you are in Shooting mode. Once you have selected this option, you are presented with a matrix containing the three screens that are shown with successive presses of the DISP. button (see Figure 4.9). You can choose among four items to be displayed on the screens: (1) shooting info, which includes things such as battery life, quality and image size settings, and general settings such as i-Contrast and the like; (2) grid lines, a set of intersecting lines that can help with composition; (3) 3:2 guide, a shaded area that shows what part of the image would print out on paper with a 3:2 aspect ratio; and (4) histogram. In daily use, you may want to have your first screen uncluttered with much of this information, and your next screen (summoned by the DISP. button) to show just grid lines. It's all a matter of how you use the information on the screen.

Reverse Display (PowerShot G11 Only)

Here's another menu item that was created just to address a very specific issue, and only on the PowerShot G11 with its swiveling screen. If you fold the LCD screen out to the side and then flip it vertically (on its horizontal axis), the screen will be folded out to the side and facing you if you are staring at the lens. This is done largely so you can take a self-portrait; in other words, the LCD shows you a mirror image of what it's aimed at, though, if you then take the picture, when you view it later it will be oriented correctly, not a mirror image. If you don't want the image in the LCD screen reversed when the screen is flipped around to the front, you can turn this setting off.

Figure 4.9
The Custom Display menu option lets you specify what information appears on the detailed shoot-ing informa-tion display.

IS Mode

The PowerShot G10/G11 comes equipped with a very capable image stabilization sys-tem, which detects camera motion and uses electronic circuitry to counteract it, thus reducing the chances your shots will be marred by blurring if the camera shakes while you're taking pictures. With image stabilization engaged (set to Continuous on this menu), you can hand-hold the camera at slower shutter speeds without ending up with ruined images, so it's a very useful feature. The problem is that it eats up battery life, so if you're out in the field without access to batteries or chargers, you may want to min-imize the use of this feature. One way to do so is by the use of a tripod, which is a good idea for any situation in which you can use one. There is nothing like a good, solid tri-pod for contributing to strong, clear photographs. If you do use a tripod, you should set this option to Off, even if battery life is not an issue, because the feature is not needed in that situation, and possibly could degrade the image slightly in some way. If turning stabilization completely off is not a viable option, you can use this menu item to switch it to Shoot Only, which means stabilization will be applied only when the shutter is pressed. The final option is Panning, in which you are using a hand-held camera to track objects moving horizontally, such as horses or runners, and you want to counteract ver-tical motion but not the horizontal motion.

Converter

This menu option is for use when you have attached the Canon TC-58D Tele-converter add-on lens to the camera. It tells the optical image stabilization system to adjust its correction for the tele-converter's magnification. When that 1.4X telephoto accessory lens is attached, you should set this menu option to indicate that fact. Otherwise, leave it set to its default setting of None. If you have set the Image Stabilization setting to None, you do not need to change the Converter menu setting, even if the converter is attached, as there is no IS to adjust.

Date Stamp (PowerShot G11 Only)

When you turn this menu option on (by setting it to Date or Date and Time, as opposed to Off), the PowerShot G11 will display the date (or date and time) in the lower-right corner of each image taken while the option is activated. The word "Date" will be shown in the lower-right corner as you are shooting to remind you that this function is set. You need to be sure you want to do this before you set the function, because the information is permanently embedded in the image, and cannot be removed unless you crop it out of the picture or otherwise alter the image. This option is not available on the PowerShot G10, although you can add the date when printing hard copies using the DPOF function.

Record RAW + Large (JPEG)

You can elect to store only JPEG versions of the images you shoot, about 5MB each at the Large Superfine resolution setting (available with the G10 only) or less than half that at Fine (with the G11). Or, you can save your photos as uncompressed, loss-free RAW files, which consume much more space on your memory card (about 16MB on the G10 and 9MB on the G11). You can also store both at once as you shoot. Many photographers elect to save *both* JPEG and a RAW file, so they'll have a JPEG version that might be usable as is, as well as the original "digital negative" RAW file in case they want to do some processing of the image later. You'll end up with two different versions of the same file: one with a .JPG extension, and one with the .CR2 extension that signifies a Canon RAW file.

If you want to enjoy this double-image storage feature, set this feature to On in the Shooting menu (see Figure 4.10). Then, when you select RAW from the FUNC. menu for your quality setting, the camera will automatically store a Large JPEG file as well. If you turn this feature off, you'll be able to shoot RAW only.

In my case, I shoot virtually everything at RAW+L. Most of the time, I'm not concerned about filling up my memory cards, as I usually have a minimum of three 8GB or 16GB memory cards with me. If I know I may fill up all those cards, I have a tiny battery-operated personal storage device that can copy an 8GB card in about 15 minutes. When shooting sports I'll shift to JPEG FINE (with no RAW file) to squeeze a little extra speed

Figure 4.10
Select Record
RAW+L to
maximize your
options for
post-processing
and image use.

out of my G10/G11's Continuous Shooting mode, and to reduce the need to wade through eight-photo bursts taken in RAW format. On my last trip to Europe, I took only RAW photos (rather than shooting both RAW and JPEG), to fit more images onto my 60GB personal storage device, as I planned on doing at least some post-processing on many of the images for a travel book I was working on.

Auto Category (PowerShot G10 Only)

On the PowerShot G11, still images are automatically placed into categories by the camera according to various criteria, including what SCN mode they were shot in, whether faces were detected, and the like. On the G10, you have the option of turning this automatic categorizing function on or off. Use this menu item to do so. I'll discuss categories further in my explanation of the items on the Playback menu.

Set Shortcut Button

This menu option lets you set the Shortcut button, at the upper left of the camera's back, to carry out one function that you want to be able to activate quickly, without going through menu options. When you choose this item on the Shooting menu, you are presented with a screen showing the possible selections. On the PowerShot G10 there are nine choices: Neutral Density Filter; White Balance; Custom White Balance

1; Custom White Balance 2; Red-eye Correction; Converter; i-Contrast; AF Lock; and Display Off. On the PowerShot G11, there are ten choices, including all the above entries and Servo AF. Or, if you want, you can just leave the Shortcut button with no setting. There's no reason not to give it some setting, though, so go ahead and pick whichever of the functions you would like to have at the touch of a finger. You can easily change it later.

Save Settings

This is a very useful, well designed function. When you choose Save Settings from the Shooting menu, you are presented with a very simple, but powerful pair of options— you can save your current settings to one of two locations in the camera, either C1 or C2 (see Figure 4.11). If you look at the mode dial on top of the camera, you will see those two settings, right along with Program, Shutter Priority, Aperture Priority, and the rest. So, in effect, you can design your own two custom Shooting modes through this very simple option. When you choose to save your current settings to either of these slots, here is what is saved: your Shooting mode (P, Tv, Av, or M); all of the items that you have set for that mode, such as shutter speed, aperture, exposure compensation, and the like; all of the items you have set through the Shooting menu; the zoom position of the lens; the manual focus position; and the inclusion of any items in the My Menu settings. You can reset either the C1 or the C2 slot to the default settings by choosing Reset

Figure 4.11
Use the Save Settings option on the Shooting menu to save a set of your favorite shooting settings to the C1 or C2 location on the mode dial.

All from the Setup menu.. Once you are comfortable with the camera's settings, you may well find some good uses for this capability. Many cameras will let you save some settings in this way, but the G10/G11 is unusually flexible in this area, and you may find it very helpful to be able to twirl the mode dial slightly and instantly have the camera set up with your favorite settings, including the amount of zoom.

Playback Menu Options

The Playback menu is where you select options related to the display, review, transfer, and printing of the photos you've taken (see Figure 4.12). The choices you'll find are:

- Slideshow
- Erase
- Protect
- Rotate
- My Category
- i-Contrast
- Red-Eye Correction
- Trimming

- Resize
- My Colors
- Scroll Display
- Resume
- Transition
- Sound Recorder (PowerShot G10 only)
- Transfer Order (PowerShot G10 only)

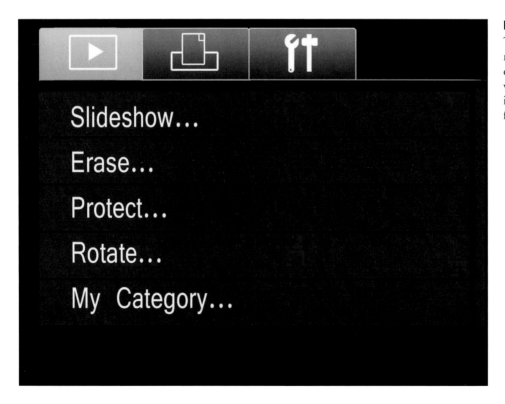

Figure 4.12
The Playback menu includes options for viewing, printing, and transferring images.

Slideshow

The Slideshow menu option is a convenient way to review images one after another, without the need to manually switch between them. To activate this feature, just choose Slideshow from the Playback menu. During playback, you can press the FUNC./SET button to pause and then restart the "slideshow" (in case you want to examine an image more closely). You also can use the left and right cross keys or the control dial during playback to move the show along. You hold down a cross key to fast forward through the images. For example, you might want to review a set of images to judge the exposure of the group of pictures. It's important to note that the Slideshow option does not include any mechanism for selecting what images to include in the show. To make that selection, you need to use the My Category option, discussed later in this section. To set up your slide show, follow these steps:

1. **Begin set up.** Choose Slideshow from the Playback menu, pressing FUNC./SET to display the screen shown in Figures 4.13 (G10) and 4.14 (G11).

2. **Choose Repeat options, Play Time, and Effect.** With the G11, next navigate to highlight Repeat and select On or Off, to determine whether the show will repeat after it ends. Move down to Play Time and select a time for each image to display, from 3 to 10, or 15 or 30 seconds. Then move to Effect, and select one of the transition effects listed. With the G10, the process is slightly different; you select Effect on the first screen, then highlight Set Up, press the FUNC./SET button, and select Repeat and Play Time options on the next screen that appears. Then G10 users should press the Menu button to get back to the first screen.

Figure 4.13 Set up your slideshow using this screen for the G10.

Figure 4.14 The G11's setup screen combines all the functions on a single page.

3. **Start the show.** Highlight Start and press FUNC./SET to begin your show. (If you'd rather cancel the show you've just set up, press Menu instead.)

4. **Use show options during display.** Press FUNC./SET to pause/restart; left and right cross keys or control dial to speed through the images; and Menu to stop the show.

Erase

As I discussed earlier, one way to delete images from the memory card in the camera is to press the AF Frame/Trash button, and then confirm the operation using the navigation keys and the FUNC./SET key. If you need to erase more than just one or two images at a time, though, you're probably better off using the Erase option on the Playback menu. Choose this menu entry on the PowerShot G11, and you'll be given three choices: Select, Select Range, and All Images (see Figure 4.15).

■ **Select.** The first option displays the most recent image. Press the left/right cross keys or use the control dial to navigate through the images, and mark or unmark various images for deletion using the FUNC./SET key (a check mark will appear in a box in the upper-left corner when an image is marked for deletion). If you try to mark a protected image for deletion, a warning Protected appears on the screen.

Figure 4.15
The Playback menu's Erase menu item on the PowerShot G11 gives you options for what images to erase.

- **Range.** To speed things up, you can select a range of images rather than marking them individually. After choosing the Select Range option, navigate to the first image in the range to be deleted, and select it with the FUNC./SET key. Then navigate to the last picture in the range (which must be higher numbered than the first one), and press FUNC./SET again.

- **All Images.** If you're ready to part with all images on your memory card, choose the All Images option and confirm with the FUNC./SET key when prompted by the menu system. This choice removes all the pictures on the card, except for those you've marked with the Protect command, and does not reformat the memory card. If you have categorized your images using the My Category option (described later), you can display images in a particular category, and use the All Images option to erase just the images from that category.

When finished marking pictures, press the Menu button, and you'll see a screen that says Erase? with two options, Stop and OK. Highlight OK, then press the Set button to erase the images, or select Cancel and press the Set button to return to the selection screen. Press the Menu button to leave your selections marked and return to the display of marked images.

With the PowerShot G10, the Erase function works in a similar way, except that you have a few more options for selecting the images to erase: by date, by category, and by folder.

Protect

If you want to keep an image from being accidentally erased (either with the Erase button or by using the Erase menu option that we just discussed), you can mark that image for protection. To protect one or more images, enter Playback mode, press the Menu button, and choose Protect. Then either select individual images or a range of images, in the same way as with the Erase procedure described above. A key icon will appear on each image when it is marked as protected, and when that image is reviewed later. To remove protection, repeat the process and use the FUNC./SET key to remove the protection from individual images or a range of images. You can also protect all images on the card, using the All Images selection. In addition, if you have used the My Category function to place images in categories, you can display images from a given category, and then use the All Images selection to protect all images in that category. Image protection will not save your images from removal when the card is reformatted.

Rotate

Both the PowerShot G10 and G11 will automatically rotate images that you take while holding the camera in the vertical position, so they will display vertically on the horizontal screen during playback. You can rotate the camera to the vertical position, and the camera will rotate the image to suit, so it's always shown in its correct orientation. (You can't change this behavior on the G11; on the G10, you can choose to disable it with the Auto Rotate option on the Setup menu.) On both camera models, you can also manually rotate an image during playback using this menu selection. Select Rotate from the Playback menu, use the left/right cross keys to page through the available images on your memory card until the one you want to rotate appears, then press FUNC./SET. The image will appear on the screen rotated 90 degrees, as shown in Figure 4.16. Press FUNC./SET again, and the image will be rotated another 90 degrees. You can keep rotating it until you achieve the desired orientation, including returning it to its original position.

When rotating an image, viewing a vertical image in correct orientation when holding the camera horizontally means that the longest dimension of the image is shown using the shortest dimension of the LCD, so the picture is reduced in size.

Figure 4.16
An image can be manually rotated in 90-degree increments using the Rotate function on the Playback menu.

My Category

This menu option is quite powerful and useful. It permits you to organize your images in the camera into several categories that are predefined for you. Choose My Category from the Playback menu and press the FUNC./SET button. Press the up/down cross keys or turn the control dial to choose a category and then press the FUNC./SET to select.

Once this has been done, you can then perform any of the following operations on all the images in a given category at once: viewing slideshows; protecting images; erasing images; and choosing images for printing directly to a printer. You can also view your images by category, using the filtered playback procedure with the Metering mode/Jump button. The PowerShot G10/11 automatically places some images into one of three categories (People, Scenery, or Events) when they are shot, basing its decisions on various factors, such as whether a face was detected, whether a scenic setting such as Sunset or Fireworks was used, and the like. In addition, you can assign (or unassign) images to any of those categories, or to any of four other categories: Categories 1, 2, and 3, and To Do. You can assign a given image to multiple categories at the same time, if you wish. Here again, as with the Erase and Protect functions discussed above, you can perform the category assignments by selecting images individually, or by selecting a range of images.

i-Contrast

We have already seen this option earlier, in our tour of the Shooting menu options. This is exactly the same procedure we talked about earlier; it gives you an opportunity to let the camera bring out additional detail in an image by tweaking the contrast. Select this option from the Playback menu, then choose the image to be adjusted. You then need to decide whether to select Auto and let the camera make the adjustment, or choose a Low, Medium, or High amount of adjustment, and then press FUNC./SET to apply the desired correction. The changed image will be saved as a new file, and the original image will still be present on the memory card. Note that you cannot make this adjustment to a RAW image. (You wouldn't need to, because RAW images are intended to be subjected to considerable post-processing through software in any event.)

Red-Eye Correction

Here is another old friend from the Shooting menu. This option lets you apply digital correction to an image of a person with the vampire stare. Just as with its counterpart on the other menu system, this procedure does not come with a guarantee of success, or even of improvement of the image, but it is worth a try. When the correction has been applied, you have the choice of saving the new version to a new file, or overwriting the original image with the altered one. As with i-Contrast, this procedure cannot be performed on a RAW image. On the G11, the process is automatic; the camera will correct red-eye if it detects it. On the G10, if the camera does not detect red-eye, you have the option of adding a frame at the area of the image that you believe needs correction, and moving it into place with the cross keys.

Trimming

This is another one of the procedures available through the G10/G11's menu system that gives you the ability to alter the images you have already taken. In this case, you can crop an image to remove unwanted parts or to emphasize certain subjects by altering the composition. Since I use software such as Adobe Photoshop, Photoshop Elements, or similar programs to perform post-processing actions like cropping, I tend to view features of this sort as not having that much value. However, there could be situations in which a photographer out in the field needs to create a slideshow quickly, without access to a computer. In such a case, this Trimming function could be a lifesaver. To use it, highlight this option on the Playback menu, then use the left/right cross keys to select the image to be trimmed. Then, follow the prompts given by the camera to change the size and location of the trimming frame. This can be done using the zoom lever, the four cross keys, the DISP. button, and the control dial. (Use that dial to switch between gray frames, which the camera will display to indicate faces in the image. Those frames can be used for trimming.) Once you have the trimming frame set the way you want it, press FUNC./SET to make the crop. The trimmed image will be saved as a new image file. This function cannot be performed on RAW images or on Small or Widescreen images.

Resize

This procedure lets you change the image size of a picture that is already saved on the camera's memory card. Note that "resize" is used here in a very specific sense; you can't really change the apparent size of the image; all you can do is cause the camera to save a new copy of the original image with a smaller file size. Here again, this is something I ordinarily would do using a computer, but there probably are situations in which it could be useful to do this in-camera. After you've selected this option from the Playback menu, navigate to the image in question, then follow the camera's prompts to select the new size, and press FUNC./SET to save the new, smaller file. As with the Trimming function, this procedure cannot be used with RAW, Small, or Widescreen images.

My Colors

This operation allows you to perform another sort of post-processing in the camera on your saved images by applying one of the camera's several built-in color settings to alter the general appearance of the picture. These are the same color settings you can apply when taking pictures using the FUNC. menu. In this case, you select My Colors from the Playback menu, and then use the left/right cross keys or the control dial to highlight the image to be changed, then press the FUNC./SET button to select it. You can then use the left/right cross keys or the control dial to select whichever of the available color settings you want to apply: Vivid; Neutral; Sepia; Black and White; Positive Film; Lighter Skin Tone; Darker Skin Tone; Vivid Blue; Vivid Green; and Vivid Red. With these PowerShot models, this transformation cannot be done with RAW images. This option is discussed in more detail in the section describing the features of the FUNC. menu.

Scroll Display (PowerShot G11 Menu Only)

This menu option lets you turn on and off the Scroll Display feature. If this feature is enabled (as it is by default), then, when the camera is in Playback mode, if you spin the control dial on the back of the camera rapidly enough, the images will display in a horizontal stream, in which you can see the images before and after the current one as they scroll by (see Figure 4.17). In addition, the camera displays the date of the image, with arrows beside the date to let you quickly change it using the up and down cross keys, thereby switching the display to select images from that date. A gray "thermometer"

Figure 4.17
When the Scroll Display feature is enabled, turning the control dial causes the images to display in a continuous stream. This illustration shows the feature on the PowerShot G11.

scroll bar appears below the image to know where you are in the stack. You might want to disable this feature if you would find it distracting to have the display suddenly switch from a conventional progression through your images to a more rapid scrolling with date selection that you don't need. In addition, the scrolling display shows the images at a slightly reduced size in order to accommodate the multiple pictures and the date selection area, so you might want to disable the feature in order to keep the images displayed at their normal sizes. The PowerShot G10 does not have a menu option to control this function, although the G10 does have the scrolling function.

Resume

This menu option is quite simple and straightforward. Its only purpose is to give you the option of which image will be displayed on the camera's screen when you go into Playback mode—either the last image you had viewed previously or the last image that was shot. Select one of these ("Last seen" or "Last shot"), and you're done with this option.

Transition

Use this selection on the Playback menu to choose from the three possible effects that are available to mark the transition from one image to the next when you are viewing single images on the camera's display. On the G11, those three effects are Fade, Scroll, and Slide. Or, you can choose Off, and the images will appear with simple "cuts" from one to the next, with no transitions between them. On the G10, the choices are not given names, but their functions are equivalent to None, Fade, and Slide.

Sound Recorder (PowerShot G10 Only)

On the PowerShot G10, as on the G11, you can record brief audio memos to attach to images in Playback mode. With the G10, though, you can go one step further and record audio files lasting up to two hours that are not attached to any image. You get access to this function through this menu option, which displays the standard recording and playback controls. Your recorded memos will be listed here for playback when you want to listen to them again. The sound recording capability is very basic, but if you're out in the field shooting pictures when the idea for the Great American Novel strikes you, you'll be able to get two hours' worth of the idea down on your memory card.

Transfer Order (PowerShot G10 Only)

This menu option lets you set which images will be transferred from the camera to a computer through a direct connection.

Print Menu Options

When the PowerShot G10/G11 is set to Playback mode, there are three menus displayed at the top of the menu screen. We've already talked about one of them—Playback—and will move quickly on to the Setup menu next. The third menu, likely to be the least-used of the three, is the Print menu, tucked between the Playback and Setup menus in Playback mode (and not visible at all when you're using Shooting mode).

The options in this menu are of use only when you have connected the camera directly to a PictBridge-compatible printer and are preparing to send images straight from the camera to the printer. I'm not going to spend a lot of time discussing these menu options, because they're essentially self-explanatory. Your choices are as follows:

- **Print.** Use this choice to begin printing once you have selected the images using the other entries in the Print menu.

- **Select Images & Qty.** This entry allows you to scroll through the images on your memory card using the left/right cross keys. Press the FUNC./SET button to activate the up/down cross keys and specify the number of prints for each image. (Leave the quantity at zero if you don't want to make any prints of a given photo.) Press the Menu button when you've finished to return to the Print menu.

- **Select Range.** As with the Erase command, to speed things up, you can select a range of images rather than marking them individually. After choosing the Select Range option, navigate to the first image in the range to be printed, and select it with the FUNC./SET key. Then navigate to the last picture in the range (which must be higher-numbered than the first one), and press FUNC./SET again.

- **Select All Images.** Use this to mark all the images on your card.

- **Clear All Selections.** This entry allows you to unmark all images and start your selection process over again.

- **Print Settings.** Choose whether to print thumbnail images, using the Index option, or full-size images, using the Standard option, and decide whether to include the dates and file numbers with the images.

To print in PictBridge mode:

1. **Connect camera.** First link the camera to the printer, using the mini-USB cable that comes with the camera. Plug it into the bottom connector inside the door on the right side of the camera, then connect it to the printer.

2. **Choose images to print.** Go into the Print menu, and you will find options for selecting the images to print, either by marking them individually using the FUNC./SET button or by selecting a range, in the same way as with the Erase and Protect functions discussed earlier.

3. **Specify print format.** When you have the images selected, choose Print Settings and specify how you want the images printed.

4. **Print selected images.** When all your choices are made, select Print, and sit back while the printer does its work.

Setup Menu Options

The Setup menu (shown in Figure 4.18 as it's accessed while in Shooting mode, where its tab is located in the middle) provides the opportunity to make adjustments on how your camera *behaves* during your shooting session, as differentiated from the Shooting menu (discussed later in this chapter), which adjusts how the pictures are actually taken, and the Playback menu, which adjusts how images are viewed. Your choices on the Setup menu include:

- Mute
- Volume
- Sound Options (PowerShot G11 only)
- Hints & Tips (PowerShot G11 only)
- LCD Brightness
- Start-up Image (PowerShot G11 only)
- Format
- File Numbering
- Create Folder
- Auto Rotate (PowerShot G10 only)
- Lens Retract
- Power Saving
- Time Zone
- Clock Display (PowerShot G10 only)
- Date/Time
- Distance Units
- Video System
- Language
- Reset All

Figure 4.18
The Setup menu gives you access to many options for controlling the camera's operations.

Mute

This first option on the Setup menu is a simple on-off selection—you can set the camera either to mute all electronic sounds, or to let them be heard. Obviously, this option can be of use if you're at a school play or other event where it's best to keep your auditory footprint to a minimum. If you set Mute to On, then the camera will not emit an electronic sound when the shutter is released, and there won't be any beeps when you move from one image to another on the screen or press a navigation key. This is not to say the camera will be so silent that you could sneak through a secret laboratory and photograph the plans of the next doomsday device without being detected; the camera still will emit some clicks and other sounds from its purely mechanical operations. But you will cut down on the general cacophony of electronic chatter.

Volume

On the PowerShot G11, this option allows you to control the volume of four operational sounds the camera makes. This menu item will be grayed out and unavailable if you have turned the Mute feature on. If Mute is off, then you can choose to set the volume from level 1 to 5 in each of four categories: the camera's Start-up sound; its

Operation sounds (essentially, beeps as you press buttons); Self-timer countdown sound; and Shutter sound. On the G10, this option also lets you control the volume of movie sounds, sound memos, and sound recorder recordings.

Sound Options (PowerShot G11 Only)

Now that we have covered how to mute the camera's operational sounds and how to adjust their volume, here is the menu option on the PowerShot G11 that lets you select what sounds are assigned to each of the four categories we discussed in connection with the Volume setting. I don't know that there's a very good way to describe these sounds in words; you just have to sample each one and decide which type of high-tech beepy noise you like the best for each category. This menu option is not available on the G10, which instead uses its My Camera menu options to set start-up images and the various operational sounds.

Hints & Tips (PowerShot G11 Only)

With this setting on the PowerShot G11, turned on by default, as you scroll through the lines of a menu, including the FUNC. menu, a line or two of explanation shows up at the bottom of the LCD screen to give a little extra information about the item that is highlighted (see Figure 4.19 for an example). I personally find this feature quite

Figure 4.19
The Hints & Tips feature on the PowerShot G11 provides information about each menu item.

useful. One nice point is that this feature is somewhat context sensitive. So, for example, if you have Mute set to Off, and highlight the Mute line, the hint at the bottom of the screen will say: "Turns on camera sounds." If you have Mute set to On, the hint line will say: "Turns off camera sounds." The reason to turn this feature off would be to regain one line of screen real estate; in other words, if Hints & Tips is turned off, one more line of the menu has room to display, so you don't have to scroll quite as much to get through the menus. This option is not available for the G10, which does not have the Hints & Tips feature.

LCD Brightness

This menu option lets you adjust the brightness of the LCD display screen within a five-point range on the G11 (and within a 14-point range on the G10). This setting will remain in effect even after the camera is turned off and then on again. An alternative way to adjust the brightness is to hold down the DISP. button for one second or more. That procedure will increase the screen's brightness to its maximum, unless it has already been set that high. Pressing and holding the DISP. button one more time will return the brightness to what it was before.

Start-up Image (PowerShot G11 Only)

With this setting on the PowerShot G11, you can select from three preset start-up screen images supplied by Canon, or you can choose to have no start-up image. The screens show the Canon logo or the PowerShot G11 logo. On the G10, this setting is on the camera's separate My Camera menu, along with settings for operational sounds.

Format

Use this item to erase everything on your memory card and set up a fresh file system ready for use. When you select Format, you'll see a display like Figure 4.20, showing the capacity of the card, how much of that space is currently in use, and two choices at the bottom of the screen to Cancel or OK (proceed with the format). A bar appears on the screen to show the progress of the formatting step. You also are presented with the option to perform a Low Level format, which is a slower, but more thorough reformatting that can help restore a memory card that has picked up some bad sectors that aren't locked out by the normal Format step.

Figure 4.20
You must con-
firm the format
step before the
camera will
erase a memory
card.

File Numbering

The PowerShot G10/G11 will automatically apply a file number to each picture you take, using consecutive numbering for all your photos over a long period of time, span-ning many different memory cards, starting over from scratch when you insert a new card, or when you manually reset the numbers. Numbers are applied from 0001 to 9999, at which time the camera creates a new folder on the card (100, 101, 102, and so forth), so you can have 0001 to 9999 in folder 100, then numbering will start over in folder 101. A given folder can hold only 2000 images, but, as discussed below, the numbering of images in a folder can still go as high as 9999.

The camera keeps track of the last number used in its internal memory. That can lead to a few quirks you should be aware of. For example, if you insert a memory card that had been used with a different camera, the G10/G11 may start numbering with the next number after the highest number used by the previous camera. (I once had a brand new camera start numbering files in the 8000 range.) I'll explain how this can happen next.

On the surface, the numbering system seems simple enough: In the menu, you can choose Continuous or Automatic Reset. Here is how each works:

- **Continuous.** If you're using a blank/reformatted memory card, the G10/G11 will apply a number that is one greater than the number stored in the camera's internal memory. If the card is not blank and contains images, then the next number will be one greater than the highest number on the card *or* in internal memory. (In other words, if you want to use continuous file numbering consistently, you must always use a card that is blank or freshly formatted.) Here are some examples.

  - You've taken 4,235 shots with the camera, and you insert a blank/reformatted memory card. The next number assigned will be 4236, based on the value stored in internal memory.

  - You've taken 4,235 shots with the camera, and you insert a memory card with a picture numbered 2728. The next picture will be numbered 4236.

  - You've taken 4,235 shots with the camera, and you insert a memory card with a picture numbered 8281. The next picture will be numbered 8282, and that value will be stored in the camera's menu as the "high" shot number (and will be applied when you next insert a blank card).

- **Automatic Reset.** If you're using a blank/reformatted memory card, the next photo taken will be numbered 0001. If you use a card that is not blank, the next number will be one greater than the highest number found on the memory card. Each time you insert a memory card, the next number will either be 0001, or one higher than the highest already on the card.

Create Folder

By default, the PowerShot G10/G11 creates new folders each month. With this option in the Setup menu, you can change this so the camera creates a new folder for each new shooting date. On the G11, just change the setting for this menu item from Monthly to Daily to accomplish this result. On the G10, there are additional options: the automatic folder creation can be set to Monthly, Daily, or any individual day of the week (Monday, Tuesday, and the rest).

Auto Rotate (PowerShot G10 Only)

This function is available only on the PowerShot G10. If you set it to On, then the camera will sense when an image was taken with the camera held vertically, and will display that image in a smaller format, so it can be oriented vertically within the standard horizontal screen of the camera. On the G11, the camera always performs this automatic rotation, so when you rotate the camera vertically, a vertically oriented image fills the screen; the only way to override it on that camera is to rotate the image manually using the Rotate function available in the Playback menu.

Lens Retract

By default, when you're in Shooting mode and you then switch to Playback mode, the camera's lens retracts back into its housing about one minute after you press the Playback button, because it appears that you won't be needing the lens for a while, and it's a good idea for it to be pulled back away from sources of possible scratches or damage. You can change this setting to zero seconds, in which case the lens will retract almost immediately after you push the Playback button while the lens is out. If you're likely to go back and forth between Shooting and Playback modes, I suggest sticking with the normal one minute wait time, to avoid overstraining the motor with the motions of a frantic turtle. This setting does not affect lens retraction when the camera is turned off while in Shooting mode.

Power Saving

This entry in the Setup menu allows you to determine whether the PowerShot G10/G11 powers itself off after not being used for about three minutes in Shooting mode, and after about five minutes in Playback mode. Your only options here are to turn the feature on or off; you don't get to select how long the camera waits before powering down (see Figure 4.21). If you leave this feature turned on, the camera will turn itself completely off after the three (or five) minutes, and you then will have to press the power

Figure 4.21
The Power Saving menu option controls whether the camera powers off after a few minutes and how soon the display goes dark when not in use.

button to turn it back on. If you leave this feature off, you have to be careful to turn the camera off when you're done with it, or you'll drain the battery before you know it.

This menu item also has a second option that involves turning off just the display screen after a certain amount of time. In this case, you do get to select the timing—you can choose to have the screen turn off automatically after 10, 20, or 30 seconds, or 1, 2, or 3 minutes. The screen power-off feature is available even if the general power-saving feature is turned off.

SAVING POWER WITH THE POWERSHOT G10 AND G11

There are three settings and several techniques you can use to help you stretch the longevity of your G10/G11's battery. The first setting is the Review option described earlier in this chapter under the Shooting menu. The big 2.8- or 3-inch LCD uses a lot of juice, so reducing the amount of time it is used (either for automatic review or for manually playing back your images) can boost the effectiveness of your battery. Power Saving turns off the camera and/or the LCD screen after defined intervals, depending on your settings. The third setting is the LCD Brightness adjustment described below. If you're willing to shade the LCD with your hand, you can often get away with lower brightness settings outdoors, which will further increase the useful life of your battery. The techniques? Use the internal flash as little as possible; no flash at all or fill flash use less power than a full blast. Turn off image stabilization if you're using a tripod or if you just feel you don't need it. When transferring pictures from your G10/G11 to your computer, use a card reader instead of the USB cable. Linking your camera to your computer and transferring images using the cable takes longer and uses a lot more power.

Time Zone

Using this entry in the Setup menu, you can set your home time zone. Then, when you travel to another time zone, you can set the camera to a travel time zone, so the images will be recorded with the correct local time. To set your Home Time Zone, follow the camera's prompts, and, using the FUNC./SET button and the left/right cross keys, move the yellow highlight over the world map to select your home base. To set the destination time zone for a trip, follow a similar procedure, highlighting the Home symbol instead of the airplane symbol. Then, when you are leaving on your trip, go into this menu option and highlight the airplane symbol, and it will then appear on the Setup menu's Time Zone line, indicating that the camera will be using the destination time zone until you reset it back to Home.

Clock Display (PowerShot G10 Only)

On both the PowerShot G10 and G11, if you hold down the FUNC./SET key for more than one second while in Shooting or Playback mode, you will trigger a display in which the screen shows a high-tech digital clock with spinning blocks showing the time down to the second. By default, this display lasts for 5 seconds or until you press a button. Using this menu item, you can change the default time between 1 second and 1 minute, or turn it completely off. The G11 does not have the option to change the default display time. On both models, you can change the background color of the clock with the left/right cross keys or the control dial.

Date/Time

Use this option to set the date and time, which will be embedded in the image file along with exposure information and other data. I showed you how to do this in Chapter 1. See Figure 1.10 if you need a refresher.

Distance Units

Use this option to select feet and inches or meters and centimeters, according to your preference. The camera will then display distances in your preferred system of notation.

Video System

This setting controls the output of the G10/G11 through the supplied AV cable when you're displaying images on an external monitor. You can select either NTSC, used in the United States, Canada, Mexico, many Central, South American, and Caribbean countries, much of Asia, and other countries; or PAL, which is used in the UK, much of Europe, Africa, India, China, and parts of the Middle East.

Language

Choose from 25 languages for menu display, rotating the control dial or using the cross keys until the language you want to select is highlighted. Press the Set button to activate. Your choices include English, German, French, Dutch, Danish, Portuguese, Finnish, Italian, Ukrainian, Norwegian, Swedish, Spanish, Greek, Russian, Polish, Czech, Magyar, Romanian, Turkish, Arabic, Thai, Simplified Chinese, Traditional Chinese, Korean, and Japanese.

If you accidentally set a language you don't read and find yourself with incomprehensible menus, don't panic. On the G10, just choose the fourth option from the bottom of the Setup menu (second from the bottom on the G11), and select the idioma, sprache, langue, or kieli of your choice.

VIEWING ON A TELEVISION

Canon makes it quite easy to view your images on a standard television screen on the PowerShot G10 and G11, and, for the G11 only, not much more difficult on a high-definition television (HDTV). (You have to buy a separate cable for HDTV.) For regular TV, just open the port cover on the right side of the camera, plug the cable supplied with the camera into the socket labeled AV Out, and connect the other end to the yellow VIDEO RCA composite jack on your television or monitor.

For HDTV display on the G11, purchase the optional HDMI Cable HTC-100 and connect it to the HDMI OUT terminal above the standard video terminal on the right side of the camera. Connect the other end to an HDMI input port on your television or monitor (my 42-inch HDTV has three of them; my 26-inch monitor has just two). Then turn on the camera and press the Playback button. The image will appear on the external TV/HDTV/monitor and will not be displayed on the camera's LCD. HDTV systems automatically show your images at the appropriate resolution for that set.

If you plug in the HD cable, be aware that you cannot also plug in the Remote cable, which goes into an adjacent port; trying to plug them both in at the same time could result in damage to the camera or the cables.

Reset All

This is a very handy function to have available if you've been fooling around with the camera's settings for hours and don't want to have to retrace all your steps to get things back to normal. Just go into the Setup menu and select this option; your only choices are to confirm the reset or cancel. This action will put most settings back to their defaults, but note that there are certain settings that will not be reset. These include date and time; language; video system; and a few others.

My Menu

The Canon PowerShot G10/G11 has a great feature that allows you to define your own menu, with just the items listed that you want. You can set up My Menu to include just the items you want, and jump to those items quickly by pressing the Menu button. To create your own My Menu set of options, you just have to select the menu items you want to include. To do so, follow these steps:

1. Press the Menu button and use the left/right cross keys or the zoom lever to highlight the My Menu tab, marked by a star. When you first begin, the personalized menu will be empty except for the My Menu Settings entry. Highlight this line and press the FUNC./SET button to select it. You'll then see a screen like the one shown in Figure 4.22.

Figure 4.22
The My Menu settings screen gives you access to the ability to select various menu items to include on your personalized My Menu list.

Figure 4.23
A typical set of options added to the My Menu list might include items such as those shown here.

2. Use the up/down cross keys to highlight Select Items, then press the FUNC./SET button.

3. Use the up/down cross keys to scroll down through the continuous list of all menu entries that can be selected to find one you would like to add. Press FUNC./SET.

4. Confirm your choice by selecting OK in the next screen and pressing FUNC./SET again.

5. Continue to select up to five of the listed menu entries for your My Menu set.

6. When you're finished, press the Menu button twice to return to the My Menu screen to see your customized menu, which might look like Figure 4.23.

In addition to selecting menu items, you can perform other functions at the My Menu Settings screen:

■ **Changing the Order.** Choose Sort to reorder the items in My Menu. Select the menu item to be moved and press the Set button. Press the up/down cross keys to move the item up and down within the menu list. When you've placed it where you'd like it, press the FUNC./SET button to lock in your selection, then press the Menu button to return to the previous screen.

■ **Set Default View.** Ordinarily, when you press the Menu button, the G10/G11 displays the menu system from the top, with the Shooting menu highlighted. However, if you enable the Set Default View option, pressing the Menu button will *always* display My Menu first. You are free to switch to another menu tab if you like, but the next time you press the Menu button, My Menu will come up again. Use this option if you work with My Menu a great deal and make settings with other menu items less frequently.

My Camera (G10 Only)

The PowerShot G10 has one additional minor-league menu that you're likely to play with when you first get the camera, and then forget about. The G11 buries these items in the Setup menu. In the G10, it's called the My Camera Menu, and is located on a tab that's next-to-last when you press the Menu button in Shooting mode, and in the very last position when you access the menus from Playback mode. It has six choices that let you select from among various canned themes, images, icons, and sounds so you can tailor your camera to your preference. The themes are about as necessary as the ability to add Black Sabbath ring tones to your cell phone (and just as much fun). These will appeal to the teenager in you:

■ **Theme.** Select from three graphics modes for your LCD. Or, if you're a no-nonsense person, choose None.

■ **Start-up Image.** This is the image you first see when the camera is powered up.

- **Start-up Sound.** You can select the sound played when your G10 comes to life. All sound options play when you scroll over them with the left/right cross keys.

- **Operation Sound.** Specifies a sound played when any button other than the shutter release is pressed.

- **Self-timer Sound.** Three sounds of varying urgency can be played while your self-timer counts down.

- **Shutter Sound.** The PowerShot has an electronic shutter, but if you'd rather hear a click, you can select an appropriate noise here.

FUNC. Menu

We have now discussed all of the "official" menus that are present in the PowerShot G10/G11: Shooting, Playback, Setup, Printing, and My Menu. Those are the only menus in the camera that look and act like traditional menus—that is, menus that take up the whole screen and present you with lines of items that you scroll through to choose various options. But we're not done yet with the menu system of this camera. The G10/G11 comes equipped with another, different sort of menu system, used only to select shooting options, which Canon calls the FUNC. menu, because it is invoked with a press of the FUNC./SET key.

The FUNC. menu is very handy and convenient to use once you get the hang of it, but it may take a little practice to get a feel for it. Here is how it works. When you're in Shooting mode, just Press the FUNC./SET key in firmly, and at the left and bottom of the LCD screen you will see two lines of symbols. The vertical list on the left, reading from top to bottom, represents the categories of settings that you can change with this system: White Balance; My Colors; Bracketing; Flash Control; Neutral Density Filter; Drive Mode (G11 only; remember that the G10 assigns Drive mode functions to the down cross key); and Image Size and Quality. These categories include some of the most important settings you can make. Let's go through them all in order.

White Balance

When you first press the FUNC./SET button to get access to the FUNC. menu, the AWB symbol will be highlighted at the top of the vertical list and at the left of the horizontal list, assuming you have not previously changed the White Balance setting (and assuming you're not in Auto mode, in which you won't be able to change the white balance setting) (see Figure 4.24). AWB stands for Automatic White Balance. In many cases, you can leave this setting alone and let the G10/G11 assess the lighting situation and set the white balance for you. If you would prefer to set the white balance to one of the predefined settings, use the right cross key or the control dial to scroll through

Figure 4.24
The FUNC. menu is called up by a press of the FUNC./ SET key. Here, the white balance item is set to AWB, for Automatic White Balance.

the list at the bottom of the screen until you find the one you want, then press FUNC./SET to select it, and the lists will disappear, leaving your setting in place. The choices are: Automatic White Balance; Daylight; Cloudy; Tungsten; Fluorescent; Fluorescent H; Flash; Underwater; and Custom 1 and 2. If you select Custom 1 or 2, you need to follow the instructions below to establish a value for that setting. That value will be retained permanently for that Custom slot until you go back and reset the value to something else.

To use the Custom settings to set the white balance to an appropriate color temperature under the current ambient lighting conditions:

1. Press the FUNC./SET key.

2. Use the up/down cross keys to highlight the top icon on the list at the left of the screen, for white balance.

3. Use the right cross key to scroll over to Custom 1 or Custom 2 on the list at the bottom of the screen.

4. Aim the camera so the screen (or viewfinder) is filled with the white (or gray) color you are using as a standard.

5. Press the DISP. key (G10) or the Menu key (G11). The camera will evaluate the correct white balance for the current lighting conditions and store that value under the Custom 1 or Custom 2 setting.

6. Set the white balance to that saved setting again whenever you need to shoot under those same lighting conditions.

On the G11 (but not the G10), you can adjust the white balance setting even further, if you want. Regardless of which setting you have used for white balance, that is, Daylight, Cloudy, Tungsten, or a Custom one, you can go on to make manual adjustments. To do so, with the current white balance setting on the screen, press the DISP. key, and you will be presented with a screen that contains a square surrounded by the letters B, G, A, and M, for Blue, Green, Amber, and Magenta (see Figure 4.25). Use the four cross keys to move the axes for these color settings higher or lower, to fine-tune your white balance setting.

Figure 4.25
On the PowerShot G11, it is possible to fine-tune any white balance setting by using the four cross keys to adjust the levels of blue, green, amber, and magenta.

My Colors

This option gives you the opportunity to exercise a bit of color-oriented creativity when you're shooting your images. Select this second option down from the top of the FUNC. menu's vertical list, and the horizontal list at the bottom of the screen will give you 11 options for altering the color cast of your images: Vivid, Neutral, Sepia, B/W (Black & White), Positive Film, Lighter Skin Tone, Darker Skin Tone, Vivid Blue, Vivid Green, Vivid Red, and Custom Color (see Figure 4.26). Or, of course, you can set this feature to Off. Most of these choices are self-explanatory; the Vivid choices emphasize the given color; Positive Film combines the effects of having all three Vivid colors together. Neutral tones down all colors. You may want to play around with these and see which ones yield results that meet your needs. Note that this feature is not available and can't be selected when shooting RAW images, because you can tweak your RAW images to produce the same effects when importing your photos into your image editor.

Although the My Colors feature is not as powerful or flexible as the Picture Styles feature introduced to the Canon EOS camera line with the Canon EOS 30D back in February, 2006, it does offer considerable benefits. Canon has set the parameters for the ten predefined selections to suit the needs of most photographers. Unlike the situation with Picture Styles, you cannot adjust the settings for those predefined selections.

Figure 4.26
The My Colors option on the FUNC. menu lets you choose from an array of adjustments to color intensity and shades. Here, the Sepia option is highlighted.

However, you can use the Custom Color option to create one brand-new selection that is all your own. If you want rich, bright colors to emulate Velvia film or the work of legendary photographer Pete Turner, you can build your own color-soaked style. If you want soft, muted colors and less sharpness to create a romantic look, you can do that, too. Perhaps you'd like a setting with extra contrast for shooting outdoors on hazy or cloudy days.

To make use of Custom Color, highlight that final option in the list of My Colors choices. (This is a good opportunity to wrap around by using the *left* cross key.) Then press the DISP. button. You will then see the word "Contrast" on the screen (see Figure 4.27). Use the left/right cross keys or the control dial to adjust the amount of contrast up or down, then use the up/down cross keys to highlight the other parameters (Contrast, Sharpness, Saturation, Red, Green, Blue, and Skin Tone, discussed next). Make your desired adjustments to each of them. When you are finished adjusting all of the parameters to your liking, press the DISP. key again and then the FUNC./SET key to exit the My Colors screen.

Figure 4.27
The My Colors option lets you adjust several parameters for each setting: contrast, sharpness, saturation, red, green, blue, and skin tone. On the screen shown here, contrast can be adjusted with the left/right cross keys.

The parameters that you can adjust with the My Colors option are as follows:

- **Contrast.** Adjust this slider to change the number of middle tones between the deepest blacks and brightest whites. Low contrast settings produce a flatter looking photo, while high contrast adjustments may improve the tonal rendition while possibly losing detail in the shadows or highlights.

- **Sharpness.** This parameter determines the apparent contrast between the outlines or edges in an image, which we perceive as image sharpness. When adjusting sharpness, remember that more is not always a good thing. A little softness is necessary to reduce or eliminate the moiré effects that can result when details in your image form a pattern that is too close to the pattern, or frequency, of the sensor itself. The default (0) level sharpening was chosen by Canon to allow most moiré interference to be safely blurred to invisibility, at the cost of a little sharpness. As you boost sharpness, moiré can become a problem, plus, you may end up with those noxious "halos" that appear around the edges of images that have been oversharpened. Use this adjustment with care.

- **Saturation.** This parameter controls the richness of the color, making, say, a red tone appear to be deeper and fuller when you increase saturation, and tend more towards lighter, pinkish hues when you decrease saturation of the reds. Boosting the saturation too much can mean that detail may be lost in one or more of the color channels, producing what is called "clipping."

- **Red.** Adjusts amount of red.

- **Green.** Adjusts amount of green.

- **Blue.** Adjusts amount of blue.

- **Skin Tone.** This adjustment has the most effect on skin tones, making them either redder or yellower.

Bracketing

Bracketing is a method for shooting several consecutive exposures using different settings, as a way of improving the odds that one of them will be exactly right, or for use in Photoshop or another application to merge images with a larger range of dark-to-bright tones. Many cameras have the ability to bracket exposures at different settings, and some cameras also can bracket other settings, such as white balance. The PowerShot G10/G11 provides bracketing for two settings: exposure and focus, through the FUNC. menu.

Navigate one icon below My Colors on the FUNC. menu and you arrive at the Bracketing option. Highlight that icon, and the list at the bottom of the screen shows three choices: Off, AEB, and Focus-BKT (see Figure 4.28). The default selection is Off.

Figure 4.28
The Bracketing
option on the
FUNC. menu
gives you access
to Auto
Exposure
Bracketing
and Focus
Bracketing.

Following are descriptions of the other two choices, each of which sets the camera up to automatically shoot a sequence of three images, one at the chosen setting, and one each at settings greater and lesser than that setting, with the goal of having one of those three images be right on the mark with its results.

Auto Exposure Bracketing

The AEB setting produces a series of shots as follows: standard exposure, underexposure, and overexposure. To use this option, follow these steps:

- **Turn the flash off.** Exposure bracketing won't work if the flash fires. To turn it off, press the Flash key (right cross key) repeatedly until you see the Flash Off icon.

- **Select Bracketing from the FUNC. menu.** Press the FUNC./SET key and navigate down to the bracketing option.

- **Select AEB.** Move the highlight to the AEB icon at the bottom of the screen to select Auto Exposure Bracketing.

- **Press the DISP. button.** This gives you access to the bracketing scale (see Figure 4.29).

Figure 4.29
The Auto Exposure Bracketing option can be set to take exposures at intervals from 1/3 EV to 2 EV.

- **Set the interval for the three exposures.** Use the left/right cross keys or the control dial to move the little colored markers (green on the G10, orange on the G11) to the desired intervals on the scale for exposure bracketing. You can select an interval of up to 2 Exposure Value (EV) units, in increments of 1/3 EV. When you've made that choice, press FUNC./SET to lock in the choice.

- **Take the picture.** Aim at your subject and hold the camera steady while it makes its three successive exposures. If you've made good choices, one of those exposures should be right on the money.

Focus Bracketing

Focus Bracketing sets up the camera to take three images: one at the manual focus position, one nearer, and one farther. The steps to take are just like those for Auto Exposure Bracketing. Again, the flash must be forced to Off. Also, of course, the camera must be set to Manual focus. Select Bracketing from the FUNC. menu and scroll over to the third icon at the bottom of the screen to select Focus Bracketing. As with Auto Exposure Bracketing, use the DISP. key to get access to the bracketing scale, then move the green (G10) or orange (G11) markers to indicate how far apart the three focus settings should be. Press FUNC./SET to lock in those settings, and press the shutter to take the three bracketed images.

Flash Exposure Compensation

In this case, unlike the other options on the FUNC. menu discussed above, the FUNC. menu provides an alternate way to accomplish something that is available from the "regular" menu system. In certain Shooting modes, Flash Exposure Compensation can be selected from the Shooting menu, under the Flash Control setting. But, if you want to get quicker access to that setting, the FUNC. menu is the way to go. Press FUNC./SET to bring up the lists of options, then select the fourth icon down on the left side—the lightning bolt with a plus and minus sign. With this setting, the scale you need is displayed immediately; all you have to do next is to use the left/right cross keys or the control dial to select as much positive or negative flash exposure compensation as you want, in 1/3-stop increments (see Figure 4.30). (Depending on the Shooting mode, the available option may be Flash Output instead of Flash Exposure Compensation.) Oh, and

Figure 4.30
Activating Flash Exposure Compensation is a simple matter of selecting it through the FUNC. menu.

in case you thought that having two distinct ways to choose this option were not enough, here are two more: press the Flash key, then the Menu key, or just hold down the Flash key, until the Flash Exposure Compensation scale appears. These work with both internal and external flash. Somebody at Canon *really* likes this feature.

Neutral Density Filter

This next option down the list on the FUNC. menu gives you the choice of using a virtual Neutral Density filter. With film cameras, you can use such a filter, which is essentially a dark piece of glass that cuts down the light reaching the film, for use when light conditions are too bright, or for when you need to use a slow shutter speed or large aperture for some reason. With the PowerShot G10/G11, the filtering is applied electronically, with the effect of reducing the light reaching the sensor to one-eighth of its actual value, resulting in an exposure setting that needs to be 3 f/stops greater. (For example, if you were shooting with your aperture at f/8.0, and you would like to change it to f/2.8 to reduce depth-of-field for selective focus with the ND turned on.) This option is easy to set. Select the ND icon on the list at the left, then move the highlight on the bottom list to ND, and you're done. See Figure 4.31, which illustrates how a neutral density filter allows using a 1/2 second exposure that normally wouldn't be available even under overcast conditions, with an ISO setting of 80 and a minimum aperture of f/8.

Figure 4.31
Dial in the neutral density filter if you want to use longer exposures than normally available with a minimum ISO setting of ISO 80 and an f/8 minimum aperture.

Drive Mode

This next option on the FUNC. menu gives you access to the continuous shooting capabilities of the PowerShot G11. (The G10's Drive mode settings are not found on the FUNC. menu; on the G10, you control the Drive mode settings through the Shooting menu, and you activate continuous shooting by pressing the down cross key.)

On the G11, select the next-to-bottom icon on the FUNC. menu's list at the left of the screen—the one that looks like a rectangle or stack of rectangles, depending on what mode is currently in effect. Then move the highlight to the one you want at the bottom of the screen. The three choices are the default, Single Shot; Continuous; and Continuous AF. With Continuous shooting, you can take about 1.1 images per second. The focus and exposure are locked as soon as the first image is taken, and they won't change after that, even if conditions change. If you choose Continuous AF, the camera autofocuses for every shot, and the speed is reduced to about 0.7 images per second. In certain modes, such as when the camera is set to Manual focus, Continuous AF will be changed to Continuous LV, and the camera will not autofocus. There's more information about the use of continuous shooting in Chapter 3.

Image Size and Quality

The final option on the FUNC. menu, and arguably the most important, is the one at the bottom of the menu's list, which gives you two choices for your shots: Image Size and Quality. After pressing the FUNC./SET key to call up the menu, move the highlight all the way down the list on the left. This action takes you to the selection area for these two choices. These choices are different on the two PowerShot models, so we'll discuss them separately in a minute. First, though, this topic needs some background.

There are really three separate choices you need to make when selecting your image size and quality. Your first decision is whether to shoot everything in RAW files, which provide the best possible quality and most post-processing options, but which take up considerably more space on your memory card than the other options. You'll sometimes be told that RAW files are the "unprocessed" image information your camera produces, before it's been modified. That's nonsense. RAW files are no more unprocessed than your camera film is after it's been through the chemicals to produce a negative or transparency. A lot can happen in the developer that can affect the quality of a film image—positively and negatively—and, similarly, your digital image undergoes a significant amount of processing before it is saved as a RAW file. Canon even applies a name (DIGIC 4) to the digital image processing (DIP) chip used to perform this magic in the PowerShot G10/G11.

A RAW file is more similar to a film camera's processed negative. It contains all the information, captured in 14-bit channels per color (and stored in a 16-bit space), with no compression, no sharpening, no application of any special filters or other settings you might have specified when you took the picture. Those settings are *stored* with the RAW file so they can be applied when the image is converted to a form compatible with your favorite image editor. However, using RAW conversion software such as Adobe Camera Raw or Canon's Digital Photo Professional, you can override those settings and apply settings of your own. You can select essentially the same changes there that you might have specified in your camera's picture-taking options.

RAW exists because sometimes we want to have access to all the information captured by the camera, before the camera's internal logic has processed it and converted the image to a standard file format. RAW doesn't save as much space as JPEG. What it does do is preserve all the information captured by your camera after it's been converted from analog to digital form.

So, why don't we always use RAW? Although some photographers do save only in RAW format, it's more common to use either RAW plus the JPEG option or just shoot JPEG and eschew RAW altogether. While RAW is overwhelmingly helpful when an image needs to be fine-tuned, in other situations working with a RAW file can slow you down significantly. RAW images take longer to store on the memory card, and require more post-processing effort, whether you elect to go with the default settings in force when the picture was taken, or make minor adjustments.

As a result, those who depend on speedy access to images or who shoot large numbers of photos at once may prefer JPEG over RAW. Wedding photographers, for example, might expose several thousand photos during a bridal affair and offer hundreds to clients as electronic proofs for inclusion in an album. Wedding shooters take the time to make sure that their in-camera settings are correct, minimizing the need to post-process photos after the event. Given that their JPEGs are so good, there is little need to get bogged down shooting RAW. Sports photographers also eschew RAW files for similar reasons.

JPEG was invented as a more compact file format that can store most of the information in a digital image, but in a much smaller size. JPEG predates most digital cameras and was initially used to squeeze down files for transmission over slow dialup connections. Even if you were using an early digital camera with 1.3 megapixel files for news photography, you didn't want to send them back to the office over a modem at 1,200 bps.

But, as I noted, JPEG provides smaller files by compressing the information in a way that loses some image data. JPEG remains a viable alternative because it offers several different quality levels. At the highest quality Fine (or, on the G10, Superfine) level, you might not be able to tell the difference between the original RAW file and the JPEG version, even though the RAW file occupies, by Canon's estimate, about 15MB on your memory card, while the Superfine JPEG takes up about 8MB and the Fine JPEG takes up only about 4MB of space. You've squeezed the image by two-thirds without losing much visual information at all. If you don't mind losing some quality, you can use more aggressive Standard compression with JPEG to cut the size in half again, to about 2.3MB.

So, using the above considerations, first decide whether to use RAW (or RAW plus JPEG) for all your shooting. If you go that route, you don't need to spend too much time thinking about other decisions regarding image quality and size, because all RAW files on a given camera (at least with these two PowerShot models) are of the same size and quality.

If you decide to shoot in one of the JPEG formats, though, you have some more decisions to make: First, what image size to select, and, second, what amount of JPEG compression to choose.

Image size is one area in which the two cameras have a fairly sharp difference in specifications, so let's break down your options for that selection according to camera model.

With the PowerShot G10, your choices are as follows:

- L (14.5 megapixels or 4,416 × 3,312 pixels)
- M1 (8.9 megapixels or 3,456 × 2,592 pixels)
- M2 (5 megapixels or 2,592 × 1,944 pixels)
- M3 (1.9 megapixels or 1,600 pixels × 1,200 pixels)
- S (0.3 megapixels or 640 × 480 pixels)
- W (Widescreen)(10.9 megapixels or 4,416 pixels × 2,480 pixels)
- RAW (14.5 megapixels or 4,416 × 3,312 pixels)

With the PowerShot G11, your choices are as follows:

- L (10 megapixels or 3,648 × 2736 pixels)
- M1 (6 megapixels or 2,816 × 2,112 pixels)
- M2 (4 megapixels or 2,272 × 1,704 megapixels)
- M3 (2 megapixels or 1,600 × 1,200 pixels)
- S (0.3 megapixels or 640 × 480 pixels)
- W (Widescreen) (7.5 megapixels or 3,648 × 2,048 pixels)
- RAW (10 megapixels or 3,648 × 2,048 pixels)

The clear difference between these two models in the area of image size is that the PowerShot G10 offers a resolution of about 14.5 megapixels, while the maximum resolution of the G11 is about 10 megapixels. Although this difference sounds fairly dramatic, in practice, with cameras using small sensors as these do, there is not a great deal of difference in the quality of the prints or computer images that can be produced by the two cameras.

Now let's look at the second choice you need to make from the FUNC. menu—the amount of compression to be used for your images, which directly affects their quality.

To reduce the size of your image files and allow more photos to be stored on a given memory card, the G10 and G11 use JPEG compression to squeeze the images down to a smaller size. This compacting reduces the image quality a little, so you're offered your choice of various levels of compression. Here again, the two models take different approaches.

The G10 provides three levels of compression, in descending quality as follows: Superfine, Fine, and Normal. The choice of Superfine compression is represented on the camera's screen by a smooth quarter-circle with the letter S inside it (see Figure 4.32). That level of compression provides the smoothest results, while Fine compression, represented by a plain quarter-circle, and Normal compression, signified on the screen by a stair-step icon, provide increasingly "jaggier" images.

Compression and image size go hand-in-hand to determine the overall quality of your images, so the camera provides you with the ability to make these two choices together in the same menu system. On the G10, the compression or quality choice (Superfine, Fine, or Normal) is made on the next-to-bottom level of the FUNC. menu's list of icons; the image size choice (L, M, S, RAW, etc.) is made on the bottom level. After pressing the FUNC./SET button, navigate with the up/down cross keys to either of those icons, then use the left/right cross keys to move the highlight to the choice you select.

Figure 4.32
The FUNC. menu's choices of image size and quality on the PowerShot G10 involve selecting a size (RAW, L, M, or S) and a quality (Superfine, Fine, or Normal).

On the PowerShot G11, your choices of image size and quality are different from those on the G10, and the method of selecting them is slightly different. As noted above, the highest resolution available on the G11, although still called L, is about 10 megapixels rather than the 14.5 megapixels of the G10. Furthermore, the G11 offers only two levels of compression: Fine and Normal; there is no Superfine. Here's how to make the choices of image size and quality on the G11 (see Figure 4.33).

After you press the FUNC./SET key to call up the FUNC. menu, and your highlight is in the list of image sizes or resolutions (L, M1, S, etc.), you will see the word DISP. on the screen. Press DISP. and you'll be shown a pair of icons showing either the quarter-circle or the stair-step icon. At this point, move the highlight to select either the quarter-circle (Fine) or the stair-step shape (Normal), then press the FUNC./SET key to confirm the selection.

In practice, on both models of camera, you'll probably want to use only the Superfine or Fine compression and the L (Large) or RAW selections for your serious photography. There are some limited advantages to using the M (Medium) and S (Small) resolution settings, and Normal JPEG compression setting. They all allow stretching the capacity of your memory card so you can shoehorn quite a few more pictures onto a single memory card. That can come in useful when on vacation and you're running out of storage,

Figure 4.33
On the PowerShot G11, the FUNC. menu lets you select between available image sizes.

or when you're shooting non-critical work that doesn't require full resolution (such as photos taken for real estate listings, web page display, photo ID cards, or similar applications). Some photographers like to record RAW+JPEG Fine so they'll have a JPEG file for review, while retaining access to the original RAW file for serious editing.

For most work, using lower resolution and extra compression is false economy. You never know when you might actually need that extra bit of picture detail. Your best bet is to have enough memory cards to handle all the shooting you want to do until you have the chance to transfer your photos to your computer or a personal storage device.

MANAGING LOTS OF FILES

The only long-term drawback to shooting everything in RAW+JPEG is that it's easy to fill up your computer's hard drive if you are a prolific photographer. Here's what I do. My most recent photos are stored on my working hard drive in a numbered folder, say G10/G11-01, with subfolders named after the shooting session, such as 090601Trees, for pictures of trees taken on June 1, 2009. An automatic utility (TrueImage Home) copies new and modified photos to a different hard drive for temporary backup four times daily.

When the top-level folder accumulates about 30GB of images, I back it up to DVDs and then move the folder to a 1.5TB (1500GB) drive dedicated solely for storage of folders that have already been backed up onto DVD. Then I start a new folder, such as G10/G11-02, on the working hard drive and repeat the process. I always have at least one backup of every image taken, either on another hard drive or on a DVD.

Part II

Getting the Most from Your Canon PowerShot G10/G11

This Part consists of five chapters designed to help get the most out of your Canon PowerShot G10 or G11, now that you've mastered the basic controls and features of the camera. After all, if all you wanted to do was point-and-shoot, you would have purchased a less versatile camera. If you, like the majority of G10/G11 owners, belong to the point-*think*-shoot crowd, you'll want to read each of the following chapters so you can get the most from the capabilities at your fingertips.

At the beginning of this book, I promised not to throw you off the dock into deep water and expect you to learn how to swim before you went under for the third time. Instead, I've helped you learn all the basic strokes, in preparation for Part II, in which, I trust, you'll master the techniques that will in turn transform you from a dog paddler to a championship swimmer.

As with Part I, you can start with any of the five chapters that follow, depending on your interests and skill level:

- **If you want to learn how to capture a full range of tonal values, every time, read:** *Chapter 5: Fine Tuning Exposure.* This chapter will show you how to handle tricky situations, such as backlighting, how to create silhouette images, how to choose from among the G10/G11's exposure and metering modes, and techniques for optimizing exposure using tools like histograms.

- **If you want to explore some cool techniques like super-long or ultra-short exposures and get up to speed on shooting movies, jump to:** *Chapter 6: Advanced Shooting and Movie-Making with Your Canon PowerShot G10/G11.* Here, I'll guide you through some specialized techniques, help you understand how focus works, and show you how to shoot movie clips and do simple editing right in the camera.

- **If you know that using your G10/G11's lens effectively involves more than just pressing the zoom lever, you'll want to go to:** *Chapter 7: Getting the Most from Your Zoom.* Discover what telephoto and wide-angle perspectives can do for your photos, and how to avoid the most common pitfalls of each end of the zoom scale. Learn about macro shooting, and discover some interesting add-ons that make your zoom even more versatile.

- **If you'd like to use light more effectively to create a mood or effect, read:** *Chapter 8: Working with Light.* Available light and electronic flash are powerful tools, but you need to understand how they work to harness their capabilities. This chapter shows you how to choose between continuous illumination and flash, and the best way to progress beyond the limitations of your PowerShot G10/G11's built-in flash.

- **If you want to jump ahead and begin working with your images on your computer, you'll want to look at** *Chapter 9: Downloading and Editing Your Images.* It's not a how-to chapter for image editing. Instead, it explains your options for transferring images and then processing them with easy-to-use, but powerful, software options, from Canon's Digital Photo Pro to Photoshop.

5

Fine Tuning Exposure

The Canon PowerShot G10/G11 offers the best of two worlds when it comes to capturing exactly the right exposure—a picture with the optimum balance of tones and colors that are neither too light nor too dark to reveal all the detail in the original subject. You can select one of the numerous predefined shooting modes suitable for your subject matter—such as portrait, landscape, underwater, sports, or night-time subjects—and the camera will do an excellent job of calculating the right settings to give you an outstanding picture with little input on your part beyond the initial mode dial selection. If you can't decide for yourself which of those specific shooting modes is best, you can select the green Auto icon instead, and the PowerShot G10/G11 will still do a fine job.

So, why do I include an entire chapter titled "Fine Tuning Exposure" in all my Canon books? As you learn to use your PowerShot G10/G11 creatively, you're going to find that the right settings—as determined by the camera's exposure meter and intelligence—need to be *adjusted* to account for your creative decisions or special situations.

For example, when you shoot with the main light source behind the subject, you end up with *backlighting*, which results in an overexposed background and/or an underexposed subject. The PowerShot G10/G11 recognizes backlit situations nicely, and can properly base exposure on the main subject, producing a decent photo. A feature like i-Contrast (introduced in Chapter 4) can fine tune exposure to preserve detail in the highlights and shadows.

But what if you *want* to underexpose the subject, to produce a silhouette effect? Or, perhaps, you might want to make use of the camera's built-in flash unit to fill in the shadows on your subject. The more you know about how to use your PowerShot G10/G11, the more you'll run into situations where you want to creatively tweak the exposure to provide a different look than you'd get with a straight shot.

This chapter shows you the fundamentals of exposure, so you'll be better equipped to override the PowerShot G10/G11's default settings when you want to, or need to. After all, correct exposure is one of the foundations of good photography, along with accurate focus and sharpness, appropriate color balance, freedom from unwanted noise and excessive contrast, as well as pleasing composition.

Understanding Exposure

Exposure determines the look, feel, and tone of an image, in more ways than one. Incorrect exposure can impair even the best composed image by cloaking important tones in darkness, or by washing them out so they become featureless to the eye. On the other hand, correct exposure brings out the detail in the areas you want to picture, and provides the range of tones and colors you need to create the desired image. However, getting the perfect exposure can be tricky, because digital sensors can't capture all the tones we are able to see. If the range of tones in an image is extensive, embracing both inky black shadows and bright highlights, the sensor may not be able to capture them all. Sometimes, we must settle for an exposure that renders most of those tones—but not all—in a way that best suits the photo we want to produce. You'll often need to make choices about which details are important, and which are not, so that you can grab the tones that truly matter in your image. That's part of the creativity you bring to bear in realizing your photographic vision.

For example, look at the two typical tourist snapshots presented side by side in Figure 5.1. The camera was mounted on a tripod for both, so the only way you can really see that they are two different images is by examining the differences in the way the water flows over the rocks. However, the pair of pictures does vary in exposure. The version on the left was underexposed, which helps bring out detail in the ridges and sky in the background, but makes the water and foreground look murky and dark. The overexposed version on the right offers better exposure for the foreground area, but now the ridges and sky are too light.

With digital camera sensors, it's tricky to capture detail in both highlights and shadows in a single image, because the number of tones, the *dynamic range,* of the sensor is limited. The solution, in this particular case, was to resort to a technique called High Dynamic Range (HDR) photography, in which the two exposures from Figure 5.1 were combined in an image editor such as Photoshop, or a specialized HDR software program. The resulting shot is shown in Figure 5.2. I'll explain more about HDR photography later in this chapter. For now, though, I'm going to concentrate on showing you how to get the best exposures possible without resorting to such tools, using only the features of your Canon PowerShot G10/G11.

To understand exposure, you need to understand the six aspects of light that combine to produce an image. Start with a light source—the sun, an interior lamp, or the glow from a campfire—and trace its path to your camera, through the lens, and finally to the sensor that captures the illumination. Here's a brief review of the things within our control that affect exposure.

■ **Light at its source.** Our eyes and our cameras—film or digital—are most sensitive to that portion of the electromagnetic spectrum we call *visible light.* That light has several important aspects that are relevant to photography, such as color, and harshness (which is determined primarily by the apparent size of the light source as it illuminates a subject). But, in terms of exposure, the important attribute of a light source is its *intensity.* We may have direct control over intensity, which might be the case with an interior light that can be brightened or dimmed. Or, we might have only indirect control over intensity, as with sunlight, which can be made to appear dimmer by introducing translucent light-absorbing or reflective materials in its path.

Figure 5.1 At left, the image is exposed for the background highlights, losing shadow detail. At right, the exposure captures detail in the shadows, but the background highlights are washed out.

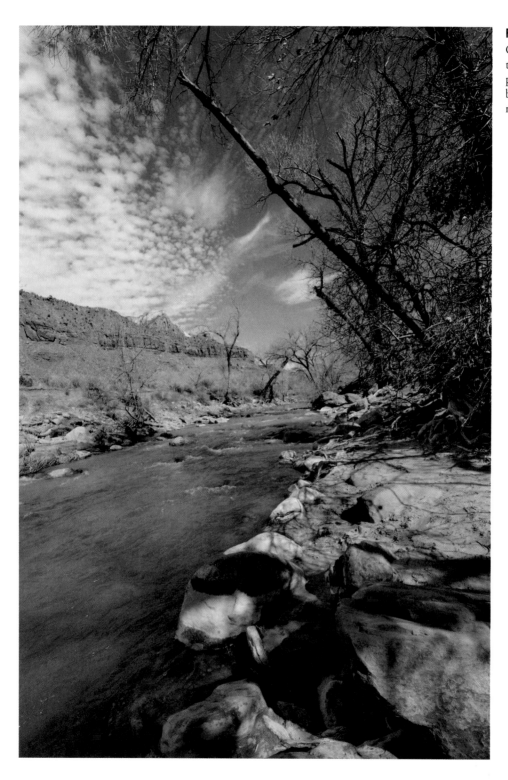

Figure 5.2
Combining the two exposures produces the best compromise image.

■ **Light's duration.** We tend to think of most light sources as continuous. But, as you'll learn in Chapter 8, the duration of light can change quickly enough to modify the exposure, as when the main illumination in a photograph comes from an intermittent source, such as an electronic flash.

■ **Light reflected, transmitted, or emitted.** Once light is produced by its source, either continuously or in a brief burst, we are able to see and photograph objects by the light that is reflected from our subjects towards the camera lens; transmitted (say, from translucent objects that are lit from behind), or emitted (by a candle or television screen). When more or less light reaches the lens from the subject, we need to adjust the exposure. This part of the equation is under our control to the extent we can increase the amount of light falling on or passing through the subject (by adding extra light sources or using reflectors), or by pumping up the light that's emitted (by increasing the brightness of the glowing object).

■ **Light passed by the lens.** Not all the illumination that reaches the front of the lens makes it all the way through. Filters can remove some of the light before it enters the lens. Inside the lens barrel is a variable-sized diaphragm called an *aperture* that dilates and contracts to control the amount of light that enters the lens. You, or the PowerShot G10/G11's autoexposure system, can control exposure by varying the size of the aperture. The relative size of the aperture is called the *f/stop*.

■ **Light passing through the shutter.** Once light passes through the lens, the amount of time the sensor receives it is determined by the PowerShot G10/G11's shutter, which can remain open for as long as 15 seconds or as briefly as 1/4000th second.

■ **Light captured by the sensor.** Not all the light falling onto the sensor is captured. If the number of photons reaching a particular photosite doesn't pass a set threshold, no information is recorded. Similarly, if too much light illuminates a pixel in the sensor, then the excess isn't recorded or, worse, spills over to contaminate adjacent pixels. We can modify the minimum and maximum number of pixels that contribute to image detail by adjusting the ISO setting. At higher ISOs, the incoming light is amplified to boost the effective sensitivity of the sensor.

These factors—the quantity of light produced by the light source; the amount reflected or transmitted towards the camera; the light passed by the lens; the amount of time the shutter is open; and the sensitivity of the sensor—all work proportionately and reciprocally to produce an exposure. That is, if you double the amount of light that's available, increase the aperture by one stop, make the shutter speed twice as long, or boost the ISO setting 2X, you'll get twice as much exposure. Similarly, you can increase any of these factors while decreasing one of the others by a similar amount to keep the same exposure.

F/STOPS AND SHUTTER SPEEDS

If you're *really* new to more advanced cameras, you might need to know that the lens aperture, or f/stop, is a ratio, much like a fraction, which is why f/2.8 is larger than f/5.6, just as 1/2 is larger than 1/4. However, f/2.8 is actually *four times* as large as f/5.6. (If you remember your high school geometry, you'll know that to double the area of a circle, you multiply its diameter by the square root of two: 1.4.)

Apertures in digital cameras are usually marked with intermediate f/stops that represent a size that's twice as much/half as much as the previous aperture. So, a lens might be marked:

f/2.8, f/4, f/5.6, f/8, with each larger number representing an aperture that admits half as much light as the one before, as shown in Figure 5.3, which illustrates a generic lens, not the one in the PowerShot G10/G11.

Shutter speeds are actual fractions (of a second), but in some cameras' displays the numerator is omitted, so that 60, 125, 250, 500, 1000, and so forth represent 1/60th, 1/125th, 1/250th, 1/500th, and 1/1000th second. In the PowerShot G10/G11, Canon actually found room to include the numerators. However, to avoid all chance of confusion, Canon uses quotation marks to signify longer exposures: For example, 0"4, 2", 2"5, 4" represent 0.4, 2.0, 2.5, and 4.0 second exposures, respectively.

Figure 5.3
Top row (left to right): f/2.8, f/4; bottom row, f/5.6, f/8.

Most commonly, exposure settings are made using the aperture and shutter speed, followed by adjusting the ISO sensitivity if it's not possible to get the preferred exposure (that is, the one that uses the "best" f/stop or shutter speed for the depth-of-field or action-stopping we want). Table 5.1 shows equivalent exposure settings using various shutter speeds and f/stops.

Table 5.1 Equivalent Exposures	
Shutter speed	**f/stop**
1/250th second	f/8
1/500th second	f/5.6
1/1000th second	f/4
1/2000th second	f/2.8

When the PowerShot G10/G11 is set for P mode, the metering system selects the correct exposure for you automatically. However, you can change quickly to an equivalent exposure by holding down the shutter release button halfway and pressing the * button ("locking" the current exposure), and then spinning the control dial (on the back of the camera) until the desired equivalent exposure combination is displayed. The equivalent exposures appear as a pairing of shutter speeds and f/stops on the LCD, which you can change using the control dial. This Program Shift mode does not work when you're using flash.

In Aperture Priority (Av) and Shutter Priority (Tv) modes, you can change to an equivalent exposure, but only by adjusting either the aperture (the camera chooses the shutter speed) or shutter speed (the camera selects the aperture). I'll cover all these exposure modes later in the chapter.

How the PowerShot G10/G11 Calculates Exposure

Your Canon PowerShot G10/G11 calculates exposure by measuring the light that passes through the lens to sensors located near the focusing surface, using a pattern you can select (more on that later) and based on the assumption that each area being measured reflects about the same amount of light as a neutral gray card with 18-percent reflectance. That assumption is necessary, because different subjects reflect different amounts of light. In a photo containing a white cat and a dark gray cat, the white cat might reflect five times as much light as the gray cat. An exposure based on the white cat will cause the gray cat to appear to be black, while an exposure based only on the gray cat will make the white cat washed out. Light-measuring devices handle this by assuming that the areas measured average a standard value of 18-percent gray—a figure that's been used as a rough standard for many years (most vendors don't calibrate their metering for exactly 18-percent gray; the actual figure may be closer to 13 or 14 percent).

In most cases, your camera's light meter will do a good job of calculating the right exposure, especially if you use the exposure tips in the next section. But if you want to double-check, or feel that exposure is especially critical, take the light reading off an object of known reflectance. Photographers sometimes carry around an 18-percent gray card (available from any camera store) and, for critical exposures, actually use that card, placed in the subject area, to measure exposure (or to set a custom white balance if needed).

You could, in many cases, arrive at a reasonable exposure by pointing your PowerShot G10/G11 at an evenly lit object, such as an actual gray card or the palm of your hand (the backside of the hand is too variable). It's more practical though, to use your camera's system to meter the actual scene, using the options available to you when using one of the more advanced shooting modes (P, Tv, Av, and M). (In the Auto and SCN modes, the metering decisions are handled by the camera's programming.)

Tip

Of course, if you use such a gray card, strictly speaking, you need to use about one-half stop *more* exposure than metered, because the PowerShot G10/G11 is calibrated for a lighter tone, rather than the 18-percent gray you just measured. If you're using a human palm instead, add one full stop more exposure.

To meter properly using the more advanced shooting modes, you'll want to choose both the *metering method* (how light is evaluated) and *exposure method* (how the appropriate shutter speeds and apertures are chosen). I'll describe both in the following sections. But first, let's clear up that black cat/gray cat/white cat conundrum, without using any actual cats. Black, white, and gray cats have been a standard metaphor for many years, so I'm going to explain this concept using a different, and more cooperative, life form: fruit.

Figure 5.4 shows three ordinary pieces of fruit. The yellow banana at left represents a white cat, or any object that is very light but which contains detail that we want to see in the light areas. The orange in the middle is a stand-in for a gray cat, because it has most of its details in the middle tones. The deep purple plum serves as our black cat, because it is a dark object with detail in its shadows.

The colors confuse the issue, so I'm going to convert our color fruit to black-and-white. For the version shown in Figure 5.5, the exposure (measured by Spot metering) was optimized for the white (yellow) banana, changing its tonal value to a medium, 18 percent gray. The dark (purple) and medium-toned (orange) fruit are now *too* dark. For Figure 5.6, the exposure was optimized for the dark (purple) plum, making most of its surface, now, fall into the middle-tone, 18 percent gray range. The light yellow banana and midtone orange are now too light.

The solution, of course, is to measure exposure from the object with the middle tones that most closely correspond to the 18-percent gray "standard." Do that, and you wind up with a picture that more closely resembles the original tonality of the yellow, orange, and purple fruit, which looks, in black-and-white, like Figure 5.7.

Figure 5.4 The yellow banana, orange, and deep purple plum represent light, middle, and dark tones.

Figure 5.5 Exposing for the light-colored banana at left renders the other two fruit excessively dark.

Figure 5.6 Exposing for the dark plum (right) causes the two fruit at left to become too light.

Figure 5.7 Exposing for the middle-toned orange produces an image in which the tones of all three subjects appear accurately.

Choosing a Metering Method

The PowerShot G10/G11 has three different schemes for evaluating the light received by its exposure sensors—Evaluative, Center Weighted, and Spot. You can choose among them by pressing the Metering mode button (directly under the * key) and rotating the control dial until the mode you want is selected. (In this case, you can't use the left/right cross keys, because pressing those keys in this context will activate their other functions—selecting Macro shooting or Flash.)

- **Evaluative.** The PowerShot G10/G11 slices up the frame into various different zones. The camera evaluates the measurements, paying special attention to the metering zones that appear to include certain levels of brightness or features such as human faces, to make an educated guess about what kind of picture you're taking, based on examination of thousands of different real-world photos. For example, if the top sections of a picture are much lighter than the bottom portions, the algorithm can assume that the scene is a landscape photo with lots of sky. This mode is the best all-purpose metering method for most pictures. It's the mode used when the camera is set to Auto shooting.

- **Spot AE Point.** This mode confines the reading to a limited (and non-specified) area in the center of the viewfinder, making up only a small percent of the image. This mode is useful when you want to base exposure on a single, limited area in the frame. If that area is in the center of the frame, so much the better. If not, you'll have to take steps to make sure the reading is accurate. One way is to make your meter reading and then lock exposure by pressing the shutter release halfway, or by pressing the AE Lock button. Another way is to use the FlexiZone focusing capability, discussed in Chapter 6, which lets you move the autofocus bracket around the screen. Using the Spot AE Point option on the Shooting menu, as discussed in Chapter 4, you can link the Spot AE Point to the AF Point. Then, when you move the FlexiZone AF Frame around the screen, you will be moving the Spot AE Point at the same time, so you can choose precisely what area of the scene is measured for your exposure. The Spot AE Point Frame and .AF frame are moved using the cross keys or the control dial after you press the frame selector button. The frame turns orange (green on the G10) and can be resized using the DISP. button. I'll explain this technique in more detail in Chapter 6.

- **Center Weighted Averaging.** In this mode, the exposure meter emphasizes a zone located roughly in the center of the frame to calculate exposure, on the theory that, for most pictures, the main subject will be located in the center. Center weighting works best for portraits, architectural photos, and other pictures in which the most important subject is located in the middle of the frame. As the name suggests, the light reading is *weighted* towards the central portion, but information is also used from the rest of the frame. If your main subject is surrounded by very bright or very dark areas, the exposure might not be exactly right. However, this scheme works well in many situations if you don't want to use one of the other modes.

Choosing an Exposure Method

If you set the PowerShot G10/G11's shooting mode dial to Auto or SCN, the camera will take care of choosing an exposure method and calculating the exposure for you. But if you're inclined to exercise more control over the exposure decision, you'll find three semi-automated methods (plus Manual) for choosing the appropriate shutter speed and aperture. Just spin the mode dial to choose the method you want to use. Your choice of which is best for a given shooting situation will depend on things like your need for lots of (or less) depth-of-field, a desire to freeze action or allow motion blur, or how much noise you find acceptable in an image. Each of the PowerShot G10/G11's exposure methods emphasizes one aspect of image capture or another. This section introduces you to all four.

Aperture Priority

In Av (Aperture Value) mode, you specify the lens opening used, and the PowerShot G10/G11 selects the shutter speed. Aperture Priority is especially good when you want to use a particular lens opening to achieve a desired effect. Perhaps you'd like to use the smallest f/stop possible to maximize depth-of-field in a close-up picture. Or, you might want to use a large f/stop to throw everything except your main subject out of focus, as in Figure 5.8, a chilling portrait of a menacing lizard, taken by talented Cleveland photographer Kris Bosworth. Maybe you'd just like to "lock in" a particular f/stop because it's the sharpest available aperture. Or, you might prefer to use, say, f/4, even though the

Figure 5.8
Use Aperture Priority to "lock in" a large f/stop when you want to blur the background.

camera's lens has a maximum aperture of f/2.8, because you want the best compromise between speed and sharpness.

Aperture Priority can even be used to specify a *range* of shutter speeds you want to use under varying lighting conditions, which seems almost contradictory. But think about it. You're shooting a soccer game outdoors with a telephoto zoom setting and want a relatively high shutter speed, but you don't care if the speed changes a little should the sun duck behind a cloud. Set your PowerShot G10/G11 to Av, and adjust the aperture until a shutter speed of, say, 1/1000th second is selected at your current ISO setting. (In bright sunlight at ISO 200, that aperture is likely to be around f/8.) Then, go ahead and shoot, knowing that your camera will maintain that f/8 aperture (for sufficient depth-of-field as the soccer players move about the field), but will drop down to 1/800th or 1/500th second if necessary should the lighting change a little.

A shutter speed of 1/4000 or 1" displaying in orange (rather than white) on the LCD indicates that the PowerShot G10/G11 is unable to select an appropriate shutter speed at the selected aperture, and that over- or underexposure will occur at the current ISO setting (see Figure 5.9). That's the major pitfall of using Av: you might select an f/stop that is too small or too large to allow an optimal exposure with the available shutter speeds. For example, if you choose f/2.8 as your aperture and the illumination is quite

Figure 5.9
When the PowerShot G10/G11 cannot achieve proper exposure in Av mode, the shutter speed will turn orange.

bright (say, at the beach or in snow), even your camera's fastest shutter speed might not be able to cut down the amount of light reaching the sensor to provide the right exposure. Or, if you select f/8 in a dimly lit room, you might find yourself shooting with a very slow shutter speed that can cause blurring from subject movement or camera shake. (However, you can eliminate this risk by turning on the Safety Shift feature through the Shooting menu, as described in Chapter 4.) In general, Aperture Priority is best used by those with a bit of experience in choosing settings. Many seasoned photographers leave their cameras set on Av all the time.

Note that there may be situations in which the expected aperture cannot be set. This can happen when the built-in flash is turned on, because, on the PowerShot G10, the fastest shutter speed available when using flash is 1/500. So, for example, if you are photographing in bright conditions and set a wide aperture such as f/2.8, and the appropriate shutter speed would be 1/2000, the G10 will reset the aperture to a value such as f/8.0, so the shutter speed can be reset to no faster than 1/500. With the G11, the fastest shutter speed available in Av mode is 1/500th second when using flash, even though it can be set to 1/2000 when using flash in Tv mode. Therefore, some aperture values may not be available if they would call for a shutter speed faster than 1/500.

Finally, note that, with both the G10 and G11, as you zoom the lens in beyond its wide-angle setting of 28mm, some apertures become unavailable. For example, when the lens is zoomed all the way in to its 120mm telephoto value, the widest aperture available is f/4.5. That's because the *effective* aperture of the f/2.8 lens becomes f/4.5 at the maximum zoom position.

Shutter Priority

Shutter Priority (Tv, for Time Value) is the inverse of Aperture Priority: you choose the shutter speed you'd like to use, and the camera's metering system selects the appropriate f/stop. Perhaps you're shooting action photos and you want to use the absolute fastest shutter speed available with your camera; in other cases, you might want to use a slow shutter speed to add some blur to a sports photo that would be mundane if the action were completely frozen. Or, you might want to give a feeling of motion, as with another Kris Bosworth image of an antique auto cruising down the parkway at dozens of miles per hour. (See Figure 5.10.) Shutter Priority mode gives you some control over how much action-freezing capability your digital camera brings to bear in a particular situation.

You'll also encounter the same problem as with Aperture Priority when you select a shutter speed that's too long or too short for correct exposure under some conditions. I've shot outdoor soccer games on sunny Fall evenings and used Shutter Priority mode to lock in a 1/1000th second shutter speed, only to find my camera refused to shoot when the sun dipped behind some trees and there was no longer enough light to shoot at that speed, even with the lens wide open.

Figure 5.10 Lock the shutter at a slow speed to introduce blur, as with this panned image of an antique automobile.

As with Av mode, it's possible to choose an inappropriate shutter speed using Tv mode. If that's the case, 2.8, the maximum aperture of your lens (to indicate underexposure) or 8.0, the minimum aperture (to indicate overexposure) will show up as orange on the LCD display (see Figure 5.11). Again, as with Av mode, you can avoid this problem by turning on Safety Shift through the Shooting menu.

Note that there may be times when you think you've set a fast shutter speed—say, 1/4000, but the camera seems to ignore your setting and changes it to 1/2000 or 1/500. Here's why this happens. With the PowerShot G10, the fastest shutter speed that can be used for flash synchronization is 1/500. So, even if you set the shutter speed to 1/640 or faster, the camera will reset the shutter speed to 1/500 if you have the flash activated (set to On, Auto, or Slow Synchro).

With the G11, the situation is slightly different. The fastest shutter speed the G11 can use with the built-in flash in Tv mode is 1/2000, and it will reset itself to that shutter speed when the flash is activated, even though it will let you set a faster speed of 1/2500, 1/3200, or 1/4000 initially. However, if the flash is activated on the G11 and Safety FE

Figure 5.11
A minimum or maximum aperture displayed in orange means the camera cannot achieve a correct exposure in Shutter Priority mode.

is turned off, then the fastest shutter speed the camera will let you set is 1/500. (Safety FE is explained in Chapter 4, and is discussed further in Chapter 8. Basically, that setting will reset the shutter speed and aperture if necessary to avoid overexposure when using flash.)

Program Mode

Program mode (P) uses the PowerShot G10/G11's built-in smarts to select the correct f/stop and shutter speed using a database of picture information that tells it which combination of shutter speed and aperture will work best for a particular photo. If the correct exposure cannot be achieved at the current ISO setting, the shutter speed and aperture indicators in the viewfinder will *both* display in orange at their extreme settings, showing 1" and 2.8 to indicate underexposure or 1/4000 and 8.0 to indicate overexposure. You can then boost or reduce the ISO to increase or decrease sensitivity.

The PowerShot G10/G11's recommended exposure can be overridden if you want. Use the exposure compensation feature (described later, because it also applies to Tv and Av modes) to add or subtract exposure from the metered value. And, as I mentioned earlier in this chapter, you can change from the recommended setting to an equivalent setting (as shown earlier in Table 5.1) that produces the same exposure, but using a different combination of f/stop and shutter speed. To accomplish this:

1. **Disable flash.** Make sure the flash is forced off by pressing the Flash button and highlighting the icon showing the lightning bolt with a line through it.

2. **Lock exposure.** Press the shutter release halfway to lock in the current base exposure, and press the AE Lock button (*) on the back of the camera (in which case the * indicator will be displayed on the screen to show that the exposure has been locked).

3. **Choose exposure combination.** A pair of slide-rule-like dials will immediately appear on the screen, with the apertures on top, and the corresponding shutter speeds below them. Spin the control dial to move the pairings of shutter speed and aperture in tandem until you find the combination you want.

4. **Take photo.** Press the shutter button to grab your shot.

Your adjustment remains in force for a single exposure; if you want to change from the recommended settings for the next exposure, you'll need to repeat those steps.

Making EV Changes

Sometimes you'll want more or less exposure than indicated by the PowerShot G10/G11's metering system. Perhaps you want to underexpose to create a silhouette effect, or overexpose to produce a high key look. It's easy to use the camera's Exposure Compensation system to override the exposure recommendations, as long as you're using the Program, Aperture Priority, or Shutter Priority shooting mode.

Exposure Compensation with the PowerShot G10/G11

One of the great features of the PowerShot G10/G11is the addition of a dial dedicated to Exposure Compensation. This is one of the functions that serious photographers really appreciate—the ability to tweak the camera's automatic exposure setting according to conditions, and, more importantly, according to the photographer's vision of how the image should look. With the addition of this dedicated dial, you have immediate access to this adjustment. So, the instructions for using this feature on the G10/G11 are quite brief—turn the exposure compensation dial to the desired value: into the + area to lighten the image, and into the – area to darken it. (See Figure 5.12.)

When using Exposure Compensation, it's important to remember that any adjustment you make to that value will remain in place even after the camera has been turned off and back on again; you have to be sure to move the Exposure Compensation dial back to zero when you no longer need the adjustment. The adjustment is not available in Manual or Auto shooting mode. However, if you turn the dial while in one of those modes, the adjustment will take effect if you later switch to a shooting mode that does permit Exposure Compensation.

Figure 5.12

If your image is too bright (top), rotate the exposure compensation dial to −1 to produce a version that's better exposed (middle). Don't go too far: −2 exposure compensation (bottom) creates an image that's too dark.

Manual Exposure

Part of being an experienced photographer comes from knowing when to rely on your PowerShot G10/G11's automation (including Auto mode, P mode, and other automated settings), when to go semiautomatic (with Tv or Av), and when to set exposure manually (using M). Some photographers actually prefer to set their exposure manually, but that doesn't leave you all on your own; the PowerShot G10/G11 provides an analog exposure scale on the right side of the LCD screen to indicate when its metering system judges your manual settings provide the proper exposure.

Manual exposure can come in handy in some situations. You might be taking a silhouette photo and find that none of the exposure modes or EV correction features give you exactly the effect you want. For example, when I shot the ballet dancer in Figure 5.13 in front of a mostly dark background highlighted by an illuminated curtain off to the right, there was no way any of my camera's exposure modes would be able to interpret the scene the way I wanted to shoot it. So, I took a couple test exposures, and set the exposure manually, using the exact shutter speed and f/stop I needed. Or, you might need to set the aperture manually when working with non-dedicated flash units, and your camera's exposure meter can't interpret the flash exposure at all.

Figure 5.13
The only way to expose this shot of a ballet dancer correctly was to use Manual exposure.

Although, depending on your proclivities, you might not need to set exposure manually very often, you should still make sure you understand how it works. Fortunately, the PowerShot G10/G11 makes setting exposure manually quite easy. Here are the steps to take:

1. **Choose Manual exposure.** Set the mode dial to M.

2. **Select setting to change.** In Manual exposure mode, pressing the Metering mode button, just above the control dial on the right, cycles among activating Metering mode, shutter speed selection, and aperture selection. Press the button until the setting you want to change is highlighted (it will have green directional arrows on either side of either the Metering mode, shutter speed, or f/stop labels in the lower row of the LCD). If you pass by the setting you wanted to change, keep pressing the button until the one you want is highlighted.

3. **Set shutter speed and aperture.** Highlight either shutter speed or aperture, and then rotate the control dial to select the shutter speed or f/stop you want. Press the Metering mode button until the other setting is highlighted, and then choose its value.

4. **Check metered exposure.** Press the shutter release halfway and the camera will determine what the metered exposure should be. Look at the vertical scale with tick marks at the right of the screen; it will have a marker on the right side of the scale that moves up and down as the manual exposure setting changes.

5. **Make corrections, if desired.** If that marker goes above the mid-point on the scale, that means the camera considers the manual exposure setting to be too bright; if the marker goes below the mid-point, the camera believes the exposure setting is too dark. If the difference becomes greater than 2 EV in either direction, the marker on the right turns orange. (See Figure 5.14.) Change shutter speed and aperture, as described in Steps 2 and 3, until the exposure you want is set.

6. **Or, let the camera correct your manual exposure settings.** If you prefer to let the camera set the exposure, you can press the AE Lock (*) and the camera will attempt to change your manual exposure setting to its own metered setting by adjusting either the aperture or the shutter speed. (If the manual settings are both too far away from the metered settings, the camera will not be able to achieve a proper exposure setting by adjusting shutter speed or aperture. You'll have to do it manually.)

7. **Take your photo.** Once you have adjusted the shutter speed and aperture to your liking, and checked them against the vertical scale on the right of the screen, press the shutter button to take the picture.

Figure 5.14
When setting exposure manually, an exposure scale shows the difference between your settings and the metered exposure.

Automatic and Scene Modes

The final tools in your exposure repertoire are the numerous automatic and scene-oriented shooting modes, which can automatically make all the basic settings needed for certain types of shooting situations, such as portraits, landscapes, sports, night portraits, "no-flash zone" pictures, and others. These "autopilot" modes are especially useful when you suddenly encounter a picture-taking opportunity and don't have time to decide exactly which of the more advanced shooting modes you want to use. Instead, you can spin the control dial to select the appropriate automatic mode and fire away, knowing that at least you have a fighting chance of getting a good or usable photo.

These modes are also helpful when you're just learning to use your PowerShot G10/G11. Once you've learned how to operate your camera, you'll probably prefer one of the advanced modes that provide more control over shooting options. The automatic or scene modes may give you few options or none at all. In some cases, the AF mode, drive mode, or metering mode will be set for you, or your options for selecting those items may be sharply limited.

Auto Mode

First, we need to mention Auto mode, because it occupies its own separate place on the mode dial. Turn the dial to that setting, and most of the time you are likely to be pleased with the results of your shots, because the camera will use its electronic intelligence to make reasonably good judgments about shutter speed, aperture, backlighting, and other factors. This is the mode to use when you hand your camera to a total stranger and ask him or her to take your picture posing in front of the Eiffel Tower. All the photographer has to do is look through the viewfinder and press the shutter release button. Just about every other decision is made by the camera's electronics. (You can still set image size and quality, exposure compensation, and a few other items, but enough basic decisions are made by the camera to result in a usable image virtually every time.) However, you should be aware that, perhaps because the PowerShot G10/G11 is intended for use by more experienced photographers, the camera does not (always) treat you like a dummy—it will let you change settings that you might not expect. For example, in Sunset mode, although the flash is set to off initially, you still have the option of turning it back on if you want to for some reason. In Fireworks mode, though, the camera *does* treat you like a dummy, and won't let you turn the flash on. However, in most SCN modes, you can choose to have the flash on, off, or automatically selected when needed. In Auto, you can choose to turn the flash on or off.

Scene Modes

Next, we come to the impressive array of specific shooting modes that Canon's engineers have devised to help you cope with the ever-changing environment that you're confronted with in the varied activities of your life. To get access to these modes, set the mode dial to the SCN setting, then turn the control dial to move to the specific scene type you want to select. As you rotate the control dial, the camera displays the name of each scene type on the screen (for example, "Foliage") so you're not left guessing what the sometimes-cryptic icons represent. And, on the G11, the camera goes so far as to display a short phrase on the screen explaining what the selected mode is designed for (for example, "shoot foliage in vivid colors"). I'll provide some brief points about each of these scene modes in the list below.

- **Portrait.** This mode tends to use wider f/stops and faster shutter speeds, providing blurred backgrounds and images with no camera shake. If you want, you can turn on continuous shooting with the Drive mode options on the Self-timer/Drive mode button (G10) or using the FUNC. menu (G11), as discussed in Chapter 4. Then, if you hold down the shutter release, the PowerShot G10/G11 will take a continuous sequence of photos, which can be useful in capturing fleeting expressions in portrait situations.

- **Landscape.** The camera tries to use smaller f/stops for more depth-of-field, and boosts saturation slightly for richer colors.

- **Night Snapshot.** This mode is similar to the Portrait setting, with wider f/stops to isolate your close-up subjects, and higher ISO, allowing higher shutter speeds to eliminate the camera shake that's accentuated at close focusing distances. However, if you have your camera mounted on a tripod, you might want to use the Aperture Priority (Av) mode instead, so you can specify a smaller f/stop with additional depth-of-field. You can force the flash off if you want to see if the camera can manage a decent image without the often glaring light of the flash.

- **Kids&Pets.** This mode is designed to capture images of quick-moving children and small pets.

- **Indoor.** In this mode, the camera adjusts the settings so that colors look more natural in the indoor environment.

- **Sports.** In this mode, the camera tries to use high shutter speeds to freeze action, switches to continuous drive to allow taking a quick sequence of pictures with one press of the shutter release, and uses Continuous AF to continually refocus as your subjects move around in the frame. You can find more information on autofocus options in Chapter 4.

- **Sunset.** This mode turns off the flash and emphasizes the red colors of a sunset.

- **Night Scene.** This mode uses a slow shutter speed by setting the flash to Slow Synchro, in order to include as much background detail as possible in an image shot in low light. You need to use a tripod or other very firm camera support with this mode. It's a good idea to turn image stabilization off when using the camera with a tripod.

- **Fireworks.** In this mode, the camera forces the flash off and sets the shutter speed to 2 seconds with a low ISO so you will catch the full effect of a fireworks burst. You should use a tripod with this mode, and turn image stabilization off.

- **Beach.** This mode is designed to take shots of people against the bright background of a beach. The camera sets the metering mode to Evaluative.

- **Underwater.** This mode is intended for use underwater, with the camera safely installed in a case that is designed for it. The ISO is increased to help deal with the reduced light, and the white balance is adjusted to allow for the bluish tone of the underwater scene.

- **Aquarium.** This mode is meant to be used for shooting natural-colored images of fish and other aquatic creatures and objects that are displayed indoors in glass aquariums. The camera adjusts the white balance in an attempt to render colors more naturally. Here again, the ISO is automatically increased to account for the loss of light from objects that are obscured by glass and water.

- **Foliage.** This mode is meant for taking shots of leaves and trees, both new, green growth and autumn leaves, with vivid colors.

- **Snow.** This mode is designed for taking natural-colored shots of people against a bright background of white snow.

- **ISO 3200. (PowerShot G10 only)** This mode is intended to let you take pictures in low light conditions without flash, with minimal effects of camera shake. It sets the camera's ISO to 3200, which is not normally available; the highest value you can set on the ISO dial of the PowerShot G10 is 1600. In this mode, the camera also selects a higher shutter speed to minimize blur caused by camera motion. The image size is automatically set to M3 (1,600 × 1,200 pixels, or about 1.9 megapixels). This mode is not available on the PowerShot G11, which has ISO settings of up to 3200, and a "low light" shooting mode that can set the ISO as high as 12800 (although at a reduced resolution).

- **Color Accent.** This is the first of three SCN mode settings that are not designed for specific scene types, but, rather, are ways to manipulate your images. They are accessed by turning the control dial in the same way as for the SCN varieties mentioned previously. The first is Color Accent, which lets you retain just one color in an image, converting the rest of the image to black-and-white. Once you have selected Color Accent, press the DISP. button, which will bring up a box at the bottom of the screen filled with a color. Then move the camera so the center frame is aimed at the one color you want to retain. Press the left cross key, and the box at the bottom of the screen will fill with that color. Then press the shutter button, and only objects of that color will retain any color in the final image (see Figure 5.15). This option is available when shooting movies, also.

Figure 5.15
With the Color Accent SCN mode option, you can tell the camera which single color to retain—in this case red; the rest of the image is transformed to black-and-white.

- **Color Swap.** This operation is similar to Color Accent, except that, rather than retain the color you first select, you change objects of that color to the second color that you select. After pressing the DISP. key, position the center frame over the object whose color you want to change, and press the left cross key. The left box at the bottom of the screen will fill with that color. Then position the center frame over the color you want to change the first object to, and press the right cross key. The right box at the bottom of the screen will fill with that color. Then take the picture, and any object of the first color will have been changed to the second color. This option is also available for movie shooting.

- **Stitch Assist.** This option assists you in putting together panoramic images fashioned out of a series of photographs that overlap to make up a large horizontal expanse, even as much as 360 degrees. On the PowerShot G11, this option is available as the last setting on the SCN menu. On the G10, Stitch Assist is accessed through its own icon on the camera's mode dial. In either case, the functioning is the same. Select Stitch Assist mode, then take a series of photographs covering the desired expanse of scenery, overlapping each image with the previous one. The view on the camera's LCD display shows the last shot on the screen to help you frame the next one to overlap it neatly. The actual work of "stitching" the images together into a final product is done later, in the software that came with the camera (or in other software designed for making panoramic images).

Low Light Mode (G11 Only)

This mode, newly introduced to this PowerShot line with the G11, was considered significant enough to be given its very own spot on the mode dial. This mode is equipped for shooting in some seriously dark locations, such as candle-lit settings and other places with very little ambient light (see Figure 5.16). The camera sets itself to a relatively slow shutter speed and to an impressively high ISO setting as necessary to achieve a proper exposure. The ISO setting is the distinguishing factor with this mode, because that setting can go higher in Low Light mode than you can set it from the ISO dial. With the dial, the highest ISO setting available is 3200, whereas, with this special mode, the camera can set the ISO as high as 12800. The camera will still allow you to turn the flash on automatic when set to Low Light mode, but you may want to turn the flash completely off if you're really trying to take an available-light shot in very low light. You also should note that the camera automatically sets the image size to M (1,824 × 1,368 pixels, or 2.5 megapixels) in this mode.

Figure 5.16
The image shown here was taken outdoors in a dimly lit plaza in Low Light mode with the PowerShot G11 hand-held; the camera set itself to ISO 3200.

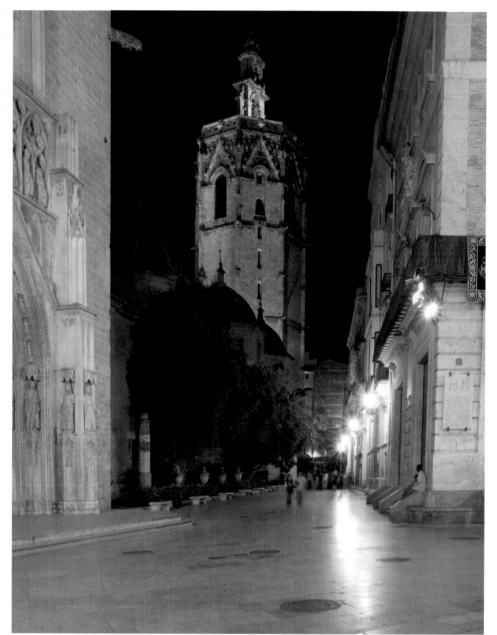

Quick Shot Mode (G11 Only)

This mode, another new feature with the PowerShot G11, offers a dramatically different shooting experience from the other shooting modes on this camera. Like Low Light mode, Quick Shot mode has its own dedicated icon on the mode dial—an image of a camera with speed lines trailing it. This mode is designed for use by the photographer who needs to snap photos very quickly, with no time to stop for elaborate compositions, or even to check the scene in the LCD display before snapping the shutter.

When you turn the dial to Quick Shot mode, the LCD display stops displaying the image seen by the lens, and switches to an information-only screen that shows several of the camera's settings. Before you press the shutter button halfway to check exposure, the screen shows settings including exposure compensation, ISO setting, flash exposure compensation, flash status (auto, on, slow synchro, off), white balance, My Colors, image size and quality, drive mode, self-timer, and a brightness histogram. Once you press the shutter button halfway to check the exposure, the display shows the selected shutter speed, aperture, and ISO (which may have just been set to Auto, so no numerical value was displayed earlier) (see Figure 5.17). You will hear the constant sound of the Continuous AF system adjusting the focus. The overall idea for this mode is that you will quickly check your settings on the highly readable information screen, and hold the camera's optical viewfinder up to your eye to quickly compose and snap each shot.

Figure 5.17
In Quick Shot mode, the PowerShot G11's screen shows only the camera's settings, not the scene itself.

The camera is set up for quick action in a setting such as that of a fast breaking news event, or perhaps for tracking small children and pets at play. It may take some adjustment to your habits to get used to having no image on the LCD screen before shooting, but if the mode's attributes work for you, it can't hurt to have this setup available.

Adjusting Exposure with ISO Settings

Another way of adjusting exposure is by changing the ISO sensitivity setting. Sometimes photographers forget about this option, because the common practice is to set the ISO once for a particular shooting session (say, at ISO 100 or 200 for bright sunlight outdoors, or ISO 800 when shooting indoors) and then forget about ISO. ISOs higher than ISO 100 or 200 are seen as "bad" or "necessary evils." However, changing the ISO is a valid way of adjusting exposure settings, particularly with the Canon PowerShot G10/G11, which produces good results at ISO settings that create grainy, unusable pictures with some other camera models.

Indeed, I find myself using ISO adjustment as a convenient alternate way of adding or subtracting EV when shooting in Manual mode, and as a quick way of choosing equivalent exposures when in automatic or semiautomatic modes. For example, suppose I've selected a manual exposure with both f/stop and shutter speed suitable for my image using, say, ISO 200. I can change the exposure in full-stop increments by turning the ISO dial one click at a time. The difference in image quality/noise at the base setting of ISO 200 is negligible if I dial in ISO 100 to reduce exposure a little, or change to ISO 400 to increase exposure. I keep my preferred f/stop and shutter speed, but still adjust the exposure.

Or, perhaps, I am using Tv mode and the metered exposure at ISO 200 is 1/500th second at f/8. If I decide on the spur of the moment I'd rather use 1/500th second at f/5.6, I can rotate the ISO dial to switch to ISO 100. Of course, it's a good idea to monitor your ISO changes, so you don't end up at ISO 1600 accidentally. ISO settings can, of course, also be used to boost or reduce sensitivity in particular shooting situations. The PowerShot G10 has direct ISO settings from ISO 80 up to 1600, with the special setting of 3200 available through SCN mode. The G11 has direct ISO settings from 80 to 3200. It can go as high as ISO 12800 with the Low Light mode (at reduced resolution), discussed earlier, but you can't make that setting with the ISO dial.

The PowerShot G10/G11 camera can also adjust the ISO automatically as appropriate for various lighting conditions. When you choose the Auto ISO setting, the camera adjusts the sensitivity dynamically to suit the subject matter. Remember that if the Auto ISO ranges aren't suitable for you, individual ISO values can also be selected in any of the more advanced shooting modes (Av, Tv, P, and Manual). However, there is one somewhat confusing aspect of the ISO settings on the PowerShot G10/G11 that you should be aware of. Even though the camera is equipped with an ISO dial, which you can turn to any setting you want at any time, in some cases what looks like a legitimate setting will have no effect. In other words, the camera can't stop you from turning the dial so it looks as if the ISO is set to, say, 100, but it *can* keep that setting from taking effect. For example, in Manual exposure mode, you cannot set the ISO to Auto. Go ahead and try this if you want—set the camera to Manual exposure, then turn the ISO dial to Auto. You will see the word Auto, slightly grayed out, outlined on the LCD screen by the ISO selector. But, you will then see that the camera has set the ISO to 80. There will not be any warning message, and, in fact, at first I thought that the Auto ISO system had chosen 80 as the correct value. I soon realized, though, that the camera is just refusing to accept Auto as the ISO setting.

Similarly, with any of the SCN mode varieties (Portrait, Night Snapshot, Fireworks, etc.), the only ISO setting the camera will accept is Auto, no matter where you set the ISO dial. Here, again, you can turn the ISO dial all you want, and you will see the numbers change, but when the dust settles, the camera will rather stubbornly leave the ISO setting at Auto, with no warning or explanation.

Bracketing

Bracketing is a method for shooting several consecutive exposures using different settings, as a way of improving the odds that one will be exactly right. Before digital cameras took over the universe, it was common to bracket exposures, shooting, say, a series of three photos at 1/125th second, but varying the f/stop from f/8 to f/11 to f/16. In practice, smaller than whole-stop increments were used for greater precision. Plus, it was just as common to keep the same aperture and vary the shutter speed, although in the days before electronic shutters, film cameras often had only whole increment shutter speeds available.

Today, cameras like the PowerShot G10/G11 can bracket exposures much more precisely, taking three shots immediately at the press of the shutter release, and bracket focusing as well. While focus bracketing is sometimes used when there is a tricky situation involving manual focus, auto exposure bracketing (AEB) is used much more often. When this feature is activated, the camera takes three consecutive photos: one at the metered "correct" exposure, one with less exposure, and one with more exposure, using an increment of your choice up to plus 2/minus 2 stops. The procedure for setting up exposure bracketing is discussed in Chapter 4, in connection with the FUNC. menu. Basically, you press the FUNC. key and scroll down to the third option, which is bracketing, and then scroll over to the right to select exposure bracketing, and press the DISP. key to get to the screen where you set the exposure interval. One key point you need to bear in mind, which the camera does not warn you about: you need to have the flash turned off for bracketing to work. So, if you have carefully set up exposure (or focus) bracketing to take three exposures at a set interval, and then press the shutter button, but hear and see only one picture taken, you may want to make sure you have forced the flash to the off position. If flash is set to On or Auto, neither type of bracketing will work.

Be sure to turn bracketing off when you're done with that feature. Bracketing, which can't be used in SCN modes, remains in effect in other modes after the first set of three images is taken, and the setting will continue to be in effect even after the camera has been turned off and then back on, until you turn the electronic flash back on, or return to the FUNC. menu to cancel bracketing. (If you turn the flash back on, you can't use bracketing while the flash is on, but bracketing will still be in effect if you then turn the flash back off. You have to use the FUNC. menu to fully cancel the bracketing setting.)

Bracketing and Merge to HDR

HDR (High Dynamic Range) photography is, at the moment, an incredibly popular fad. There are even entire books that do nothing but tell you how to shoot HDR images. If you aren't familiar with the technique, HDR involves shooting two or three or more images at different bracketed exposures, giving you an "underexposed" version with lots of detail in highlights that would otherwise be washed out; an "overexposed" rendition that preserves detail in the shadows; and several intermediate shots. These are combined to produce a single image that has an amazing amount of detail throughout the scene's entire tonal range.

I call this technique a fad because the reason it exists in the first place is due to a (temporary, I hope) defect in current digital camera sensors. It's presently impossible to capture the full range of brightness that we perceive; digital cameras, including the PowerShot G10/G11, can't even grab the full range of brightness that *film* can see, as I showed you in Figures 5.1 and 5.2 at the beginning of this chapter.

But as the megapixel race slows down, sensor designers have already begun designing capture electronics that have larger density (dynamic) ranges, and I fully expect to see cameras within a few years that can produce images similar to what we're getting now with HDR manipulation in image editors.

HDR works like this: Suppose you wanted to photograph a dimly lit room that had a bright window showing an outdoors scene. Proper exposure for the room might be on the order of 1/60th second at f/2.8 at ISO 200, while the outdoors scene probably would require f/11 at 1/400th second. That's almost a 7 EV step difference (approximately 7 f/stops) and well beyond the dynamic range of any digital camera, including the PowerShot G10/G11.

When you're using Merge to HDR, a feature found in Adobe Photoshop (similar functions are available in other programs, including Photomatix [www.hdrsoft.com; free to try, $99 to buy]), you'd take several pictures. As I mentioned earlier, one would be exposed for the shadows, one for the highlights, and perhaps one for the midtones. Then, you'd use the Merge to HDR command (or the equivalent in other software) to combine all of the images into one HDR image that integrates the well-exposed sections of each version. You can use the PowerShot G10/G11's exposure bracketing feature to produce those images.

The images should be as identical as possible, except for exposure. So, it's a good idea to mount the camera on a tripod, use a remote release, and take all the exposures in one burst. Just follow these steps:

1. **Set up your camera on a sturdy support.** Mount the PowerShot G10/G11 on a tripod and connect a remote release switch (such as the optional Canon RS60-E3), if available.

2. **Specify RAW.** Set the camera to shoot RAW images, as described in Chapter 4.

3. **Choose bracketing.** Set exposure bracketing to a two-stop increment, as described earlier in this chapter and in Chapter 4.

4. **Focus.** Manually focus or autofocus the camera.

5. **Take your shots.** Trigger the camera to expose your set of three images.

6. **Process the photos.** Copy your images to your computer and continue in Photoshop with the Merge to HDR steps listed next.

The next steps show you how to combine the separate exposures into one merged High Dynamic Range image. The sample images shown in Figures 5.18, 5.19, and 5.21 show the results you can get from a two-shot bracketed sequence. I merged only two pictures for simplicity, because the differences between three or more bracketed exposures, even when taken at exposures that are two stops apart, may not show up well on the printed page.

1. If you use an application to transfer the files to your computer, make sure it does not make any adjustments to brightness, contrast, or exposure. You want the real raw information for Merge to HDR to work with. If you do everything correctly, you'll end up with at least two photos like the ones shown in Figures 5.18 and 5.19.

2. Load the images into Photoshop using your preferred RAW converter.

3. Save as .PSD files.

4. Activate Merge to HDR by choosing File > Automate > Merge to HDR.

5. Select the photos to be merged, as shown in Figure 5.20, where I have specified the two PSD files. You'll note a checkbox that can be used to automatically align the images if they were not taken with the camera mounted on a rock-steady support.

6. Once HDR merge has done its thing, you must save in .PSD, to retain the file's full color information, in case you want to work with the HDR image later. Otherwise, you can convert to a normal 24-bit file and save in any compatible format.

Figure 5.18 Make one exposure for the shadow areas.

Figure 5.19 Make a second exposure for the highlights, such as the sky.

Figure 5.20
Use the Merge
to HDR com-
mand to com-
bine the two
images.

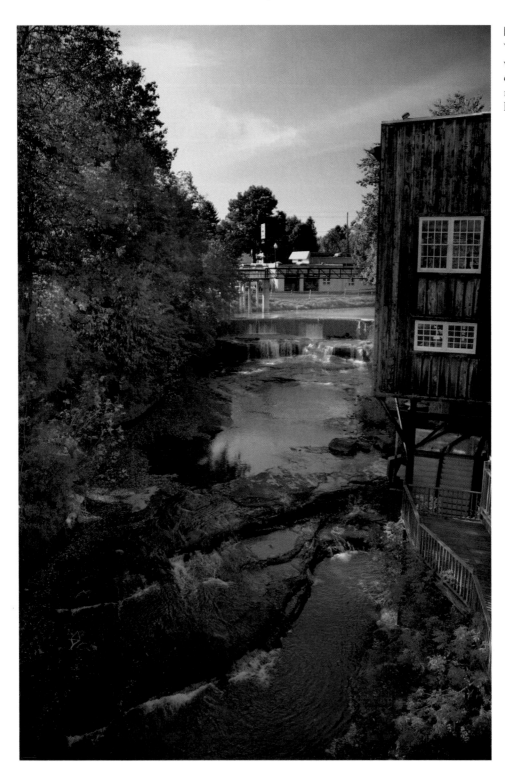

Figure 5.21
You'll end up with an extended dynamic range photo like this one.

If you do everything correctly, you'll end up with a photo like the one shown in Figure 5.21, which has the properly exposed foreground of the first shot, and the well-exposed sky of the second image. Note that, ideally, nothing should move between shots. In the example pictures, the river is moving, but the exposures were made so close together that, after the merger, you can't really tell.

What if you don't have the opportunity, inclination, or skills to create several images at different exposures, as described? If you shoot in RAW format, you can still use Merge to HDR, working with a *single* original image file. What you do is import the image into Photoshop several times, using Adobe Camera Raw to create multiple copies of the file at different exposure levels.

For example, you'd create one copy that's too dark, so the shadows lose detail, but the highlights are preserved. Create another copy with the shadows intact and allow the highlights to wash out. Then, you can use Merge to HDR to combine the two and end up with a finished image that has the extended dynamic range you're looking for.

Dealing with Noise

Image noise is that random grainy effect that some like to use as a visual effect, but which, most of the time, is objectionable because it robs your image of detail even as it adds that "interesting" texture. Noise is caused by two different conditions: high ISO settings and long exposures.

High ISO noise commonly appears when you raise your camera's sensitivity setting above ISO 400. With the Canon G10 camera, noise may become visible at ISO 800, and is usually fairly noticeable at ISO 1600. The G11 does a much better job at higher ISO settings. This kind of noise appears as a result of the amplification needed to increase the sensitivity of the sensor. While higher ISOs do pull details out of dark areas, they also amplify non-signal information randomly, creating noise.

A similar noisy phenomenon occurs during long time exposures, which allow more photons to reach the sensor, increasing your ability to capture a picture under low light conditions. However, the longer exposures also increase the likelihood that some pixels will register random phantom photons, often because the longer an imager is "hot" the warmer it gets, and that heat can be mistaken for photons.

Fortunately, Canon's electronics geniuses have done a good job minimizing noise from all causes in the PowerShot G10 and a better job with the G11. You can also apply noise reduction to some extent using Photoshop or similar software, and when converting RAW files to some other format, using your favorite RAW converter, or an industrial-strength product like Noise Ninja (www.picturecode.com) to wipe out noise after you've already taken the picture.

Fixing Exposures with Histograms

While you can often recover poorly exposed photos in your image editor, your best bet is to arrive at the correct exposure in the camera, minimizing the tweaks that you have to make in post-processing. However, you can't always judge exposure just by viewing the image on your PowerShot G10/G11's LCD before or after the shot is made. Ambient light may make the LCD difficult to see, and the brightness level you've set can affect the appearance of the playback image.

Instead, you can use a histogram, which is a chart displayed on the PowerShot G10/G11's LCD that shows the number of tones being captured at each brightness level. You can use the information to provide correction for the shot you are about to take, or for the next shot you take. The G10/G11 offers a histogram that shows overall brightness levels for an image, which can be displayed during Shooting mode or Playback mode.

DISPLAYING HISTOGRAMS

To view histograms on your screen, press the DISP. button while an image is shown on the LCD, either before shooting or during playback. Keep pressing the button until the histogram is shown. The display will cycle between several levels of information, one of which will include the histogram. If you don't see the histogram while in Shooting mode, go to Custom Display on the Shooting menu and change that setting. The histogram will display only in Program, Shutter Priority, Aperture Priority, and Manual shooting modes, as well as in Quick Shot mode on the PowerShot G11. You also can display the histogram on the review image that displays right after you have taken a picture. Set that option by choosing Review Info from the Shooting menu, and then selecting Detailed.

A brightness histogram like that used in the PowerShot G10/G11 is a chart that includes a representation of up to 256 vertical lines on a horizontal axis that show the number of pixels in the image at each brightness level, from 0 (black) on the left side to 255 (white) on the right. (The 2.8-inch or 3-inch LCD of these PowerShot models doesn't have enough pixels to show each and every one of the 256 lines, but, instead, provides a representation of the shape of the curve formed.) The more pixels at a given level, the taller the bar at that position. If no bar appears at a particular position on the scale from left to right, there are no pixels at that particular brightness level.

A typical histogram produces a mountain-like shape, with most of the pixels bunched in the middle tones, with fewer pixels at the dark and light ends of the scale. Ideally, though, there will be at least some pixels at either extreme, so that your image has both a true black and a true white representing some details. Learn to spot histograms that represent over- and underexposure, and add or subtract exposure using an EV modification to compensate.

For example, Figure 5.22 shows the histogram for an image that is badly underexposed. You can guess from the shape of the histogram that many of the dark tones to the left of the graph have been clipped off. There's plenty of room on the right side for additional pixels to reside without having them become overexposed. Or, a histogram might look like Figure 5.23, which is overexposed. In either case, you can increase or decrease the exposure (either by changing the f/stop or shutter speed in Manual mode or by adding or subtracting an EV value in Program mode) to produce the corrected histogram shown in Figure 5.24, in which the tones "hug" the right side of the histogram to produce as many highlight details as possible. See "Making EV Changes," earlier in this chapter for information on dialing in exposure compensation.

The histogram can also be used to aid in fixing the contrast of an image, although gauging incorrect contrast is more difficult. For example, if the histogram shows all the tones bunched up in one place in the image, the photo will be low in contrast. If the tones are spread out more or less evenly, the image is probably high in contrast. In either case, your best bet may be to switch to RAW (if you're not already using that format) so you can adjust contrast in post processing. However, you can also change to a user-defined setting using the My Colors feature (not available when shooting RAW), with contrast set lower or higher as required.

Figure 5.22
This histogram shows an underexposed image.

Figure 5.23
This histogram reveals that the image is over-exposed.

Figure 5.24
A histogram for a properly exposed image should look like this.

6

Advanced Shooting and Movie-Making with Your Canon PowerShot G10/G11

Getting the right exposure is one of the foundations of a great photograph, but a lot more goes into a compelling shot than good tonal values. A sharp image, proper white balance, good color, and other factors all can help elevate your image from good to exceptional. So, now that you've got a good understanding of exposure tucked away, you'll want to learn how to use the automatic and manual focusing controls available with the Canon PowerShot G10/G11, and master some of the many ways you can fine tune your images. We'll also discuss some creative ways to use exposure, including using very short or long exposures, and we'll look at techniques to improve your movie-making with this camera.

Getting into Focus

Learning to use the Canon PowerShot G10/G11's autofocus system is easy, but you do need to fully understand how the system works to get the most benefit from it. Once you're comfortable with autofocus, you'll know when it's appropriate to use the manual focus option, too. The important thing to remember is that focus isn't absolute. For example, some things that appear to be in sharp focus at a given viewing size and distance might not be in focus at a larger size and/or closer distance. In addition, the goal of optimum focus isn't always to make things look sharp. Not all of an image will be or should be sharp. Controlling exactly what is sharp and what is not is part of your creative palette. Use of depth-of-field characteristics to throw part of an image out of focus while other parts are sharply focused is one of the most valuable tools available to a photographer. But selective focus works only when the desired areas of an image are in focus properly. For the digital camera photographer, correct focus can be one of the trickiest parts of the technical and creative process.

Your camera's autofocus sensors require a certain minimum amount of light to operate. If necessary, the AF assist beam built into the PowerShot G10/G11 and Canon's dedicated flash units provide additional light that helps assure enough illumination for autofocus.

Focus Modes and Options

As you've come to appreciate by now, the PowerShot G10/G11 offers many options for how it approaches photography. Focus is no exception. Of course, as with other aspects of this camera, you can set the shooting mode to Auto, and the camera will do just fine in its focusing in most situations. (Actually, the G10 will still let you choose an AF mode even if the shooting mode is Auto.) But, if you want more creative control, the choices are there for you to make. The PowerShot's focus options actually provide you with more choices than any other aspect of the camera's operation.

Assuming you're not going to set the shooting mode to Auto, your first choice is whether to use autofocus or manual focus. Manual focus, of course, was the only choice available to photographers from the nineteenth century days of daguerreotypes until about the 1980s, when autofocus started becoming available. Manual focus presents you with great flexibility along with the challenge of keeping the image in focus under what may be challenging conditions, such as rapid motion of the subject, darkness of the scene, and the like. We'll talk more about manual focus later in this chapter. For now, we'll assume you're going to rely on the camera's AF capabilities.

The PowerShot G10/G11 has two basic AF modes: Continuous AF and Continuous AF off (also known as Single Autofocus and Single-Shot AF). Beyond those two basic modes, there is a more specialized mode called Servo AF that is designed for one particular type of situation. Once you have decided on which AF mode to use, you also need to tell the camera how to set the AF Frame. In other words, after you tell the camera how to autofocus, you also have to tell it where to direct its focusing attention. I'll explain each of the three focus modes, and other aspects of focus in more detail later in this section.

MANUAL FOCUS

With Manual focus activated by pressing the up cross key, your PowerShot G10/G11 lets you set the focus yourself by turning the control dial. There are some advantages and disadvantages to this approach. While your batteries will last slightly longer in Manual focus mode, it will take you longer to focus the camera for each photo, a process that can be tricky. Modern digital cameras depend so much on autofocus that the viewfinders are no longer designed for optimum manual focus. The optical viewfinder on your PowerShot, for example, can't be used for manual focusing at all—you must rely on the view (magnified or otherwise) on the LCD. So, although manual focus is still an option for you to consider in certain circumstances, it's not as easy to use as it once was. I recommend that you try to use the camera's various AF options first, and switch to Manual focus only if AF is not working for you.

Focus Pocus

Although Canon began adding autofocus capabilities to its film cameras in the 1980s, prior to that focusing was always done manually. Honest. Imagine what it must have been like to focus manually under demanding, fast-moving conditions such as sports photography.

Focusing was problematic because our eyes and brains have poor memory for correct focus, which is why your eye doctor must shift back and forth between sets of lenses and ask "Does that look sharper—or was it sharper before?" in determining your correct prescription. Similarly, manual focusing involves jogging the focus ring back and forth as you go from almost in focus, to sharp focus, to almost focused again. The little clockwise and counterclockwise arcs decrease in size until you've zeroed in on the point of correct focus. What you're looking for is the image with the most contrast between the edges of elements in the image.

The PowerShot G10/G11's autofocus mechanism, like all such systems found in modern digital cameras, also evaluates these increases and decreases in sharpness, but it is able to remember the progression perfectly, so that autofocus can lock in much more quickly and, with an image that has sufficient contrast, more precisely. Unfortunately, while the PowerShot's focus system finds it easy to measure degrees of apparent focus at each of the focus points in the viewfinder, it doesn't really know with any certainty *which* object should be in sharpest focus. Is it the closest object? The subject in the center? Something lurking *behind* the closest subject? A person standing over at the side of the picture? Many of the techniques for using autofocus effectively involve telling the PowerShot G10/G11 exactly what it should be focusing on.

Adding Circles of Confusion

But there are other factors in play, as well. You know that increased depth-of-field brings more of your subject into focus. But more depth-of-field also makes autofocusing (or manual focusing) more difficult because the contrast is lower between objects at different distances. So, autofocus with the camera's lens set to its maximum 120mm focal length may be easier than at the minimum 28mm focal length (or zoom setting), because at the longer focal length the lens has less apparent depth-of-field.

To make things even more complicated, many subjects aren't polite enough to remain still. They move around in the frame, so that even if the PowerShot is sharply focused on your main subject, the subject may change position and require refocusing. An intervening subject may pop into the frame and pass between you and the subject you meant to photograph. You (or the PowerShot) have to decide whether to lock focus on this new subject, or remain focused on the original subject. Finally, there are some kinds of subjects that are difficult to bring into sharp focus because they lack enough contrast to allow the PowerShot's AF system (or our eyes) to lock in. Blank walls, a clear blue sky, or other subject matter may make focusing difficult.

If you find all these focus factors confusing, you're on the right track. Focus is, in fact, measured using something called a *circle of confusion*. An ideal image consists of zillions of tiny little points, which, like all points, theoretically have no height or width. There is perfect contrast between the point and its surroundings. You can think of each point as a pinpoint of light in a darkened room. When a given point is out of focus, its edges decrease in contrast and it changes from a perfect point to a tiny disc with blurry edges (remember, blur is the lack of contrast between boundaries in an image). (See Figure 6.1.)

If this blurry disc—the circle of confusion—is small enough, our eye still perceives it as a point. It's only when the disc grows large enough that we can see it as a blur rather than a sharp point that a given point is viewed as out of focus. You can see, then, that enlarging an image, either by displaying it larger on your computer monitor or by making a large print, also enlarges the size of each circle of confusion. Moving closer to the

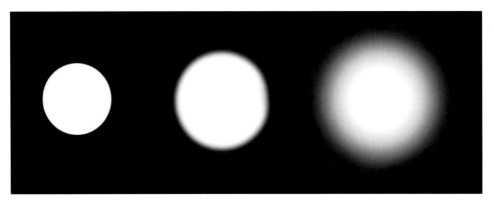

Figure 6.1
When a pinpoint of light (left) goes out of focus, its blurry edges form a circle of confusion (center and right).

image does the same thing. So, parts of an image that may look perfectly sharp in a 5×7-inch print viewed at arm's length, might appear blurry when blown up to 11×14 and examined at the same distance. Take a few steps back, however, and the image may look sharp again.

To a lesser extent, the viewer also affects the apparent size of these circles of confusion. Some people see details better at a given distance and may perceive smaller circles of confusion than someone standing next to them. For the most part, however, such differences are small. Truly blurry images will look blurry to just about everyone under the same conditions.

Technically, there is just one plane within your picture area, parallel to the back of the camera (or sensor, in the case of a digital camera), that is in sharp focus. That's the plane in which the points of the image are rendered as precise points. At every other plane in front of or behind the focus plane, the points show up as discs that range from slightly blurry to extremely blurry. (See Figure 6.2.) In practice, the discs in many of these planes

Figure 6.2
The model is in focus, but the area behind her appears blurry because the depth-of-field is limited.

will still be so small that we see them as points, and that's where we get depth-of-field. Depth-of-field is just the range of planes that includes discs that we perceive as points rather than blurred splotches. The size of this range increases as the aperture is reduced in size and is allocated roughly one-third in front of the plane of sharpest focus, and two-thirds behind it. The range of sharp focus is always greater behind your subject than in front of it.

Using Manual Focus

As I noted earlier, manual focus is not as attractive an option nowadays as it used to be when cameras were designed for that method of focusing and were equipped with readily visible focusing aids. But Canon's designers have done a good job of letting you exercise your initiative in the focusing realm, so you certainly should become familiar with the technique for those occasions when it makes sense to take control in this area. Here are the basic steps:

- **Select a shooting mode other than Auto.** If you set the mode to Auto, you'll be pressing the MF button in vain; it just won't respond, because manual focus is not available in that mode.

- **Press the MF button (top cross key).** The large letters MF will appear on the screen, then fade to a small icon at the bottom of the screen (top of the screen on the G11).

- **Aim at your subject and turn the control dial to focus.** The focusing block in the center of the screen will enlarge to help you assess whether the image is in focus. (That is, unless you turned off this feature, called MF-point Zoom, through the Shooting menu.) Turn the dial until the subject appears to be in the sharpest possible focus.

- **Use the Safety MF feature to fine tune the focus.** After you have made your focus adjustments with the control dial, you can press either the shutter button or the AF Frame/Trash button to "fine tune" the focus. Actually, this just means that after going through all the trouble of using manual focus, you're going to punt and use autofocus after all, which may seem a bit strange. But, in some circumstances this could be a useful procedure, because you are getting the focus system started by showing it exactly where to focus, then letting it finish up the process. It also may help you get used to the manual focus procedure by practicing and comparing your results to those of the autofocus mechanism. This Safety MF feature is not available if you turn it off through the Shooting menu.

- **If your subject is a particular, small area of the overall scene, set the camera to Single-Shot AF (Continuous AF off), and set the AF Frame to FlexiZone.** Then set the focus frame to its smallest size and move it over the area of the scene that needs to be in sharpest focus.

Hyperfocal Distance—A Tool for Quick Candid Shots

There is one somewhat specialized area in which you might want to consider a particular advantage of using manual focus—to grab quick shots without using any of the autofocus options at all, and without having to manually focus the camera. In effect, this technique lets you convert your sophisticated autofocusing camera into something like a Kodak Brownie from days of old—a box camera that shoots with a fixed focus, but still manages to take quite presentable pictures.

The key here is to use Manual focus, and preset it to what is called the camera's *hyperfocal distance*, which is defined as the focusing distance at which everything from half that distance to infinity will appear to be in sharp focus. Note that I say things will "appear" to be in sharp focus. As I discussed earlier in this chapter, there is only one mathematical plane in which images will actually be in perfectly sharp focus for a given lens, taking into account factors such as focal length and aperture. However, because of our old friends the circles of confusion, even though images may not be in perfect focus, if those circles are small enough, they will still appear to be in sharp enough focus to pass our visual inspection.

If you aspire to what some call "street photography"—snapping candid shots of people and other subjects on city streets (or in other public locations) when you see something that catches your eye, you may want to try this technique. With the camera's focus preset, you don't have to fiddle with any controls or settings; you can just fire away at anything that catches your interest within the zone of sharp focus. There are many varied approaches taken by different photographers in this area, and you will need to experiment to find a system that works for you. Following is one possible way to set up the PowerShot G10/G11 for quick, candid shots using the hyperfocal distance:

- **Set up the camera's other shooting options.** I suggest setting the shooting mode to Aperture Priority (Av) and using as small an aperture as you can manage, given the prevailing lighting conditions. Try to use at least f/4.5 to widen the depth-of-field. I suggest using Evaluative exposure metering, auto white balance, and RAW + L image size and quality to leave your options open for post-processing. Set the flash to forced off. Set Continuous AF on, so you can snap lots of shots when the right moment comes. You may want to turn off the camera's operational sounds to avoid attracting attention. With the PowerShot G11, consider using the swivel screen at an angle so you don't have to face in the direction you're shooting.

- **Set the camera to Manual focus at the hyperfocal distance.** This step requires that you do some homework before you go out on your candid-shooting expedition. You can go to www.dofmaster.com to find tools to calculate the camera's hyperfocal distance. You have to base the calculation on the actual focal length of the camera's lens. In our case, although the 35mm equivalent focal length of the PowerShot G10/G11's lens at its wide-angle setting is 28mm, its actual focal length (marked on the lens) is 6.1mm. Using that value, and f/4.5 as our aperture, the answer is that the hyperfocal distance for the PowerShot's lens is 3.9 feet. This means that, if you set the camera's manual focus to 3.9 feet and leave it there, everything you shoot, from a distance of about 2 feet (half of 3.9 feet) to infinity will appear sharp, as long as you're using the full wide-angle setting for your lens. Of course, the PowerShot camera does not have a focusing scale that shows exactly where 3.9 feet is. If you want to be as exact as possible, get a measuring tape and set the camera up exactly 3.9 feet from a subject, then adjust the Manual focus control until focus is sharp, and note exactly where the focusing bar reaches on the camera's scale.

■ **Save all of these settings to C2.** Once all of the above settings are just the way you want them, choose Save Settings from the Shooting menu and save all of them to C2 on the mode dial. (I suggest C2 just because it's the last setting on the dial, and might be easier to turn to in a hurry than C1.)

■ **When you see a likely subject, turn to C2 and fire away.** Try these settings for a while and check out the results. If they don't measure up, change various settings until you have created the perfect instrument for super street photography.

Your Autofocus Mode Options

Choosing the right autofocus mode and the way in which focus points are selected is your key to success. Using the wrong mode for a particular type of photography can lead to a series of pictures that are all sharply focused—on the wrong subject. When I first started shooting sports with an autofocus camera (back in the film camera days), I covered one baseball game alternating between shots of base runners and outfielders with pictures of a promising young pitcher, all from a position next to the third base dugout. The base runner and outfielder photos were great, because their backgrounds didn't distract the autofocus mechanism. But all my photos of the pitcher had the focus tightly zeroed in on the fans in the stands behind him. Because I was shooting with film instead of a digital camera, I didn't know about my gaffe until the film was developed. A simple change, such as locking in focus or focus zone manually, or even manually focusing, would have done the trick.

To save battery power, your PowerShot ordinarily doesn't start to focus the lens until you partially depress the shutter release. But, autofocus isn't some mindless beast out there snapping your pictures in and out of focus with no feedback from you after you press that button. There are several settings you can modify that return a fair amount of control to you. Your first decision should be whether you set the PowerShot G10/G11to Continuous or Continuous Off (what the rest of the world calls One-Shot AF/Single Autofocus).

1. Press the Menu button and navigate to the Shooting menu.

2. Scroll to the entry called AF Mode (G10) or Continuous AF (G11, shown in Figure 6.3).

Figure 6.3

Press the left/right cross keys until the AF choice you want is selected.

3. Set AF mode to Continuous or Single (G10) or set Continuous AF to On or Off (G11).

4. Press the Menu button again to exit.

Here are what each of the available autofocus modes do:

Single Autofocus/Continuous AF Off

If you've chosen Single autofocus (G10) or elected to leave Continuous AF turned off (G11, which is the same thing, but with misleading terminology), you'll be using the mode also called *Single Autofocus* by most of the universe. In this mode, focus is set when you press the shutter button halfway and remains locked at that focus setting until the button is fully depressed, taking the picture, or until you release the shutter button without taking a shot. For non-action photography, this option is usually your best choice, as it minimizes out-of-focus pictures, at the expense of spontaneity, because the camera will not take a picture at all while it is seeking focus. You're locked out of shooting until the autofocus mechanism is happy with the current focus setting. Continuous AF off/Single-Shot AF/Single Autofocus is sometimes referred to as *focus priority* for that reason. Because of the small delay while the camera zeroes in on correct focus, you might experience slightly more shutter lag. This mode uses less battery power than Continuous AF.

When sharp focus is achieved, the focus frame will turn green and you'll hear a little beep (assuming you have normal shooting and setup options enabled). By keeping the shutter button depressed halfway, you'll find you can reframe the image by moving the camera to aim at another angle while retaining the focus (and exposure) that's been set.

Continuous AF

Continuous AF is a mode you might want to use when photographing sports, young kids at play, and other fast-moving subjects. In this mode, the autofocus system continues to operate all the time, even when the shutter button is not depressed halfway. In other words, the camera always attempts to focus the image. When you use this mode, the camera will be ready to fine tune its focus quickly once you decide on a final subject at which to aim the camera, because the focusing apparatus is doing its best to be ready for the current focusing conditions. Of course, this option drains battery power quite quickly, so turn it off unless you have a definite need for it (or have an endless supply of batteries). In addition, this option can have the drawback of the camera's switching its focus to any subject that enters the focus frame, thereby drawing the focus away from a subject you were interested in. That's where the next AF mode comes into play.

Servo AF

Servo AF is another option that can be turned on from the Shooting menu on either the G10 or the G11 (see Figure 6.4) and can be used alone, or with Continuous AF activated. This option tells the camera to lock autofocus on the subject in the focus

Figure 6.4
Select Servo AF from the Shooting menu when you want to keep the focus on a particular moving subject.

frame when you press the shutter release halfway, and then continue to keep that subject in focus, as long as it remains within the focus frame.

The focus frame in the center turns blue when you lock on to a subject in this way, and the camera will continue to lock its focus on the subject within that blue frame, as long as you are able to keep the subject in the focus frame. This option is designed for situations such as tracking a particular athlete at a sporting event, a particular performer at a concert, or a particular child racing around on a playground. This focus mode addresses the situation we just discussed in connection with Continuous AF mode, in which a new subject moves into the frame and steals the focus away from the subject you are most interested in, by ensuring that the subject you want to focus on stays in focus (as long as you keep it within the blue frame). Again, as with Continuous AF (which can be used at the same time as Servo AF), this option puts a strain on your battery supply, so preserve it for occasions when it is of definite use.

I know these three focus options can be confusing, so Table 6.1 is a summary of when to use each of them.

Table 6.1 Autofocus Modes

Mode	What it does	When to use
Continuous AF off (G11)/ Single-Shot Autofocus (G10)	Locks focus only when shutter release is pressed halfway, and does not refocus if subject moves. Camera will shoot picture only when focus is achieved.	When shooting subjects that are not in motion, when you want to minimize number of out-of-focus shots.
Continuous AF	Tries to focus at all times, even before shutter release is pressed halfway. Camera will shoot picture even if focus is not achieved.	Moving subjects, when you want the camera to focus and refocus for a possible shot.
Servo AF	Locks focus on subject within focus frame when shutter release is pressed halfway, and refocuses if the subject moves but remains within the focus frame. Camera will shoot picture even if focus is not achieved.	Use when you want to lock focus on a particular subject that may be moving, and want the camera to ignore other moving objects that come into the frame *after* you've pressed the shutter release button halfway. Use with or without Continuous AF, so the camera will/will not also focus *before* pressing the shutter halfway.

Setting the AF Frame

You're not done yet with choosing the settings for autofocus on these PowerShot models. The settings already discussed—Continuous AF off/Single-Shot AF, Continuous AF, Servo AF, and Manual focus, all tell the camera *how* to focus. But, with the AF modes, the camera needs to be told not only how to focus, but *where* to focus. That is the subject of our next discussion—telling the camera where to focus, by setting the options for the AF Frame. (This function is not available in Movie or Auto modes.)

Both the PowerShot G10 and G11 offer a fairly impressive array of autofocus frame options, which help you dictate exactly where in the scene the sharpest focus should be. To select the AF Frame mode, follow these steps:

1. Press the Menu button, navigate to the Shooting menu, select the top entry (AF Frame), and press the left/right cross keys to select from among the choices available with your current shooting mode. (With some modes, the choice will be either On or Off.) Press Menu again to exit.

   Or:

2. Press the AF Frame/Trash button on the back right of the camera, followed by the * button located to the right of the AF Frame button.

3. As you press the * button, the AF Frame mode cycles among the modes available using your current shooting mode setting. When you've selected the mode you want to use, press the AF Frame button again to confirm it. You can move the frame with the cross keys or the control dial.

The G10 and G11 take slightly different approaches to handling AF Frames, so I'll discuss the operations individually for each camera.

PowerShot G10

On the G10, you have up to four choices for how the AF Frame works, depending on shooting mode: Face Detect, AiAf, Center, and FlexiZone:

- **Face Detect.** When you press the shutter button down halfway, the camera will detect what it believes to be human faces and place AF Frames on up to three of them. The camera will place a white frame over what it believes to be the main subject, and a gray frame over up to two additional faces. (See Figure 6.5.) If you are satisfied with the camera's choice, press the shutter button down fully to take the picture. The camera will use the selected face to calculate focus, exposure, white balance, and flash exposure (if flash is used).

  To move the focus frame to a different face, press the AF Frame button, then use the left/right cross keys or the control dial to move the focus frame to another face. Then press the AF Frame button again to lock in this choice.

Figure 6.5

In Face Detect
mode, the
PowerShot
G10 will detect
up to three
faces, placing a
white block
around the
main subject's
face, and gray
blocks around
additional
faces.

Tip

If only gray frames are placed (no main face is selected), or the G10 is unable to select a face (usually because the faces are too small, too large, located at the edge of the frame, or are turned sideways), then focus frame mode switches to AiAF if Continous AF off/Single-Shot autofocus is active; or to Center if Continuous AF or Servo AF are active. You can activate/deactivate Face Detect by pressing the AF Frame button and using the up/down cross keys to toggle between On and Off.

■ **AiAF.** The camera uses a matrix of up to 9 frames to determine focus using computer intelligence. When you first press the shutter button halfway to focus with this mode, you may see only one block, or you may see more. To see the whole matrix of 9 blocks, press the AF Frame button. (See Figure 6.6).

You can then change the size of this AF block between large and small with presses of the DISP. button, and, when the block is small, you can move it around the screen with the control dial or with the four cross keys. This method of focusing lets the camera use its computations to determine the optimum focus, while giving you a certain degree of control by letting you change the size and location of the measuring grid.

Figure 6.6
In AiAF mode, the PowerShot G10 uses a block of nine AF Frames that can be moved around the screen and resized.

- **Center.** This is the simplest of the AF Frame choices. The focusing frame is locked in the center of the screen. This choice is available only in Auto shooting mode and in the various Scene modes. (One exception: The Center AF Frame mode is available in other shooting modes [P, Av, Tv, and M] when you have turned off the LCD display with the DISP. button.)

- **FlexiZone.** In this mode, the AF Frame starts out as a normal-sized rectangle in the center of the screen, but, after pressing the AF Frame button, you can change the frame's size to very small with the DISP. button, and you can move either size frame around the screen with the four cross keys or the control dial. I personally like this focusing option for many situations, particularly where there is no need for speed of focusing, because it lets you focus quite precisely on a very small area of your scene, thereby relying more on your judgment as a photographer than on the machine intelligence of the camera.

PowerShot G11

With the G11, Canon has streamlined and consolidated the AF Frame choices somewhat. With this newer PowerShot model, the only two choices on the Shooting menu in most shooting modes are Face AiAF and FlexiZone.

■ **Face AiAF.** Face AiAF combines the functions of Face Detect and AiAF from the G10. The camera will display frames for up to 9 detected faces. Here again, as with the G10, you can press the AF frame button to enter Face Select mode, in which the camera places a frame over what it believes to the be main subject, and up to two additional faces. (Similar to Figure 6.5.) You can move this frame to another face by pressing the AF frame button, and then pressing the left/right cross keys. Or, hold down the AF frame button again to deselect the face. Then take the picture.

In Auto shooting mode, only Face AiAF is available. In other shooting modes, if FlexiZone is selected, it is changed to Center if the LCD display is turned off. (That makes sense, because you would have a hard time moving the focus frame around the screen if you couldn't see the screen!)

Tip

If, as with the G10, only gray frames are placed (no main face is selected), or the G11 is unable to select a face (usually because the faces are too small, too large, located at the edge of the frame, or are turned sideways), then the camera will try to select a main subject and display up to nine green frames when the shutter release is pressed halfway.

■ **FlexiZone.** This mode on the G11 works similarly to the way it does on the G10. The AF Frame starts out as a rectangle in the center of the screen, but, after pressing the AF Frame button, you can change the frame's size to very small with the DISP. button. Press the DISP. button again to toggle back to the original size. You can move either size focus frame around the screen with the four cross keys or the control dial. (See Figure 6.7).

So, what should a photographer do when faced with all of these focusing options? Following are some general guidelines based on my own preferences. You very well may develop a different set of guidelines that are more suitable for your own situations.

■ If you're taking casual snapshots or are in a hurry and don't have time to make detailed settings, set the shooting mode to Auto and the chances are very good that the pictures will be in focus.

■ If your subject is an orderly group of people standing still, set the focus mode to Single-Shot AF (Continuous AF off) and set the AF Frame to Face Detect (Face AiAF on the G11).

Figure 6.7
The FlexiZone autofocus frame can be moved around the screen and resized by pressing the DISP. button.

- If your subject is a general group of people, animals, or other objects in constant motion, set the camera to Continuous AF and set the AF Frame to AiAF (Face AiAF on the G11).

- If your subject is a particular person or other object among a general group of people, animals, or objects in constant motion, set the camera to Continuous AF and to Servo AF; set the AF Frame to AiAF (Face AiAF on the G11). Then aim the AF Frame at your particular subject and press the shutter button halfway, and keep the blue focus frame locked on your subject until you take the picture.

- If your subject is a particular, small area of the overall scene, set the camera to Single-Shot AF (Continuous AF off), and set the AF Frame to FlexiZone. Then set the focus frame to its smallest size and move it over the area of the scene that needs to be in sharpest focus.

Locking Manual Focus

When you have composed your image and pressed the shutter button down halfway so that the camera's autofocus system has locked in its exposure and focus, press the MF button (up cross key.) Now the MF icon will appear on the screen, and the focus will be locked at this distance until you either take the picture or press the MF button again to release the lock. This procedure could be useful if you need to preset the focus distance for a subject that isn't available yet but will need to be shot quickly, and you know in advance at what distance it will be from the camera.

Macro Shooting

Shooting with the macro focusing option, which means shooting extreme close-ups, is an entire branch of photography in itself. The most serious practitioners of macro photography use highly specialized equipment, including special lenses, extension tubes, bellows, racks, tripods, lights, and on and on. But, with the PowerShot G10/G11, you actually have an amazingly capable instrument for general macro photography, which can be of considerable use to you even if you don't join the ranks of the true macro-philes.

Although macro shooting is not something you're likely to do every day unless you're a coin collector, student of insects, or aficionado of other very small things, the chances are you will have some occasion to use the remarkable capabilities of the PowerShot G10/G11 to focus down to a vanishingly small distance from your subject (see Figure 6.8). Without the use of any add-on lenses or other extra equipment, both of these

Figure 6.8
These crayons were photographed from just three inches away.

models can focus down to 1 centimeter from the end of the lens—that is just four-tenths of an inch, or about the thickness of my little finger! And the camera can achieve this marvel of focusing while still using its various autofocus modes, though, of course, several of them (Face Detect, Servo AF, etc.) would not be useful while shooting at that range, or anywhere close to it. Note that the 1-centimeter distance is available only when the PowerShot's lens is zoomed back to its wide-angle setting; when it's zoomed in to its full telephoto focal length of 120mm, the closest it can focus in macro mode is 30 centimeters (about 12 inches).

Before I detail the steps for successful use of the macro focusing mode, here are some ideas for how you might make use of it:

- Document the contents of coin and stamp collections, or collections of any small items.

- Take close-up shots of flowers and plants while they're in full bloom. Explore them in different lighting conditions and from various angles to uncover different aspects of their beauty.

- Get close enough to insects, reptiles, and other living creatures to capture their activities and appearances in documentary-like detail.

- Unleash your creative side by putting together elaborate (or simple) tabletop still-life tableaus in the spirit of Salvador Dali, or that are just fun to look at.

- Take sharply focused close-ups from various angles to illustrate items you are selling on eBay or other online auction sites.

- If you need a quick copy of a receipt, instruction sheet, check, or other document and don't have access to a copy machine, pull out your trusty PowerShot G10/G11 and make a perfectly serviceable photographic copy. You can view the image on your camera's display (magnified to show details if need be), display it on a computer screen, send it by e-mail, or print it out.

Chances are there's something in that list that you may want to do at some point. So let's go through the steps that will accomplish a solid macro photograph. Of course, if you're in a hurry you won't have time to carry out all of these steps, but here's the full list for when you do have time:

1. Secure the camera firmly on a solid tripod. Turn Image Stabilization off.

2. Arrange for lighting that will not be blocked by the camera itself, which is likely to cast a shadow because of its extreme proximity to the subject. If you can't achieve shadowless lighting with available fixtures or natural light, consider obtaining a ring flash—a unit like Canon's Macro Ring Lite MR-14EX, designed for macro photography, which fits on or around the camera's lens, so the camera cannot cast a shadow.

3. Select a shooting mode that fits the situation at hand. Consider using Aperture Priority and setting the aperture as small as possible with the lighting available, to achieve the greatest depth-of-field you can so as to keep the subject in sharp focus.

4. Turn Continuous AF off, so the camera focuses only once. In the alternative, use Manual focus, with Safety MF turned on.

5. Set the AF Frame mode to FlexiZone and set the AF Frame to its smallest size.

6. Press the Macro button (left cross key) to engage Macro mode.

7. Press the AF Frame button, then press the DISP. button to make the frame as small as possible. Use the cross keys to move the AF Frame to cover the part of the subject that needs to be in sharpest focus.

8. Activate the self-timer or use the remote Switch RS60-E3 so the shutter will be tripped without your pressing the shutter button and possibly shaking the camera.

9. Compose the shot, check the focus, press the shutter button, and stand clear while the self-timer counts down, to make sure that you don't cast any shadows over the subject and that you don't touch the camera while it's making the exposure.

More Exposure Options

In Chapter 5, you learned techniques for getting the *right* exposure, but I haven't explained all your exposure options just yet. You'll want to know about the *kind* of exposure settings that are available to you with the Canon PowerShot G10/G11. There are options that let you control when the exposure is made, or even how to make an exposure that's out of the ordinary in terms of length. The sections that follow explain your camera's special exposure features, and even discuss a few it does not have, to put the others in context.

A Tiny Slice of Time

Exposures that seem impossibly brief can reveal a world we didn't know existed. In the 1930s, Dr. Harold Edgerton, a professor of electrical engineering at MIT, pioneered high-speed photography using a repeating electronic flash unit he patented called the *stroboscope.* As the inventor of the electronic flash, he popularized its use to freeze objects in motion, and you've probably seen his photographs of bullets piercing balloons and drops of milk forming a coronet-shaped splash.

Electronic flash freezes action by virtue of its extremely short duration—as brief as 1/50,000th second or less. Although the PowerShot G10/G11's built-in flash unit can give you these ultra-quick glimpses of moving subjects, an external flash, such as one of the Canon Speedlites, offers even more versatility. You can read more about using electronic flash to stop action in Chapter 8.

Of course, the PowerShot is fully capable of immobilizing all but the fastest movement using only its shutter speeds, which range all the way up to a speedy 1/4,000th second. Indeed, you'll rarely have need for such a brief shutter speed in ordinary shooting. If you wanted to use an aperture of f/2.8 at ISO 100 outdoors in bright sunlight, for some reason, a shutter speed of 1/4,000th second would more than do the job. You'd need a faster shutter speed only if you moved the ISO setting to a higher sensitivity (but why would you do that?). Under less than full sunlight, 1/4,000th second is more than fast enough for any conditions you're likely to encounter.

Most sports action can be frozen at 1/2,000th second or slower, and for many sports a slower shutter speed is actually preferable—for example, to allow the wheels of a racing automobile or motorcycle, or the propeller on a classic aircraft to blur realistically. But if you want to do some exotic action-freezing photography without resorting to electronic flash, the PowerShot's top shutter speed is at your disposal. Here are some things to think about when exploring this type of high-speed photography:

- **You'll need a lot of light.** High shutter speeds cut very fine slices of time and sharply reduce the amount of illumination that reaches your sensor. To use 1/4,000th second at an aperture of f/6.3, you'd need an ISO setting of 800—even in full daylight. To use an f/stop smaller than f/6.3 or an ISO setting lower than 1600, you'd need *more* light than full daylight provides. (That's why electronic flash units work so well for high-speed photography when used as the sole illumination; the short duration of the flash—1/1,000th second or less -- provides both the effect of a brief shutter speed and the high levels of illumination needed.)

- **Forget about reciprocity failure.** If you're an old-time film shooter, you might recall that very brief shutter speeds (as well as very high light levels and very *long* exposures) produced an effect called *reciprocity failure,* in which given exposures ended up providing less than the calculated value because of the way film responded to very short, very intense, or very long exposures of light. Solid-state sensors don't suffer from this defect, so you don't need to make an adjustment when using high shutter speeds (or brief flash bursts).

- **No elongation effect.** This is another old bugaboo that has largely been solved through modern technology, but I wanted to bring it to your attention anyway. In olden times, cameras used shutters that traveled horizontally. To achieve faster shutter speeds, focal plane shutters (located just in front of the focal plane) open only a smaller-than-frame-sized slit so that, even though the shutter is already traveling at its highest rate of speed, the film/sensor is exposed for a briefer period of time as the slit moves across the surface. At very short shutter speeds, and with subjects moving horizontally at very fast velocities, it was possible for the subject to partially "keep up" with the shutter if it were traveling in the same direction as the slit, producing an elongated effect. Conversely, subjects moving in the opposite direction of shutter motion could be compressed. Today, shutters like those in the PowerShot move vertically and at a higher maximum rate of speed. So, unless you're photographing a rocket blasting into space, and holding the camera horizontally to boot (or shooting a racing car in vertical orientation), it's almost impossible to produce unwanted elongation/compression.

Working with Short Exposures

You can have a lot of fun exploring the kinds of pictures you can take using very brief exposure times, whether you decide to take advantage of the action-stopping capabilities of your built-in or external electronic flash or work with the Canon PowerShot G10/G11's faster shutter speeds. Here are a few ideas to get you started:

■ **Take revealing images.** Fast shutter speeds can help you reveal the real subject behind the façade, by freezing constant motion to capture an enlightening moment in time. Legendary fashion/portrait photographer Philippe Halsman used leaping photos of famous people, such as the Duke and Duchess of Windsor, Richard Nixon, and Salvador Dali to illuminate their real selves. Halsman said, "*When you ask a person to jump, his attention is mostly directed toward the act of jumping and the mask falls so that the real person appears.*" Try some high-speed portraits of people you know in motion to see how they appear when concentrating on something other than the portrait.

■ **Create unreal images.** High-speed photography can also produce photographs that show your subjects in ways that are quite unreal. A helicopter in mid-air with its rotors frozen or a motocross cyclist leaping over a ramp, but with all motion stopped so that the rider and machine look as if they were frozen in mid-air, make for an unusual picture. The college basketball players never stopped to pose for the tableaux you see in Figure 6.9, but a fast shutter speed froze them in place.

■ **Capture unseen perspectives.** Some things are *never* seen in real life, except when viewed in a stop-action photograph. Edgerton's balloon bursts were only a starting point. Freeze a hummingbird in flight for a view of wings that never seem to stop. Or, capture the splashes as liquid falls into a bowl, as shown in Figure 6.10. No electronic flash was required for this image (and wouldn't have illuminated the water in the bowl as evenly). Instead, a clutch of high intensity lamps and an ISO setting of 1600 allowed the camera to capture this image at 1/2,000th second.

Figure 6.9
This basketball shot captures a brief moment in time.

Figure 6.10 A large amount of artificial illumination and an ISO 1600 sensitivity setting allowed capturing this shot (taken with the G11's Sepia color toning option) at 1/2,000th second without use of an electronic flash.

Long Exposures

Longer exposures are a doorway into another world, showing us how even familiar scenes can look much different when photographed over periods measured in seconds. At night, long exposures produce streaks of light from moving, illuminated subjects like automobiles or amusement park rides. Extra-long exposures of seemingly pitch-dark subjects can reveal interesting views using light levels barely bright enough to see by. At any time of day, including daytime (in which case you'll often need the help of the neutral density filter to make the long exposure practical), long exposures can cause moving objects to vanish entirely, because they don't remain stationary long enough to register in a photograph.

Three Ways to Take Long Exposures

There are actually three common types of lengthy exposures: *timed exposures, bulb exposures*, and *time exposures*. The PowerShot G10/G11 offers only the first one of these, but it's helpful to understand what other options exist, to put this camera's capability into context. Because of the length of the exposure, all of the following techniques should be used with a tripod to hold the camera steady.

- **Timed exposures.** These are long exposures from 1 second to 15 seconds, measured by the camera itself. To take a picture in this range with the PowerShot G10/G11, simply use Manual or Tv mode and use the control dial to set the shutter speed to the length of time you want, choosing from preset speeds of 1.0, 1.3, 1.6, 2.0, 2.5, 3.2, 4.0, 5.0, 6.0, 8.0, 10.0, 13.0, or 15.0 seconds. The advantage of timed exposures is that the camera does all the calculating for you. There's no need for a stopwatch. If you review your image on the LCD and decide to try again with the exposure doubled or halved, you can dial in the correct exposure with precision. The disadvantage of timed exposures is that you can't take a photo with this camera for longer than 15 seconds.

- **Bulb exposures.** This type of exposure, not available with the G10/G11, is so-called because in the olden days the photographer squeezed and held an air bulb attached to a tube that provided the force necessary to keep the shutter open for the desired period of time.

- **Time exposures.** This is a setting found on some cameras to produce longer exposures. With cameras that implement this option, the shutter opens when you press the shutter release button, and remains open until you press the button again.

The PowerShot G10/G11 does not have a built-in time exposure capability.

Working with Long Exposures

Because the PowerShot G10/G11 produces such good images at longer exposures, and there are so many creative things you can do with long-exposure techniques, you'll want to do some experimenting. Get yourself a tripod or another firm support and get started. Here are some things to try:

- **Make people invisible.** One very cool thing about long exposures is that objects that move rapidly enough won't register at all in a photograph, while the subjects that remain stationary are portrayed in the normal way. That makes it possible to produce people-free landscape photos and architectural photos at night or, even, in full daylight if you use the neutral density filter (set from the FUNC. menu) to allow an exposure of at least a few seconds. If you find the technique isn't working, you may need to wait for an overcast day to allow for a long enough exposure, if daylight people-vanishing is your goal. They'll have to be walking *very* briskly and across the field of view (rather than directly toward the camera) for this to work. At

Figure 6.11 This alleyway is thronged with people, as you can see in this two-second exposure using only the available illumination.

Figure 6.12 With the camera still on a tripod, a longer exposure rendered the passersby almost invisible.

night, it's much easier to achieve this effect with the 15-second exposures that are possible, as you can see in Figures 6.11 and 6.12.

- **Create streaks.** If you aren't shooting for total invisibility, long exposures with the camera on a tripod can produce some interesting streaky effects, as shown in Figure 6.13. You don't need to limit yourself to indoor photography, however. Depending on the light conditions, using the neutral density filter may darken the scene sufficiently to allow you to take photographs outdoors with a shutter speed slow enough to paint streaks on your image.

- **Produce light trails.** At night, car headlights and taillights and other moving sources of illumination can generate interesting light trails. Your camera doesn't even need to be mounted on a tripod; hand-holding the PowerShot for longer exposures adds movement and patterns to your trails. If you're shooting fireworks, a longer exposure may allow you to combine several bursts into one picture, as shown in Figure 6.14.

- **Blur waterfalls, etc.** You'll find that waterfalls and other sources of moving liquid produce a special type of long-exposure blur, because the water merges into a fantasy-like veil that looks different at different exposure times, and with different waterfalls. Cascades with turbulent flow produce a rougher look at a given longer exposure than falls that flow smoothly.

- **Show total darkness in new ways.** Even on the darkest, moonless nights, there is enough starlight or glow from distant illumination sources to see by, and, if you use a long exposure, there is enough light to take a picture, too.

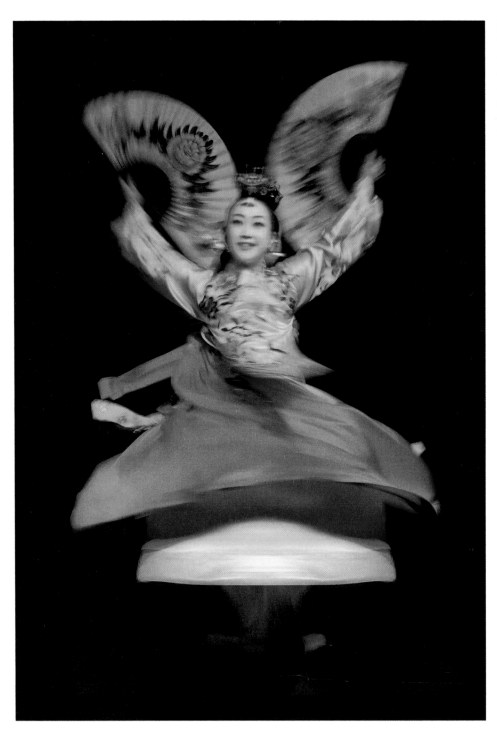

Figure 6.13
This Korean dancer produced a swirl of color as she spun during the 1/4 second exposure.

Figure 6.14 A long exposure allows capturing several bursts of fireworks in one image.

Delayed Exposures

Sometimes it's desirable to have a delay of some sort before a picture is actually taken. Perhaps you'd like to get in the picture yourself, and would appreciate it if the camera waited 10 seconds after you press the shutter release to actually take the picture. Maybe you want to give a tripod-mounted camera time to settle down and damp any residual vibration after the release is pressed to improve sharpness for an exposure with a relatively slow shutter speed. It's possible you want to explore the world of time-lapse photography.

Self-Timer

The PowerShot G10/G11 has a built-in self-timer with a range of delay options from 1 to 30 seconds. Your camera also has a Self-timer/Multiple shot setting that allows taking 1 to 10 shots after the delay. You call the self-timer into action by pressing the Self-timer button, which doubles as the bottom cross key on both cameras, and also acts as the Drive mode button on the G10. The operation of the self-timer is easy to follow from the camera's prompts, but if you need a refresher, see Chapter 3.

Forget to bring along your tripod, but still want to take a close-up picture with a precise focus setting? Set your digital camera to the Self-timer function, then put the camera on any reasonably steady support, such as a fence post or a rock. When you're ready to take the picture, press the shutter release. The camera might totter back and forth for a second or two, but it will settle back to its original position before the self-timer activates the shutter.

Beyond Visible Light with Infrared

Congratulations—you have won the Infrared Lottery! What I mean by that is, by your wise choice of purchasing a PowerShot G10/G11, you have acquired one of the modern digital cameras that is capable of using infrared light to take some very interesting and unusual-looking photographs. Not every digital camera can take infrared photographs in this way. Many cameras nowadays have an infrared-blocking filter built into them, so they can't take advantage of the exotic-looking properties of infrared images.

You can test any digital camera for infrared picture-taking ability by aiming an infrared remote control at the camera's lens and clicking any button on the remote a few times, or holding it down. If the camera is sensitive to infrared light, you will see a bright light being emitted from the remote, though it's invisible to the naked eye. Both the G10 and G11 PowerShot models pass this test quite nicely. This camera is not designed for infrared picture taking, and may not be as good at it as some other cameras that are built (or converted) for that purpose, but I consider this model to do a pretty decent job in this esoteric area.

So, what do you do with your newfound power to take infrared photographs? If you want, you can delve quite deeply into the topic and become immersed in lots of arcane information about how infrared works. An internet search on "infrared digital photography" will get you going on that endeavor.

The purpose of this book, though, is to give you enough practical information to get you started without bogging you down. So, to give you a sample of what the PowerShot G10/G11 can do in this area, I'll give you a set of steps you can take to enter the world of infrared photography. These steps represent just one approach, but they will work. Here is my suggested scenario:

■ **Get an infrared filter.** In order to take interesting looking infrared photographs, you need not only to have a camera like the PowerShot G10/G11 which can "see" infrared light, you also need to have a way to block the normal, humanly visible light. If you don't take that step, the visible light will overwhelm the infrared light and the resulting photograph will look rather ordinary. Some people use exposed, developed photographic film as a makeshift infrared filter. You would be better off, though, with a commercially available photographic filter such as the Hoya R72, available from good photo supply firms. Then you need to find a way to secure it in front of the lens. You could try cobbling together a holder from a cardboard tube or the like, or you could get a more permanent device such as a filter adapter sold by lensmateonline.com. Or you could start out by just holding it firmly in front of the lens.

■ **Set the camera on a tripod.** This is required because the infrared filter is quite dark, and you will need a long exposure, possibly of more than one second, to get a usable image.

■ **Use custom white balance.** If you need a refresher on the procedure, see Chapter 4. But there is a twist here: instead of aiming the camera at a white (or gray) surface to get the white balance set, for infrared, I suggest you aim at green foliage, if possible (trees, grass, bushes), because those make some of the best subjects for infrared photos, which render green objects in white in dramatic contrast to their normal appearance.

■ **Use Aperture Priority (Av) mode.** Because the camera is on a tripod, you don't have to worry about having a long exposure. Try f/4.5 for a start. The camera will probably select a long exposure.

■ **Find a suitable subject.** As I noted above, you might want to start with green trees and plants outdoors. Include sky and clouds as well, if possible, for contrasty, dramatic images. Once you've gotten started, though, experiment with a variety of subjects.

■ **Use the self-timer.** This isn't a strong requirement, but I like to use the self-timer when possible, to avoid camera shake for long exposures.

See Figure 6.15 for an example of a photograph shot with the PowerShot G11 using the above technique.

Figure 6.15 This infrared shot was taken with the PowerShot G11 in Aperture Priority mode with a Hoya R72 filter, exposed at f/3.5 for 0.4 second at ISO 800. Custom white balance was set based on the color of the green bushes.

Making Movies

The Canon PowerShot G10/G11 can shoot movies with monaural sound at 640 × 480 pixels resolution (standard VGA) or 320 × 240 resolution, both at 30 frames per second. These are fairly rudimentary capabilities in these days when many digital still cameras, including some of the "point-and-shoot" models otherwise similar to these PowerShots, can capture super-high-quality HD (high-definition video).

Some of the high-end Canon still cameras, which have advanced video capabilities, have even been used to put together video projects that rival anything Hollywood can produce. But don't sell the PowerShot G10/G11 short in the video realm. This camera can record up to an hour's worth of video in one continuous shot, at the full capture rate of professional equipment. If you're out and about and develop a sudden need to make a video recording of an event, from a school sports event to a breaking news story, these cameras will get the footage down on your SD card with very acceptable quality.

You'll want to keep the following things in mind before you start:

■ **Choose your resolution.** Use the FUNC. menu, discussed in Chapter 4, to choose the resolution for your movie. There are not many choices to be made; select either 640 × 480 pixels or the smaller-sized 320 × 240 pixels. At both resolutions, the camera will record at the full video frame rate of 30 fps and will record monaural sound through the camera's tiny microphone.

■ **Choose a movie shooting mode.** There still is one more shooting mode choice to be made after you have selected one of the two available resolutions. If you look at the movie camera icon at the upper right of the camera's screen, you will see two little green arrows, meaning you can spin the control dial to make a selection (see Figure 6.16). Choose Standard, Color Accent, or Color Swap. The Standard mode is straight shooting of what the camera sees. Color Accent and Color Swap work the same as their counterparts on the SCN menu, discussed in Chapter 5. (With Color Accent, you retain only one color from the scene; with Color Swap, you convert objects of one color to another color.)

Figure 6.16
The green arrows near the movie camera icon mean that there is still a choice that can be made of a particular type of movie mode: Standard, Color Accent, or Color Swap.

- **Use the right card.** You'll want to use an SD Class 6 memory card or better to store your clips; slower cards may not work properly. Choose a memory card with at least 4GB capacity (8GB or 16GB are even better).

- **Use a fully charged battery.** Canon says that a fresh battery will allow about one hour of filming at normal (non-Winter) temperatures.

- **Be prepared for shooting limitations.** With the PowerShot G10, your optical zoom level and focus are fixed at the points they are at when you first press the shutter button, so you need to plan ahead and not expect to film subjects that will require changes of focus or optical zoom. (Digital zoom is still available.) These limitations don't apply with the G11, but bear in mind that zooming while shooting a movie scene is something that should be done sparingly, if at all. Both cameras will adjust exposure while filming.

- **Press the shutter button.** You don't have to hold it down. Press it again when you're done.

MOVIE TIME

I've standardized on 16GB SDHC cards when I'm shooting movies; one of these cards will hold about 3 hours of video at the higher 640 × 480 resolution and about 9 hours at the lower 320 × 240 quality. However, the camera cannot shoot a continuous movie scene for more than one hour or create a file greater than 4GB. Therefore, one solid hour of video without pausing is your practical limit. (Though you could start right back in again to record a second hour-long scene, if you still had space on your memory card and still had battery power.)

GETTING INFO

The information display shown on the LCD screen when shooting movies is quite sparse; the screen will show time elapsed and the REC indicator to show that you are shooting a movie. The only other option is to display grid lines, if you have selected that feature through the Shooting menu under Custom Display.

Editing Movies in the Camera

The PowerShot G10/G11 provides a very basic capability for editing movies in the camera. This is not a technique I would recommend for general use in editing your videos, and you won't be doing a lot of post-production work with this simple tool, but there may be a situation in which you have no computer available and you need to trim the beginning or end of a video by a few seconds so you can show it on a TV set, perhaps at a conference. Here's how to do it:

- **Get the video on the screen.** Press the Playback button and press the Jump key, then move with the down cross key to the icon for movies. Turn the control dial to find the movie you're looking for.

- **Press the FUNC./SET key twice.** Once to select the movie you want, and again to call up the playback and editing controls (see Figure 6.17).

- **Select the scissors icon.** Scroll with the control dial over to the icon of a pair of scissors. Press FUNC./SET to select it.

Figure 6.17
The movie editing screen provides tools for moving through the movie and performing basic edits by trimming the beginning and end of the movie clip.

■ **Select beginning or end to trim.** At the top left of the screen, scroll to either the icon showing the scissors before a frame of film (trim beginning) or the scissors after a frame of film (trim end).

■ **Scroll to select the portion to trim.** Using the right cross key (if trimming beginning) or left cross key (if trimming end), or the scroll wheel for faster selection, move the orange marker along the bar at the bottom of the screen that represents the length of the film.

■ **Select and use the trimming tool.** Use the down cross key to move down the column of icons at the top left of the screen to the next-to-last icon, labeled "Save." Select it, and the camera will prompt you with three choices: New File, Overwrite, and Cancel. Your safest option is to choose New File, unless you're 100% sure that it's safe to overwrite the existing movie with the new, shorter version.

7

Getting the Most from Your Zoom

The 28-140mm f/2.8 zoom lens mounted on your Canon PowerShot G10 or G11 is the "eye" of your camera. It captures the light that's focused on the sensor to produce the image. Through its zooming capability, the lens changes the magnification of the image, and, indirectly, the perspective of your photograph. The maximum aperture (or f/stop) of your lens also affects your ability to shoot under varying light conditions. The size of the lens opening you choose helps determine the range of sharpness (depth-of-field) and the absolute *amount* of sharpness.

Those aspects are very important to your picture taking. With a camera like the G10/G11, the lens is fixed and cannot be interchanged (although you can adjust its characteristics with add-on attachments). So, the quality and features of the lens itself is one of the most crucial factors you should consider in choosing a camera. Fortunately, the lens mounted on the G10/G11 is a very good one, and to a large extent, one of the key reasons why these cameras are so popular.

It's true that the predecessor to the G10/G11, the PowerShot G9, did have a 6X (rather than 5X) zoom lens with a range of 35mm to 210mm, and that many dedicated PowerShot owners miss the extra telephoto power. However, Canon giveth and Canon taketh away, and while depriving you of focal lengths from 141-210mm, the company did improve the wide-angle perspective of the PowerShot G-series with that new 28-34mm focal length range. In addition, the optional TC-DC58D tele-converter gives you back some of that missing telephoto reach with the equivalent of 196mm of zoom range.

This chapter explains some of the things you should keep in mind when using your zoom, how to select the best focal lengths for the kinds of photography you want to do, and things you can do to increase the versatility of your camera's built-in optics.

How Lenses Affect Your Pictures

The first thing to get out of the way is the notion of absolute and equivalent focal lengths. Your 28-140mm zoom lens is actually a 6.1-30.5mm zoom in absolute terms, because those are the true focal lengths available from the optics built into the camera. The effective focal lengths in use, however, are customarily given in the form of the *equivalent* focal length compared to a 35mm film camera or "full frame" digital camera. Because the sensor on the G10/G11 measures just 5.7×7.6mm, rather than the 24×36mm of a full frame camera, the smaller sensor in your PowerShot requires shorter focal lengths to produce the same field of view.

That is, at 6.1mm, your lens has the same field of view as a 28mm lens on a full frame camera; at 30.5mm, it has the same field of view as a 140mm telephoto on a full frame camera. Because various cameras in this class have sensors of varying sizes, it makes sense to always convert their "real" focal lengths to the full frame equivalent. So, in specifications for digital cameras, and throughout this book, I'll always refer to the *equivalent* focal lengths, and ignore the "real" focal lengths, because the latter have little meaning to the average photographer.

Focal length equivalents aside, as I noted in the introduction to this chapter, your lens and its characteristics have significant effects on the quality of your images, and even the types of pictures you can take. Here's a quick rundown of the most important aspects.

- **Change magnification.** Zooming in and out changes the magnification of your image in the viewfinder, on the LCD, and in the final image captured by your sensor. With the G10/G11, this magnification factor is 1X to 5X. In Figure 7.1 you can see that the image at the 140mm maximum zoom position (bottom) is five times larger than the image produced at the 28mm setting (top).

- **Change perspective.** As you move closer or farther away from your subject, your perspective changes. At closer distances, with the lens zoomed out wider, objects in the foreground become exaggerated in size and more prominent compared to shots taken from a greater distance, and the lens zoomed in to telephoto settings. This change in perspective is intertwined with the magnification of your zoom. To keep an image the same size in the frame, you can zoom in or out, changing the magnification, or you can move closer or farther away, changing the perspective.

Figure 7.1
At its 28mm setting, the PowerShot's zoom lens provides a true wide-angle view (top); at 140mm, the zoom offers a telephoto perspective.

- **Control exposure.** The aperture built into your lens controls the exposure, as well as what exposures you can use. For example, with the G10/G11, the maximum aperture is f/2.8 (at the wide-angle setting) and the smallest f/stop available is f/8. So, you can use only exposure combinations that call for f/2.8 to f/8. For example on a bright day with an ISO setting of ISO 200, you could shoot at 1/800th second at f/8, 1/1600th second at f/5.6, or 1/3200th second at f/4. To use other combinations, you'd need to reduce the ISO setting to less than ISO 200 (the G10/G11 goes down to ISO 80), or turn on the built-in neutral density filter. (Note that 1/6400th second at f/2.8 is unavailable in bright sunlight, anyway, because neither camera *has* a 1/6400th second setting; 1/4000th second is tops.) Keep in mind that at the maximum zoom position, the f/2.8 aperture becomes an effective f/4.5.

- **Affects depth-of-field.** The range of sharpness of your image, also called depth-of-field (DOF) is affected by the size of the f/stop. Your camera has the least amount of DOF at f/2.8, and the most at f/8. Fortunately (and unfortunately), the smaller sensor and smaller sensor size means that the 6.1-30.5 *true* focal lengths of your lens provide vast amounts of depth-of-field at any of these f/stops at normal shooting distances. Whether you're using f/2.8 or f/8 you'll probably have more than enough DOF, except when shooting macro pictures a few inches from the lens, when even the DOF provided at f/8 may not be enough. The *unfortunate* part comes from having so much DOF in most instances that selective focus techniques may be more difficult or impossible.

- **Affects sharpness.** The f/stop built into your lens affects the absolute sharpness, too, not just the range of sharpness. As with most camera lenses, the largest f/stop does not produce the best image quality; f/2.8 is good, but not as good as f/4 or f/5.6. At f/8 and smaller, lenses start to lose a little sharpness because of a phenomenon called *diffraction*. (The light entering the lens is scattered slightly by the edges of the aperture's diaphragm.) Diffraction grows worse as lens focal lengths become shorter, which is one of the reasons why the G10/G11's lens stops at f/8 and doesn't continue on to smaller stops, such as f/11 or f/16, found in lenses for other types of cameras, including digital SLRs.

So, what can you do with the zoom built into your Canon PowerShot G10/G11? Here's what you need to know:

- **Bring you closer.** A longer focal length brings distant subjects closer to you, offers better control over depth-of-field, and avoids the perspective distortion that wide-angle lenses provide. They compress the apparent distance between objects in your frame. The optional Tele-converter TC-DC58D has a focal length equivalent of 196mm, offering a 1.4x increase in magnification over the PowerShot's maximum 140mm focal length.

■ **Wider perspective.** Sometimes you need the widest view that your lens offers. Often, your back is up against a wall and you *can't* take a step backwards to take in more subject matter. Perhaps you're standing on the rim of the Grand Canyon, and you want to take in as much of the breathtaking view as you can. You might find yourself just behind the baseline at a high school basketball game and want an interesting shot with a little perspective distortion tossed in the mix. In all these cases, you'll need to use the widest focal length that your lens offers.

■ **Bring your camera closer.** The macro setting of your lens allows you to autofocus from 0.39 inches to 1.6 feet at the wide-angle zoom position, and 12 inches to 1.6 feet at the telephoto position. In Manual focus mode you can focus from 0.39 inches to infinity when set to wide angle, or 12 inches to infinity at the telephoto setting. This provides quite a bit of flexibility when you want to vary your subject distance (say, to avoid spooking a skittish creature).

■ **More speed.** Your lens's f/2.8 maximum aperture at 28mm (f/4.5 at 140mm) means you can shoot many scenes in available light, using reasonable ISO speeds of ISO 1600 or below. ISO 3200 (G10) or ISO 12800 (G11) can be used only at reduced resolution. You have to evaluate whether the image you want to capture is worth the noise penalty of higher IS settings.

■ **Special features.** The optical image stabilization built into your lens makes your lens "faster" by allowing you to shoot at a slower shutter speed. For example, if 1/30th second at f/2.8 won't cut it, and raising the ISO isn't an option (say, you're already at ISO 1600), you can often grab your shot at an even slower shutter speed, assuming that it's camera shake and not subject movement you're trying to freeze. Your PowerShot can often get good images at 1/15th second or even 1/8th second, if you've turned on the Image Stabilization feature in the Shooting menu.

Using the Wide-Angle Zoom Settings

The zoom settings from 28mm to about 45mm are considered wide angle with your PowerShot G10/G11. To use these focal lengths effectively, you need to understand how they affect your photography. Here's a quick summary of the things you need to know.

■ **More depth-of-field.** Practically speaking, even with the copious amounts of depth-of-field that your camera's true 6.1-30mm focal length range offers, wide-angle settings still offer more depth-of-field at a particular subject distance and aperture. (But see the sidebar below for an important note.) You'll find that helpful when you want to maximize sharpness of a large zone, but not very useful when you'd rather isolate your subject using selective focus (telephoto focal lengths are better for that).

■ **Stepping back.** Wide-angle focal lengths have the effect of making it seem that you are standing farther from your subject than you really are. They're helpful when you don't want to back up, or can't because there are impediments in your way.

- **Wider field of view.** While making your subject seem farther away, as implied above, a wide-angle lens also provides a larger field of view, including more of the subject in your photos.

- **More foreground.** As background objects retreat, more of the foreground is brought into view by a wide-angle lens. That gives you extra emphasis on the area that's closest to the camera. Photograph your home with a medium zoom setting, and the front yard probably looks fairly conventional in your photo (that's why these medium focal lengths are called "normal"). Switch to a wider setting and you'll discover that your lawn now makes up much more of the photo. So, wide-angle focal lengths are great when you want to emphasize that lake in the foreground, but problematic when your intended subject is located farther in the distance.

- **Perspective distortion.** When you tilt the camera so the plane of the sensor is no longer perpendicular to the vertical plane of your subject, some parts of the subject are now closer to the sensor than they were before, while other parts are farther away. So, buildings, flagpoles, or NBA players appear to be falling backwards, as you can see in Figure 7.2. While this kind of apparent distortion (it's not caused by a defect in the lens) can happen with any focal length, it's most apparent when a wide angle is used.

- **Super-sized subjects.** The tendency of a wide-angle lens to emphasize objects in the foreground, while de-emphasizing objects in the background can lead to a kind of size distortion that may be more objectionable for some types of subjects than others. Shoot a bed of flowers up close with a wide-angle setting, and you might like the distorted effect of the larger blossoms nearer the lens. Take a photo of a family member with the same lens from the same distance, and you're likely to get some complaints about that gigantic nose in the foreground. Figure 7.3 shows a dry creek bed using a medium focal length at top. At bottom, a wide-angle setting emphasizes the rocks in the foreground, making them appear huge, and making the background trees (and even the horizon) seem farther away.

- **Steady cam.** You'll find that you can hand-hold a wide-angle focal length at slower shutter speeds, without need for image stabilization, than you can with a telephoto lens. The reduced magnification of the wide-zoom setting doesn't emphasize camera shake like a telephoto lens does.

- **Interesting angles.** Many of the factors already listed combine to produce more interesting angles when shooting with wide-angle focal lengths. Raising or lowering a telephoto lens a few feet probably will have little effect on the appearance of the distant subjects you're shooting. The same change in elevation can produce a dramatic effect for the much-closer subjects typically captured with a wide-zoom setting.

Figure 7.2
When you tilt the camera upwards, tall buildings appear to be falling backward.

Figure 7.3 At top, a normal view of a dry creek bed. At bottom, the wide-angle perspective from a slightly lower angle makes the small rocks in the foreground appear to be huge.

DOF IN DEPTH

The depth-of-field (DOF) advantage of wide-angle focal lengths is diminished when you enlarge your picture; believe it or not, a wide-angle image enlarged and cropped to provide the same subject size as a telephoto shot would have the *same* depth-of-field. Try it: take a wide-angle photo of a friend from a fair distance, and then zoom in to duplicate the picture in a telephoto image. Then, enlarge the wide shot so your friend is the same size in both. The wide photo will have the same DOF (and will have much less detail, too).

Avoiding Potential Wide-Angle Problems

Wide-angle focal lengths have a few quirks that you'll want to keep in mind when shooting so you can avoid falling into some common traps. Here's a checklist of tips for avoiding common problems:

- **Symptom: converging lines.** Unless you want to use wildly converging lines as a creative effect, it's a good idea to keep horizontal and vertical lines in landscapes, architecture, and other subjects carefully aligned with the sides, top, and bottom of the frame. That will help you avoid undesired perspective distortion. Sometimes it helps to shoot from a slightly elevated position so you don't have to tilt the camera up or down.

- **Symptom: color fringes around objects.** Lenses are often plagued with fringes of color around backlit objects, produced by *chromatic aberration*, which comes in two forms: *longitudinal/axial*, in which all the colors of light don't focus in the same plane; and *lateral/transverse*, in which the colors are shifted to one side. Lens designers must use special techniques to reduce these effects.

- **Symptom: lines that bow outward.** Some wide-angle focal lengths cause straight lines to bow outwards, with the strongest effect at the edges. You can minimize barrel distortion simply by framing your photo with some extra space all around, so the edges where the defect is most obvious can be cropped out of the picture.

- **Symptom: light and dark areas when using polarizing filter.** If you know that polarizers work best when the camera is pointed 90 degrees away from the sun and have the least effect when the camera is oriented 180 degrees from the sun, you know only half the story. With focal lengths in the 28mm vicinity, the angle of view (75 degrees diagonally, or 44 degrees horizontally) is extensive enough to cause problems. Think about it: when a 28mm lens is pointed at the proper 90-degree angle from the sun, objects at the edges of the frame will be oriented at 112 to 68 degrees, with only the center at exactly 90 degrees. Either edge will have much less of a polarized effect. The solution is to avoid using a polarizing filter with focal lengths having an equivalent focal length of less than about 35mm. Zoom out, if necessary, and avoid extreme wide-angle shots.

Using Telephoto Settings

Telephoto focal lengths also can have a dramatic effect on your photography. Here are the most important things you need to know. In the next section, I'll concentrate on telephoto considerations that can be problematic—and how to avoid those problems.

- **Selective focus.** Long focal lengths have reduced depth-of-field within the frame, allowing you to use selective focus to isolate your subject. You can open the lens up as wide as possible to create shallow depth-of-field, or close it down a bit to allow more to be in focus. The flip side of the coin is that when you *want* to make a range of objects sharp, you'll need to use a smaller f/stop to get the depth-of-field you need. Like fire, the depth-of-field of a telephoto lens can be friend or foe. Figure 7.4 shows a photo of a statue with an ugly background, so I photographed it using the 140mm setting and the widest f/stop available to de-emphasize the background.

- **Getting closer.** Telephoto focal lengths bring you closer to wildlife, sports action, and candid subjects. No one wants to get a reputation as a surreptitious or "sneaky" photographer (except for paparazzi), but when applied to candids in an open and honest way, a long lens can help you capture memorable moments while retaining enough distance to stay out of the way of events as they transpire.

- **Reduced foreground/increased compression.** Telephoto focal lengths have the opposite effect of wide angles: they reduce the importance of things in the foreground by squeezing everything together. This compression even makes distant objects appear to be closer to subjects in the foreground and middle ranges. You can use this effect as a creative tool.

- **Accentuates camera shakiness.** Telephotos also magnify any camera shake. It's no wonder that image stabilization is popular in longer focal lengths, because the telephoto range is where the anti-shake effects do the most good.

- **Interesting angles require creativity.** Telephoto focal lengths require more imagination in selecting interesting angles, because the "angle" you do get on your subjects is so narrow. Moving from side to side or a bit higher or lower can make a dramatic difference in a wide-angle shot, but raising or lowering a telephoto lens a few feet probably will have little effect on the appearance of the distant subjects you're shooting.

Figure 7.4
A wide f/stop and telephoto focal length helped isolate this statue from its background.

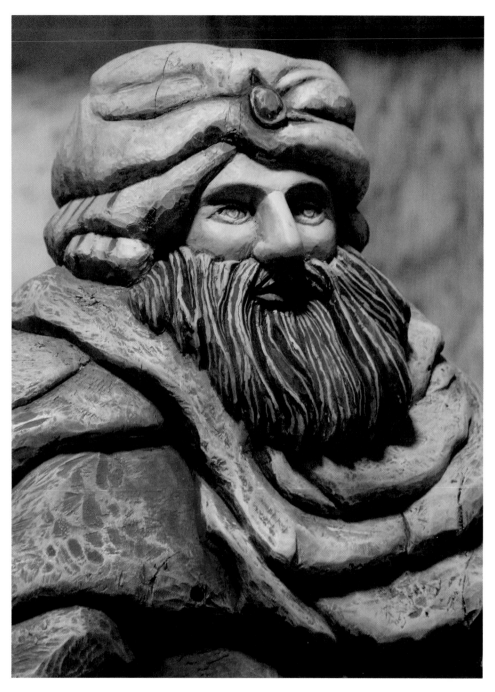

Avoiding Telephoto Lens Problems

Many of the "problems" that telephoto focal lengths pose are really just challenges and not that difficult to overcome. Here is a list of the seven most common picture maladies and suggested solutions.

- **Symptom: flat faces in portraits.** Head-and-shoulders portraits of humans tend to be more flattering when a focal length in the 50mm to 85mm range is used. Longer focal lengths compress the distance between features like noses and ears, making the face look wider and flat. A wide-angle might make noses look huge and ears tiny when you fill the frame with a face. So stick with 50mm to 85mm focal length ranges, going longer only when you're forced to shoot from a greater distance, and wider only when shooting three-quarters/full-length portraits, or group shots.

- **Symptom: blur due to camera shake.** Use a higher shutter speed (boosting ISO if necessary), and image stabilization, or mount your camera on a tripod, monopod, or brace it with some other support. Of those three solutions, only the first will reduce blur caused by *subject* motion; IS or a tripod won't help you freeze a race car in mid-lap.

- **Symptom: color fringes.** Chromatic aberration is the most pernicious optical problem found in telephoto focal lengths. There are others, including spherical aberration, astigmatism, coma, curvature of field, and similarly scary-sounding phenomena. Your only solution may be to correct the fringing in your favorite RAW conversion tool or image editor. Photoshop's Lens Correction filter (found in the Distort menu) offers sliders that minimize both red/cyan and blue/yellow fringing.

- **Symptom: lines that curve inwards.** Pincushion distortion is sometimes found at many telephoto focal lengths. You might find after a bit of testing that it is worse at certain focal lengths with your particular zoom lens. Like chromatic aberration, it can be partially corrected using tools like Photoshop's Lens Correction filter.

- **Symptom: low contrast from haze or fog.** When you're photographing distant objects, a long lens shoots through a lot more atmosphere, which generally is muddied up with extra haze and fog. That dirt or moisture in the atmosphere can reduce contrast and mute colors. Some feel that a skylight or UV filter can help, but this practice is mostly a holdover from the film days. Digital sensors are not sensitive enough to UV light for a UV filter to have much effect.

- **Symptom: low contrast from flare.** To reduce flare from bright light sources at the periphery of the picture area, or completely outside it, avoid pointing your camera directly at the sun. Because telephoto focal lengths often create images that are lower in contrast in the first place, you'll want to be especially careful, and perhaps shade the front of the lens with your hand.

- **Symptom: dark flash photos.** A long lens might make a subject that's 50 feet away look as if it's right next to you, but your camera's flash isn't fooled. You'll need extra power for distant flash shots, and probably more power than your built-in flash provides. The shoe-mount Canon 580EX II Speedlite, for example, can automatically zoom its coverage down to that of a medium telephoto lens, providing a theoretical full-power shooting aperture of about f/8 at 50 feet and ISO 400. (Try *that* with the built-in flash!) Of course, this flash is expensive and larger than your entire camera. One of the other Canon external flash units might be all you need, however. I'll explain more about flash in Chapter 8.

Image Stabilization

Image stabilization provides you with camera steadiness that's the equivalent of at least two or three shutter speed increments. This extra margin can be invaluable when you're shooting under dim lighting conditions or hand-holding with the camera set for its longest optical focal length of 140mm. Perhaps that shot of a foraging deer calls for a shutter speed of 1/250th second at f/5.6, and you fear that the image will be blurry. Relax, with image stabilization turned on, you can shoot at 1/250th second and get virtually the same results as if you had used 1/500th or even 1/100th second, as long as the deer doesn't decide to bound off.

Or, maybe you're shooting a high school play without a tripod or monopod, and you'd really, really like to use 1/15th second at f/4. Assuming the actors aren't flitting around the stage at high speed, your PowerShot and its IS feature can let you grab the shot at the wide-angle position. However, keep these facts in mind:

- **IS doesn't stop action.** Unfortunately, no image stabilization is a panacea to replace the action-stopping capabilities of a higher shutter speed. Image stabilization applies only to camera shake. You still need a fast shutter speed to freeze action. IS works great in low light, when you're using long focal lengths, and for macro photography. It's not always the best choice for action photography, unless there's enough light to allow a sufficiently high shutter speed. If so, IS can make your shot even sharper.

- **IS slows you down.** The process of adjusting the lens elements takes time, just as autofocus does, so you might find that IS adds to the lag between when you press the shutter and when the picture is actually taken. That's another reason why image stabilization might not be a good choice for sports.

- **Use when appropriate.** In some situations, IS can produce worse results if used while you're panning the camera from side to side during exposure. The camera can confuse the motion with camera shake and overcompensate. You might want to switch off IS when panning or when your camera is mounted on a tripod (or set the Image Stabilization to Panning mode on the G10/G11).

- **Do you need IS at all?** Remember that an inexpensive monopod might be able to provide the same additional steadiness as an IS lens. If you're out in the field shooting wild animals or flowers and think a tripod isn't practical, try a monopod first.

Lens Add-Ons

For those looking for a super-compact camera, one of the advantages of a camera like the G10/G11 is that it *doesn't* have interchangeable lenses. Its fixed, all-in-one zoom lens, designed to handle *most* of the shooting situations you're likely to encounter, allows for a very small, virtually pocket-sized design. Of course, the type of avid photographer that the PowerShots appeal to are the same kind who will, eventually, want to push their camera to its limits and do a few things that aren't quite possible with the G10/G11's unadorned zoom lens.

That's where lens add-ons come in. To look at the G10/G11's trim, retractable zoom lens, devoid of any sort of thread to allow attaching so much as a filter, you'd think that expansion is out of the question. Not true! The ring around the base of the lens comes off as easy as 1-2-3, revealing a bayonet mount that can be used to attach various adapters that allow using several useful accessories, including filters.

Filters and other lens attachments change the way your lens views the world. Filters are add-on disks or squares of glass, gelatin, or some other transparent/translucent material that you fasten to the front of your lens. They modify the light in some way, changing its color, reducing the amount of light that reaches the sensor (frequently both at the same time), or, in the case of *polarizing* filters, wholly or partially eliminating glare. Other kinds of lens attachments do different things in changing the characteristics of light before it passes through the lens. Some change the magnification of the lens, producing a more pronounced telephoto or wide-angle effect. Lens attachments can also allow you to focus more closely, or, distort your image in some way.

As far as the 1-2-3 goes, just look at Figure 7.5 to see how to remove this ring from the front of your camera. Press the release button (1.), rotate the ring in a counterclockwise direction, as you face the camera (2.), and slide it forward (3.). The bayonet mount will be revealed.

You can attach to this bayonet the Canon Conversion Lens Adapter LA-DC58K, a sort of tube that has threads on the front that allow attaching the Canon Tele-converter TC-DC58D. They are sold separately, which is a good thing, because that leaves you free to purchase more useful adapters from Lensmate (www.lensmateonline.com) instead. Go ahead and get the TC-DC58D tele-converter if you want to increase the telephoto range of your camera, but strongly consider the versatile Lensmate adapters if you also want to use filters and other accessories with your G10/G11. All Lensmate adapters fit both the G10 and G11.

The adapter consists of three parts, each available separately. Part A is a base ($24.95), which is always used in conjunction with Parts B or C ($22.95 each) and has a 58mm thread on its outer edge. You can use Part A alone, but only with a low profile 58mm polarizing filter like the Kenko Pro1 Digital Circular Polarizer. In that case, the zoom

Figure 7.5

Remove the ring around the lens to reveal the bayonet mount.

range of the combo is limited to 28-50mm, because at longer focal lengths, the lens will strike the filter.

Part B, when attached to the Part A base, flares outwards enough to allow using large 72mm filters with no vignetting in the corners at any focal length (although you must use one of the filters tested and recommended by Lensmate to ensure no vignetting). (See Figure 7.6.)

Part C is used instead of Part B, to allow attaching the Canon TC-DC58D tele-converter (see Figure 7.7) (or, alternately, a Raynox DCR250 macro attachment with the recommended 58-52mm step-down ring) (Figure 7.8.). Unlike the plastic LA-DC58K adapter, the Lensmate G11/G10 adapters are custom-made of machined aluminum, and fit more snugly. While Canon's adapter uses an odd-ball 57mm thread, the basic Lensmate adapter has a standard 58mm or 72mm thread to accept two of the most common filter sizes.

If you already use the Cokin P filter system with your dSLR, Lensmate offers an adapter to attach the Cokin filter holder to the 72mm Part B adapter, so you can work with 84mm-wide Cokin filters, too. The company also has an adapter for Lee 100mm wide square filters.

Figure 7.6
Lensmate's
Part B adapter
attaches to
Part A to allow
use of 72mm
filters.

Figure 7.7 The Canon Tele-converter TC-DC58D increases the maximum focal length of your lens to 192mm.

Figure 7.8 The Raynox Super Macro Conversion lens also fits on the Lensmate to allow closer focusing at any focal length setting.

Working with Filters

Filters add a lot of versatility. Just among Cokin-style filters alone, there are hundreds of different filter models offered for special effects, color correction, neutral density, diffusion, and other applications. As you investigate the Cokin system, you'll see that its flexibility accounts for much of its popularity.

There are more than 200 different Cokin filters, but other manufacturers also produce filters and holders in the standard Cokin sizes. You can place two different square filters in the pair of slots on the holder. They're held in place by friction, so you can move them up and down to partially or fully cover the lens when you want to vary your effect. A third, circular filter, can be dropped into a special slot that's closest to the camera lens. These include star filters, polarizers, and other filters, and they can be rotated within the slot to produce a particular effect (say, to vary the amount of polarization).

Polarizers

Polarizing filters are a type of filter that can provide richer and more vibrant colors while reducing some of the reflective glare that affects many photos taken in bright daylight. Polarizing filters operate in much the same way as polarized sunglasses. The polarizer itself consists of two rings; one is attached to the lens, while the outer ring rotates the polarizing glass. This lets you selectively filter out different light waves. You can rotate the ring until the effect you want is visible. The amount of glare reduction depends heavily on the angle from which you take the photograph, and the amount of scattered light in the reflections (which is determined by the composition of the subject). Polarizers work best when the sun is low in the sky and at a 90-degree angle from the camera and subject (that is, off to your left or right shoulder). Blue sky and water, which can contain high amounts of scattered light, can be made darker and more vibrant as glare is reduced. You can also reduce or eliminate reflections from windows and other nonmetallic surfaces. Figure 7.9 shows an example of how an image can be improved with a polarizing filter.

Neutral Density Filters

Although your G10/G11 has a built-in electronic ND filter, found in the FUNC. menu, sometimes you can use a little more filtration. In such cases, you'll want to use an add-on filter, attached using an adapter, like the Lensmate adapters described in the previous section. Neutral density filters are one of those high-concept tools with a function that's easy to grasp: they add nothing to the image except density (by preventing some of the light from reaching the sensor), and they are neutral (so the colors remain the same). A straight gray ND (neutral density) filter increases the amount of exposure required, so that you'll need to use a larger aperture, slower shutter speed, or higher ISO setting to achieve correct exposure with the filter in place. You can even use all three in

Figure 7.9
If the sky is too light (top), a polarizing filter can darken it and enrich the other colors in your image.

appropriate proportions, if you like. The net effect is the same as if there were less light illuminating the subject, so extra exposure is required.

The exact amount of neutral density supplied can be found in the filter's name, which usually includes either the *filter factor* or *optical density* of the particular filter. For example, you might see neutral density filters labeled ND2, ND4, and ND8 which would signify that these filters would require 1-stop (2X), 2-stops (4X), and 3-stops (8X), of additional exposure, respectively. If you think about the relationship between f/stops—a one-stop difference requires twice as much exposure, a two-stop difference calls for four times as much exposure—the nomenclature makes sense. Your camera's built-in filter is an 8X ND filter, and will reduce exposure by three stops; add-on filters offer different amounts of filtration.

Given the eternal quest for faster and more sensitive sensors, what good are neutral density filters? You'll find them useful anytime you want to use a slower shutter speed or a larger f/stop in a situation in which your camera's lowest ISO setting won't allow the use of one or the other. A slow shutter speed (for creative blurring purposes) *and* wide f/stop (also for creative selective focus applications) may be almost impossible to achieve. Proper use of ND filters can give you both options. As I mentioned, you can *split* the effects among all the exposure factors: an ND8 filter (like the one built into the G10/G11) has three stops of light-blocking power that will let you use a shutter speed that is half as fast, an f/stop that is twice as large, and an ISO setting that is twice as sensitive, all in the same photograph if that's what you want.

- **Slower shutter speeds.** Your G10/G11 has a minimum ISO setting of ISO 80. Your lens has a minimum f/stop of f/8. So, outdoors in bright daylight you may find it impossible to use a shutter speed longer than 1/50th or even 1/100th second. If your mountain stream is not in bright sunlight, it's still unlikely you'll be able to use a shutter speed any longer than about 1/30th to 1/15th second. That's a shame when you have a beautiful waterfall or crashing ocean waves in your viewfinder and want to add a little creative motion blur. An ND8 filter can give you the 1/2 second to several-second exposures you'll need for truly ethereal water effects.

- **Larger f/stops.** Frequently there is too much light to use the large f/stop you want to apply to reduce depth-of-field. The wide-open f/stop you prefer for selective focus applications might demand shutter speeds of 1/4000th second or higher. With a 2X or 4X ND filter, you can use the widest f/stop available at 1/4000th second.

- **Countering overwhelming electronic flash.** I have several older manual studio flash units that are simply too powerful for *both* my available range of f/stops and ISO settings, even when switched from full power to half power. (Newer units generally offer 1/4, 1/8, 1/16, and 1/32 power options and may be continuously variable over that or an even larger range.) An ND filter allows me to shoot flash pictures with these strobes at my camera's lowest ISO setting and apertures larger than f/8.

- **Vanishing act.** Create your own ghost town despite a fully populated image by using a longer shutter speed. With an ND8 filter and a shutter speed of 15 seconds, moving vehicular and pedestrian traffic doesn't remain in one place long enough to register in your image. With enough neutral density, you can even make people and things vanish in full daylight.

■ **Sky and foreground balance.** A special kind of neutral density, the split ND, or graduated ND filter, is a special tool for landscape photographers. In the average scene, the sky is significantly brighter than the foreground and well beyond the ability of most digital camera sensors to capture detail in both. An ND filter that is dark at the top and clear at the bottom can even out the exposure, restoring the puffy white clouds and clear blue sky to your images. There are other types of split and graduated filters available, as you'll learn from the next section.

Split density and graduated filters are available in both traditional round screw-in filter types as well as in square versions that can be slipped into a Cokin or similar filter holder. The most useful variety is the graduated neutral density filter, which is a "must have" filter that belongs in any serious photographer's kit.

A graduated ND filter (or its kin, the non-graduated split density filter) has gray coloration in its "top" half, and clear glass in its "bottom" region. In practice, though, the filter can be rotated in use so that the neutral density is placed in the bottom or left/right orientations. The filter holds back light in the neutral density region, while allowing all the light to pass through the clear portion. The most common usage is to darken the sky in landscape photos shot in horizontal format (which would otherwise be overexposed) and allow the foreground area of the scene to be exposed normally. Because the filter can be rotated, you can use it for this purpose when shooting vertical landscape photos, as well, or, simply to darken the left, right, or bottom of an image when taking pictures in any orientation.

Infrared Filters

One of the most exciting emerging applications for digital cameras is infrared photography, which provides a new and eerie perspective on many familiar subjects. The majority of cameras are fully capable of taking photographs using only infrared illumination when equipped with a *cut-off* filter that blocks visible light and allows only IR light to continue on to the sensor. An IR filter will let you produce images with dramatic dark skies, vivid puffy white clouds, and ghostly foliage on trees. IR can be used on subjects other than landscapes, too, to image humans with strange, pale complexions, and architecture quite unlike anything you may have seen before. However, because your camera itself includes a filter designed to *pass* visible light and *block* most (but not all) infrared illumination, you'll have to shoot using very slow shutter speeds, because so little light is left for the exposure once the majority of both visible and infrared light have been removed.

Even though an IR filter seems virtually black to the human eye, and will obscure your image on the LCD, the G10/G11 are perfect for infrared photography, because you can view, unhindered, through the camera's optical viewfinder.

To use an IR filter, you'll almost always want to mount the camera on a tripod. First, set your white balance manually—but point the lens at a subject that reflects a lot of

IR, such as grass or foliage. Then, set up the camera, frame your image, focus, and select exposure with the camera set on Manual (start with ISO 200 and about 1/4th second at f/8). You might want to use the self-timer to avoid residual camera shake that can result from pressing the shutter release button.

Review your image on the camera's LCD. If you've set the white balance correctly, the image will appear in a black-and-white or sandstone-and-gray color scheme. (See Figure 7.10.) Otherwise, the image may be tinted slightly red. You can remove color casts later in your image editor (see my book *David Busch's Digital Infrared Pro Secrets* for detailed instructions on post-processing IR photos). The most important thing to look for during the shooting session is proper exposure. If the image appears too dark or light, change the exposure appropriately. It might be a good idea to bracket your shots (making several exposures of more and less than your first guesstimate) in any case.

Figure 7.10
Infrared photography provides otherworldly effects.

Special Effects Filters

You can make your own special effects filters. With a little work, you can sometimes duplicate the effects of filters that would be quite costly to buy, or create brand-new filters that have never been seen before outside your imagination. It's easy to manufacture new filters out of ordinary, otherwise-useless filters like skylight or UV filters. You can use a Cokin-style filter holder and make square filters.

Here are some ideas for some do-it-yourself special effects filters:

- **Glamour filter.** Take an old UV filter (it doesn't even matter if it is scratched), and carefully smear the outer edges with petroleum jelly. Such a filter is a great tool for romantic portraits of females who want to be seen with flawless skin. The smaller the center spot, the larger the area of diffusion.

- **More glamour.** A piece of stocking material or other material with texture can be used to provide even more diffusion over the entire image—or cut a hole in the middle to allow the central portion of the image to remain sharp. Many years ago, Hollywood cinematographers photographed aging stars through a chicken feather to provide the needed softening effect. (One wag pointed out that a certain actress was so wrinkled that it would be advisable to use an entire chicken, instead.)

- **Starry night.** A piece of window screen material can produce a star-point effect. The advantage of going the do-it-yourself route is that your screen "filter" can be fitted even to lenses that don't normally accept filters. Just use a large enough piece.

- **Split filters.** Get yourself a sample book of Lee or Roscoe lighting filter swatches and use pieces to construct a split neutral density filter (use gray swatches) or split color filters. While lighting filters may not have the optical quality you need for super sharp photos, you may find them good enough for experimentation.

- **Go wild.** Anything that you can fit in front of your lens, from a kaleidoscope with the colored-speckle end removed, to diffraction gratings can be used to produce a special effects filter. You can try out various possibilities just by holding them in front of the camera lens, then convert the ones that work best into permanent makeshift filters.

8

Making Light Work for You

Successful photographers and artists have an intimate understanding of the importance of light in shaping an image. Rembrandt was a master of using light to create moods and reveal the character of his subjects. Artist Thomas Kinkade's official tagline is "Painter of Light." The late Dean Collins, co-founder of Finelight Studios, revolutionized how a whole generation of photographers learned and used lighting. It's impossible to underestimate how the use of light adds to—and how misuse can detract from—your photographs.

All forms of visual art use light to shape the finished product. Sculptors don't have control over the light used to illuminate their finished work, so they must create shapes using planes and curved surfaces so that the form envisioned by the artist comes to life from a variety of viewing and lighting angles. Painters, in contrast, have absolute control over both shape and light in their work, as well as the viewing angle, so they can use both the contours of their two-dimensional subjects and the qualities of the "light" they use to illuminate those subjects to evoke the image they want to produce.

Photography is a third form of art. The photographer may have little or no control over the subject (other than posing human subjects) but can often adjust both viewing angle *and* the nature of the light source to create a particular compelling image. The direction and intensity of the light sources create the shapes and textures that we see. The distribution and proportions determine the contrast and tonal values: whether the image is stark or high key, or muted and low in contrast. The colors of the light (because even "white" light has a color balance that the sensor can detect), and how much of those colors the subject reflects or absorbs, paint the hues visible in the image.

As a PowerShot G10/G11 photographer, you must learn to be a painter and sculptor of light if you want to move from *taking* a picture to *making* a photograph. This chapter provides an introduction to using the two main types of illumination: *continuous* lighting (such as daylight, incandescent, or fluorescent sources) and the brief, but brilliant snippets of light we call *electronic flash.*

Continuous Illumination versus Electronic Flash

Continuous lighting is exactly what you might think: uninterrupted illumination that is available all the time during a shooting session. Daylight, moonlight, and the artificial lighting encountered both indoors and outdoors count as continuous light sources (although all of them can be "interrupted" by passing clouds, solar eclipses, a blown fuse, or simply by switching a lamp off). Indoor continuous illumination includes both the lights that are there already (such as incandescent lamps or overhead fluorescent lights indoors) and fixtures you supply yourself, including photoflood lamps or reflectors used to bounce existing light onto your subject.

The surge of light we call electronic flash is produced by a burst of photons generated by an electrical charge that is accumulated in a component called a *capacitor* and then directed through a glass tube containing xenon gas, which absorbs the energy and emits the brief flash. Electronic flash is notable because it can be much more intense than continuous lighting, lasts only a brief moment, and can be much more portable than supplementary incandescent sources. It's a light source you can carry with you and use anywhere.

Indeed, your PowerShot G10/G11 has an electronic flash unit built in, as shown in Figure 8.1. But you can also use an external flash, either mounted on the camera's accessory shoe or used off-camera and linked with a cable to the accessory shoe with an adapter, or triggered by a slave light (which sets off a flash when it senses the firing of another unit). Studio flash units are electronic flash, too, and aren't limited to "professional" shooters, as there are economical "monolight" (one-piece flash/power supply) units available in the $200 price range. A serious PowerShot G10/G11 photographer (or someone who uses a G10/G11 as a backup to a digital SLR) might want to buy a couple to store in a closet and use to set up a home studio, or use as supplementary lighting when traveling away from home.

There are advantages and disadvantages to each type of illumination. Here's a quick checklist of pros and cons:

- **Lighting preview—Pro: continuous lighting.** With continuous lighting, you always know exactly what kind of lighting effect you're going to get and, if multiple lights are used, how they will interact with each other. With electronic flash, the general effect you're going to see may be a mystery until you've built some experience, and you may need to review a shot on the LCD, make some adjustments, and then reshoot to get the look you want. (In this sense, a digital camera's review capabilities replace the Polaroid test shots pro photographers relied on in decades past.)

Figure 8.1

One form of light that's always available is the built-in flash on your PowerShot G10/G11.

■ **Lighting preview—Con: electronic flash.** While some external flash units have a modeling light function (consisting of a series of low-powered bursts that flash for a period of time), your PowerShot G10/G11 lacks such a capability in its internal flash, and, in any case, this feature is no substitute for continuous illumination, or an always-on modeling lamp like that found in studio flash. As the number of flash units increases, lighting previews, especially if you want to see the proportions of illumination provided by each flash, grow more complex.

■ **Exposure calculation—Pro: continuous lighting.** Your PowerShot G10/G11 has no problem calculating exposure for continuous lighting, because the illumination remains constant and can be measured through a sensor that interprets the light reaching the viewfinder. The amount of light available just before the exposure will, in almost all cases, be the same amount of light present when the shutter is released. The PowerShot G10/G11's Spot metering mode can be used to measure and compare the proportions of light in the highlights and shadows, so you can make an adjustment (such as using more or less fill light) if necessary. You can even use a hand-held light meter to measure the light yourself and set the exposure in Manual mode.

■ **Exposure calculation—Con: electronic flash.** Electronic flash illumination doesn't exist until the flash fires, and so can't be measured by the PowerShot G10/G11's exposure sensor during the exposure. Instead, the light must be measured by interpreting the intensity of a preflash triggered an instant before the main flash, as it is reflected back to the camera and through the lens. If you have a do-it-yourself bent, there are hand-held flash meters, too, including models that measure both flash and continuous light.

- **Evenness of illumination—Pro/con: continuous lighting.** Of continuous light sources, daylight, in particular, provides illumination that tends to fill an image completely, lighting up the foreground, background, and your subject almost equally. Shadows do come into play, of course, so you might need to use reflectors or fill-in light sources to even out the illumination further, but barring objects that block large sections of your image from daylight, the light is spread fairly evenly. Indoors, however, continuous lighting is commonly less evenly distributed. The average living room, for example, has hot spots and dark corners. But on the plus side, you can *see* this uneven illumination and compensate with additional lamps.

- **Evenness of illumination—Con: electronic flash.** Electronic flash units (like continuous light sources such as lamps that don't have the advantage of being located 93 million miles from the subject) suffer from the effects of their proximity. The *inverse square law*, first applied to both gravity and light by Sir Isaac Newton, dictates that as a light source's distance increases from the subject, the amount of light reaching the subject falls off proportionately to the square of the distance. In plain English, that means that a flash or lamp that's eight feet away from a subject provides only one-quarter as much illumination as a source that's four feet away (rather than half as much). (See Figure 8.2.) This translates into relatively shallow "depth-of-light."

- **Action stopping—Con: continuous lighting.** Action stopping with continuous light sources is completely dependent on the shutter speed you've dialed in on the camera. And the speeds available are dependent on the amount of light available and your ISO sensitivity setting. Outdoors in daylight, there will probably be enough sunlight to let you shoot at 1/2,000th second and f/6.3 with a non-grainy sensitivity setting of ISO 400. That's a fairly useful combination of settings if you're not using a super-telephoto with a small maximum aperture. But inside, the reduced illumination quickly has you pushing your PowerShot G10/G11 to its limits. For example, if you're shooting indoor sports, there probably won't be enough available light to allow you to use a 1/2,000th second shutter speed (although I routinely shoot indoor basketball at ISO 1600 and 1/500th second at f/4). In many indoor sports situations, you may find yourself limited to 1/500th second or slower.

- **Action stopping—Pro: electronic flash.** When it comes to the ability to freeze moving objects in their tracks, the advantage goes to electronic flash. The brief duration of electronic flash serves as a very high "shutter speed" when the flash is the main or only source of illumination for the photo. Your PowerShot G10/G11's shutter speed may be set for 1/200th second during a flash exposure, but if the flash

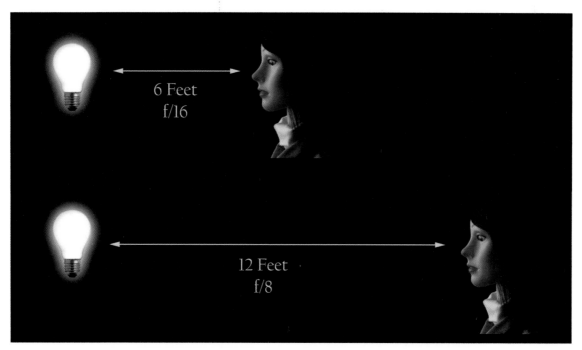

Figure 8.2 A light source that is twice as far away provides only one-quarter as much illumination.

illumination predominates, the *effective* exposure time will be the 1/1000th to 1/50000th second or less duration of the flash, because the flash unit reduces the amount of light released by cutting short the duration of the flash. Figure 8.3 shows an eye-catching "hammer breaks bulb" photo by Cleveland photographer Kris Bosworth, who reports that syncing the flash with the event was the trickiest part of the whole experiment. The only fly in the ointment is that, if the ambient light is strong enough, it may produce a secondary, "ghost" exposure, as I'll explain later in this chapter.

■ **Cost—Pro: continuous lighting.** Incandescent or fluorescent lamps are generally much less expensive than electronic flash units, which can easily cost several hundred dollars. I've used everything from desktop hi-intensity lamps to reflector floodlights for continuous illumination at very little cost. There are lamps made especially for photographic purposes, too, priced up to $50 or so. Maintenance is economical, as well; many incandescent or fluorescent lamps use bulbs that cost only a few dollars.

■ **Cost—Con: electronic flash.** Electronic flash units aren't particularly cheap. The lowest-cost dedicated flash designed specifically for the Canon digital cameras is about $110. (I'll tell you about specific flash units later in this chapter.) Such units are limited in features, however. Plan to spend some money to get the features that a sophisticated electronic flash offers.

Figure 8.3
A switch that was closed by the impact of the hammer on the bulb triggered the electronic flash that froze this action.

- **Flexibility—Con: continuous lighting.** Because incandescent and fluorescent lamps are not as bright as electronic flash, the slower shutter speeds required (see Action stopping, above) mean that you may have to use a tripod more often, especially when shooting portraits. The incandescent variety of continuous lighting gets hot, especially in the studio, and the side effects range from discomfort (for your human models) to disintegration (if you happen to be shooting perishable foods like ice cream). The heat also makes it more difficult to add filtration to incandescent sources.

- **Flexibility—Pro: electronic flash.** Electronic flash's action-freezing power allows you to work without a tripod in the studio (and elsewhere), adding flexibility and speed when choosing angles and positions. Flash units can be easily filtered, and, because the filtration is placed over the light source rather than the lens, you don't need to use high quality filter material. For example, a couple sheets of unexposed, processed Ektachrome film can make a dandy infrared-pass filter for your flash unit. Roscoe or Lee lighting gels, which may be too flimsy to use in front of the lens, can be mounted or taped in front of your flash with ease.

Continuous Lighting Basics

While continuous lighting and its effects are generally much easier to visualize and use than electronic flash, there are some factors you need to take into account, particularly the color temperature of the light. (Color temperature concerns aren't exclusive to continuous light sources, of course, but the variations tend to be more extreme and less predictable than those of electronic flash.)

Color temperature, in practical terms, is how "bluish" or how "reddish" the light appears to be to the digital camera's sensor. Indoor illumination is quite warm, comparatively, and appears reddish to the sensor. Daylight, in contrast, seems much bluer to the sensor. Our eyes (our brains, actually) are quite adaptable to these variations, so white objects don't appear to have an orange tinge when viewed indoors, nor do they seem excessively blue outdoors in full daylight. Yet, these color temperature variations are real and the sensor is not fooled. To capture the most accurate colors, we need to take the color temperature into account in setting the color balance (or *white balance*) of the PowerShot G10/G11—either automatically using the camera's smarts, or manually, using our own knowledge and experience.

Color temperature can be confusing, because of a seeming contradiction in how color temperatures are named: warmer (more reddish) color temperatures (measured in degrees Kelvin) are the *lower* numbers, while cooler (bluer) color temperatures are *higher* numbers. It might not make sense to say that 3,400K is warmer than 6,000K, but that's the way it is. If it helps, think of a glowing red ember contrasted with a white-hot welder's torch, rather than fire and ice.

The confusion comes from physics. Scientists calculate color temperature from the light emitted by a theoretical object called a black body radiator, which absorbs all the radiant energy that strikes it, and reflects none at all. Such a black body not only *absorbs* light perfectly, but it *emits* it perfectly when heated (and since nothing in the universe is perfect, that makes it theoretical).

At a particular physical temperature, this imaginary object always emits light of the same wavelength or color. That makes it possible to define color temperature in terms of actual temperature in degrees on the Kelvin scale that scientists use. Incandescent light, for example, typically has a color temperature of 3,200K to 3,400K. Daylight might range from 5,500K to 6,000K. Each type of illumination we use for photography has its own color temperature range—with some cautions. The next sections will summarize everything you need to know about the qualities of these light sources.

Daylight

Daylight is produced by the sun, and so is moonlight (which is just reflected sunlight). Daylight is present, of course, during daytime hours, even when you can't see the sun. When sunlight is direct, it can be bright and harsh. If daylight is diffused by clouds, softened by bouncing off objects such as walls or your photo reflectors, or filtered by shade, it can be much dimmer and less contrasty.

Daylight's color temperature can vary quite widely. It is highest (most blue) at noon when the sun is directly overhead because the light is traveling through a minimum amount of the filtering layer we call the atmosphere. The color temperature at high noon may be 6,000K. At other times of day, the sun is lower in the sky and the particles in the air provide a filtering effect that warms the illumination to about 5,500K for most of the day. Starting an hour before dusk and for an hour after sunrise, the warm appearance of the sunlight is even visible to our eyes when the color temperature may dip to 5,000–4,500K, as shown in Figure 8.4.

Because you'll be taking so many photos in daylight, you'll want to learn how to use or compensate for the brightness and contrast of sunlight, as well as how to deal with its color temperature. I'll provide some hints later in this chapter.

Incandescent/Tungsten Light

The term incandescent or tungsten illumination is usually applied to the direct descendants of Thomas Edison's original electric lamp. Such lights consist of a glass bulb that contains a vacuum, or is filled with a halogen gas, and contains a tungsten filament that is heated by an electrical current, producing photons and heat. Tungsten-halogen lamps are a variation on the basic light bulb, using a more rugged (and longer-lasting) filament that can be heated to a higher temperature, housed in a thicker glass or quartz envelope, and filled with iodine or bromine ("halogen") gases. The higher temperature

Figure 8.4 At dawn and dusk, the color temperature of daylight may dip as low as 4,500K.

allows tungsten-halogen (or quartz-halogen/quartz-iodine, depending on their construction) lamps to burn "hotter" and whiter. Although popular for automobile headlamps today, they've also been popular for photographic illumination.

Although incandescent illumination isn't a perfect black body radiator, it's close enough that the color temperature of such lamps can be precisely calculated and used for photography without concerns about color variation (at least, until the very end of the lamp's life).

The other qualities of this type of lighting, such as contrast, are dependent on the distance of the lamp from the subject, type of reflectors used, and other factors that I'll explain later in this chapter.

Fluorescent Light/Other Light Sources

Fluorescent light has some advantages in terms of illumination, but some disadvantages from a photographic standpoint. This type of lamp generates light through an electro-chemical reaction that emits most of its energy as visible light, rather than heat, which is why the bulbs don't get as hot. The type of light produced varies depending on the phosphor coatings and type of gas in the tube. So, the illumination fluorescent bulbs produce can vary widely in its characteristics.

That's not great news for photographers. Different types of lamps have different "color temperatures" that can't be precisely measured in degrees Kelvin, because the light isn't produced by heating. Worse, fluorescent lamps have a discontinuous spectrum of light that can have some colors missing entirely. A particular type of tube can lack certain shades of red or other colors (see Figure 8.5), which is why fluorescent lamps and other alternative technologies such as sodium-vapor illumination can produce ghastly looking human skin tones. Their spectra can lack the reddish tones we associate with healthy skin and emphasize the blues and greens popular in horror movies.

Figure 8.5
The fluorescent lighting in this gym added a distinct greenish cast to the image.

Adjusting White Balance

I showed you how to adjust white balance in Chapter 4, using the PowerShot G10/G11's built-in presets and custom white balance capabilities.

In most cases, however, the PowerShot G10/G11 will do a good job of calculating white balance for you, so Auto can be used as your choice for the white balance setting most of the time. Use the preset values or set a custom white balance that matches the current shooting conditions when you need to. The only really problematic light sources are likely to be fluorescents. Some lighting vendors, such as GE and Sylvania, may actually provide a figure known as the *color rendering index* (or CRI), which is a measure of how accurately a particular light source represents standard colors, using a scale of 0 (some sodium-vapor lamps) to 100 (daylight and most incandescent lamps). Daylight fluorescents and deluxe cool white fluorescents might have a CRI of about 79 to 95, which is perfectly acceptable for most photographic applications. Warm white fluorescents might have a CRI of 55. White deluxe mercury vapor lights are less suitable, with a CRI of 45, while low-pressure sodium lamps can vary from CRI 0-18.

Remember that if you shoot RAW, you can specify the white balance of your image when you import it into Photoshop, Photoshop Elements, or another image editor using your preferred RAW converter. While color-balancing filters that fit on the front of the lens exist, they are primarily useful for film cameras, because film's color balance can't be tweaked as extensively as that of a digital camera's sensor.

Electronic Flash Basics

Until you delve into the situation deeply enough, it might appear that serious photographers have a love/hate relationship with electronic flash. You'll often hear that flash photography is less natural looking, and that the built-in flash in most cameras should never be used as the primary source of illumination because it provides a harsh, garish look. Indeed, most "pro" cameras like the Canon EOS 1D Mark III and 1Ds Mark III don't have a built-in flash at all. Available ("continuous") lighting is praised, and built-in flash photography seems to be roundly denounced.

In truth, however, the bias is against *bad* flash photography. Indeed, flash has become the studio light source of choice for pro photographers, because it's more intense (and its intensity can be varied to order by the photographer), freezes action, frees you from using a tripod (unless you want to use one to lock down a composition), and has a snappy, consistent light quality that matches daylight. And even pros will concede that the built-in flash of the Canon PowerShot G10/G11 has some important uses as an adjunct to existing light, particularly to fill in dark shadows.

But electronic flash isn't as inherently easy to use as continuous lighting. As I noted earlier, electronic flash units are more expensive, don't show you exactly what the lighting effect will be (unless you use a second source called a *modeling light* for a preview), and the exposure of electronic flash units is more difficult to calculate accurately.

How Electronic Flash Works

The built-in flash is somewhat limited in range (Canon rates it effective out to 23 feet); you'll see why external flash units are often a good idea later in this chapter.

An electronic flash (whether built in or connected to the PowerShot G10/G11 through its hot shoe) is triggered at the instant of exposure, during a period when the sensor is fully exposed by the shutter. The PowerShot G10/G11 has a combination mechanical and electronic shutter. The shutter completely opens, at which point the flash can be triggered. This is called *1st-curtain sync*, although in the case of the G10/G11 there is no "curtain" (the term refers to the pair of curtains that travel across the sensor frame with so-called *focal plane* shutters. The flash fires, then, after a delay that can vary from 15 seconds to 1/2,000th second with the PowerShot G11 or 1/500th second with the G10, the shutter closes. If the flash is triggered just before the shutter starts to close, then *2nd-curtain sync* is used. In both cases, though, a shutter speed of 1/2,000th second (G11) or 1/500th (for the G10) is the maximum that can be used to take a photo. If you try to set the PowerShot G10/G11's shutter to a faster speed in Tv or M mode while using flash, the camera will automatically adjust the shutter speed down to that model's maximum shutter speed when using flash.

Ghost Images

The difference between triggering the flash when the shutter just opens, or just when it begins to close might not seem like much. But whether you use 1st-curtain sync (the default setting) or 2nd-curtain sync (an optional setting) can make a significant difference to your photograph *if the ambient light in your scene also contributes to the image.*

At faster shutter speeds, particularly 1/500th second or faster, there isn't much time for the ambient light to register, unless it is very bright. It's likely that the electronic flash will provide almost all the illumination, so the choice of 1st-curtain sync or 2nd-curtain sync isn't very important. However, at slower shutter speeds, or with very bright ambient light levels, there is a significant difference, particularly if your subject is moving, or the camera isn't steady.

In any of those situations, the ambient light will register as a second image accompanying the flash exposure, and if there is movement (of camera or subject), that additional image will not be in the same place as the flash exposure. It will show as a ghost image and, if the movement is significant enough, as a blurred ghost image trailing in front of or behind your subject in the direction of the movement.

As I noted, when you're using 1st-curtain sync, the flash's main burst goes off the instant the shutter opens fully (a preflash that is used to measure exposure in auto flash modes fires *before* the shutter opens). This burst produces an image of the subject on the sensor. Then, the shutter remains open for an additional period (in the range of 15 seconds to 1/2,000th second, as I said). If your subject is moving, say, towards the right side of the frame, the ghost image produced by the ambient light will produce a blur on the right side of the original subject image, making it look as if your sharp (flash-produced) image is chasing the ghost. For those of us who grew up with lightning-fast superheroes who always left a ghost trail *behind them*, that looks unnatural (see Figure 8.6).

Figure 8.6 1st-curtain sync produces an image that trails in front of the flash exposure (top), while 2nd-curtain sync creates a more "natural looking" trail behind the flash image.

So, Canon uses 2nd-curtain sync to remedy the situation. In that mode, the shutter opens, as before. The shutter remains open for its designated duration, and the ghost image forms. If your subject moves from the left side of the frame to the right side, the ghost will move from left to right, too. *Then*, about 1.5 milliseconds before the second shutter curtain closes, the flash is triggered, producing a nice, sharp flash image *ahead* of the ghost image. Voilà! We have monsieur *Speed Racer* outdriving his own trailing image.

Avoiding Sync Speed Problems

In the past, before cameras and flash units became as sophisticated as they are today, photographers sometimes ran into problems when the camera's shutter speed was too fast to synchronize properly with the flash. Nowadays, I generally end up with sync speed problems only when shooting using third-party flash units, rather than my PowerShot G10/G11's built-in flash or a Canon dedicated Speedlite. That's because if you're using either type of "smart" flash, the camera knows that a strobe is attached, and remedies any unintentional goof in shutter speed settings. That luxury is not available when using non-dedicated, "dumb" flash units.

In addition, the PowerShot G10/G11 can sync with the flash at any speed up to 1/500th second, and the G11, in some circumstances, can sync at speeds up to 1/2,000th second. If you happen to set the PowerShot G10/G11's shutter to a faster speed in Tv or M mode, the camera will automatically adjust the shutter speed down to 1/500th second on the G10 and 1/2,000th on the G11. In Av, P, or any of the more automatic shooting modes, where the PowerShot G10/G11 selects the shutter speed, it will never choose a shutter speed higher than 1/500th second for the G10 and 1/2,000th for the G11 when using flash.

Determining Exposure

Calculating the proper exposure for an electronic flash photograph is a bit more complicated than determining the settings by continuous light. The right exposure isn't simply a function of how far away your subject is (which the PowerShot G10/G11 can figure out based on the autofocus distance that's locked in just prior to taking the picture). Various objects reflect more or less light at the same distance so, obviously, the camera needs to measure the amount of light reflected back and through the lens. Yet, as the flash itself isn't available for measuring until it's triggered, the PowerShot G10/G11 has nothing to measure.

The solution is to fire the flash twice. The initial shot is a preflash that can be analyzed, then followed by a main flash that's given exactly the calculated intensity needed to provide a correct exposure. As a result, the primary flash may be longer for distant objects and shorter for closer subjects, depending on the required intensity for exposure. This through-the-lens evaluative flash exposure system operates whenever the built-in internal flash is used, or if you have attached a Canon dedicated flash unit to the PowerShot G10/G11.

Guide Numbers

Guide numbers, usually abbreviated GN, are a way of specifying the power of an electronic flash in a way that can be used to determine the right f/stop to use at a particular shooting distance and ISO setting. In fact, before automatic flash units became prevalent, the GN was actually used to do just that. Today, guide numbers are most useful for comparing the power of various flash units, and Canon doesn't even provide GN figures for the G10/G11's built-in flash. They are available for external flash units, described later in this chapter, and you can use the guide numbers to directly compare how powerful these add-on flashes are.

Using the Built-In Flash

The Canon PowerShot G10/G11's built-in flash is a handy accessory because it is available as required, without the need to carry an external flash around with you constantly. This section explains how to use the built-in flash in the various shooting modes. This explanation is not as quick and easy as you might expect, because this camera, as you've already seen, is quite sophisticated in its general shooting capabilities, and it's also no slouch in the area of flash control options. There are numerous features and functions that I need to describe before I get into the nitty-gritty of which settings to use when. I also need to make a few general points about the nature of your camera's built-in flash.

The Always-Ready Flash

Although this is an obvious point, it's worth emphasizing. The built-in flash of the PowerShot G10/G11 is always available for use without any physical movement of the flash mechanism. In other words, unlike the built-in units on some other Canon cameras, including both dSLRs and compacts, you don't have to pop up the flash unit with a switch or other mechanism. This fact has a couple of important implications.

First, you need to be sure you have the flash set the way you want it, especially if you're in a location where flash should not be used, such as certain museums, theaters, or other locations or gatherings. With some other cameras, you can close the built-in flash unit physically and be certain it cannot fire. With the PowerShot G10/G11, there's no way to be certain from looking at the camera that the flash will not fire; you need to check the settings to make sure there's no chance it will go off just when its brilliant discharge is least welcome. One bit of good news in this area: as I'll discuss a bit later in this section, with the PowerShot G10/G11, unlike some other cameras in this class, you can *always* force the flash to its Off setting, even when shooting in the Auto mode.

Another point about the PowerShot G10/G11's always-ready flash is that you never have to worry about fumbling for a switch or button to get the flash into position to fire; it's constantly ready to do its job, if you have the camera's settings arranged so it will fire. So, in that sense, the always-deployed flash can provide a considerable boost to the speed of your shooting in situations where flash suddenly becomes necessary. If you need to use it to fill in dark shadows as fill flash when shooting in sunlight, set the flash to on, and it's ready to go. (See Figure 8.7.)

Range and Angle of View

The PowerShot G10/G11's built-in flash unit has several virtues, but extensive range is not one of them. As I mentioned above, the G11 flash's effective range is no more than about 23 feet, which is less powerful than the larger external flash units available for the PowerShot. Therefore, you need to be mindful of the fact that the built-in flash can be

Figure 8.7
The G10/ G11's built-in flash is instantly ready for fill-flash duties to brighten shadows in daylight shots.

a useful tool for filling in shadows and grabbing snapshots indoors, but it's not a substitute for a stronger, dedicated unit such as those used by photojournalists and wedding photographers.

When you're deciding whether the built-in flash is likely to be of use in a particular situation, here are a couple of important factors to keep in mind: distance and ISO setting. The farther away your subject is from the camera, the greater the light fall-off, thanks to the inverse square law discussed earlier. Keep in mind that a subject that's twice as far away receives only one-quarter as much light, which is two f/stops' worth. Also, the higher the ISO sensitivity, the more photons captured by the sensor. So, doubling the sensitivity from ISO 100 to 200 produces the same effect as, say, opening up your lens from f/8 to f/5.6.

There's one other factor that often affects the performance of built-in flash units, but that is not as big an issue with the PowerShot G10/G11 as with many other cameras: the focal length or angle of view of the lens for any given shot. With many other compact cameras (and even some dSLRs), the built-in flash unit does not have a variable angle of view. In other words, every time the flash fires, it sends out the same size or width beam of light; it does not vary the shape of the beam to match the zoom factor of your shot. So, if you are taking a wide-angle shot, the flash may not fully cover the area in the scene, or, if you have zoomed your lens in for a telephoto shot, a good portion of the flash's coverage may be "wasted" by falling outside of the field of view of the lens. The PowerShot G10/G11, though, has what Canon calls the Light Guide Zoom Flash, whose angle of view changes as the lens zooms in and out. So, with this flash unit, there is a relatively close match between the coverage by the lens and the coverage by the flash, resulting in a more efficient use of this resource than with some other cameras.

Available Settings for the Built-In Flash

Now it's just about time to get into the details of how to work with the settings for the PowerShot G10/G11's built-in flash. As I've indicated, though, the flash system with this camera is remarkably sophisticated for a compact camera, and I need to go over a few general points about how the flash settings are structured before I discuss the details of the various settings.

The main point to bear in mind when working with the built-in flash is that your choices of flash settings will change, depending on other choices you have made in setting up the camera for your shot. There are three levels of decisions you can make when you're deciding how the built-in flash should operate, and all three decisions, one after the other, have an impact on how the flash will operate when you press the shutter button to take the picture.

First, you choose a shooting mode; second, you can press the Flash button to choose a general status for the flash; and third, if you're using flash, you can use the Flash Control submenu to make further choices about how the flash will operate when and if it fires. Of course, you don't have to consciously make all three of those choices; if you don't think about them yourself, the camera will use its default settings and make the choices for you. But I'm assuming you are the sort of photographer who wants to take control over such decisions. So let's look at those three choices in more detail now.

Mode Dial: Shooting Mode

The shooting mode you select with the mode dial can have considerable influence over the behavior of the flash. In some modes (for example, the Fireworks and Sports versions of SCN mode), the flash is forced off and there's nothing you can do to turn it on—except switch out of Fireworks or Sports mode. In many of the SCN modes and Auto mode, the camera will initially set the flash to Auto, but will let you override that choice. However, in those more automatic shooting modes, although you can choose whether the flash is on or off, your other choices of flash behavior, such as controlling flash output and shutter sync, are limited. In the most advanced shooting modes, M, Av, Tv, and P, most of the decisions about the use of flash are completely within your control. With the G11, and P mode, you can select Auto, On, Slow Synchro, and Off; with Tv you can choose On or Off; with Av, the selections are On, Slow Synchro, and Off. In Manual mode, you can choose Off or On.

Flash Button: On, Off, or Auto (and Sometimes Slow Synchro)

After selecting the shooting mode, the next stage of control you have over the flash is exercised with the Flash button, which also acts as the right cross key. In rare cases (Fireworks and Sports types of SCN mode on both the G10 and G11, as discussed previously, and also the ISO 3200 type of SCN mode on the G10), the Flash button is disabled. You can press it until you have a lightning bolt imprinted on your thumb, and nothing will happen (except to your thumb). (Also, it should go without saying, the Flash button has no effect when the camera is set to Movie mode.)

But, in every other shooting mode, the camera lets you make choices with the Flash button. These choices vary with your shooting mode and they vary somewhat between the G10 and G11. For example, on the G11, for the few shooting modes for which Slow Synchro flash is a possible choice, you select Slow Synchro with the Flash button (see Figure 8.8). (On the G10, Slow Synchro is activated from the Flash Control submenu of the Shooting menu and not from the Flash button.) In most cases on both models, the only choices available through the Flash button are setting the flash to On, Auto, or Off (see Figure 8.9). In some cases, only two of those three choices are available.

Figure 8.8
On the PowerShot G11, pressing the Flash button can give you access to as many as four choices for setting the built-in flash: Auto, On, Slow Synchro, and Off.

Figure 8.9
On the PowerShot G10, the Flash button can give you access to three choices for setting the built-in flash: Auto, On, and Off.

Now, what do those three settings mean? If the built-in flash is set to On, you will see a downward lightning bolt on the LCD screen, with nothing added to it (see Figure 8.10). That means that the flash will fire, no matter what. It is "forced on." It's up to you to control the camera's other settings to produce the effect you want in the final image, but you can be guaranteed that, unless there's a system failure, the PowerShot's internal flash will fire.

Conversely, if the built-in flash is set to Off, the flash will not fire, even if a solar eclipse takes place while you're shooting. The screen will show the lightning bolt inside the universal negative symbol—a circle with a line through the center. If you make that setting, of course, no other flash settings come into play. This is the setting you use in that museum with a $500 fine for using flash.

Finally, if you use the Flash button to set the flash to Auto, putting the lightning bolt with the letter "A" beside it on the LCD screen, then the camera will use its autoexposure circuitry to determine whether the flash needs to fire in order to expose the scene properly. In that case, you're telling the camera, in effect, "I'm not sure if we're going to need flash—you decide."

Figure 8.10
The lightning bolt on the LCD display means that the built-in flash unit is forced to its "On" setting and will definitely fire when the shutter button is pressed.

Flash Control Menu: Other Settings

Okay, let's assume you have chosen your shooting mode and you have used the Flash button to set the flash to Auto or On, so there's a good chance it will fire. Now, you have a third set of choices to make. You can call up the Flash Control submenu (see Figure 8.11) and pick from an array of further options for how the flash will operate if it does fire. This array of options will vary according to the other choices you have made. Right now, I'm going to discuss all of the possible choices that can be made from this submenu, even though you're never going to see all of the choices at any one time.

Figure 8.11
The Flash Control submenu can be accessed from the Shooting menu, by pressing and holding the Flash button, or by pressing the Flash button and then pressing the Menu button.

As a reminder, there are three ways to get to the Flash Control submenu: select Flash Control from the Shooting menu; press the Flash button once lightly, then the Menu button; or hold down the Flash button until the Flash Control submenu appears. If you just need the Flash Output/Flash Exposure Compensation setting, you can select that item by pressing the FUNC./SET key and selecting the fourth item down on the FUNC. menu.

Here are all the choices that may be available on the Flash Control submenu, depending on the context:

- **Flash Mode.** This option can be set to either Manual or Auto (see Figure 8.12). Now, here's a slightly tricky point to be aware of: This is one of two uses of the term "Auto" in connection with the operation of the flash, with two different meanings. Here is what "Auto" means in this case: Unlike the setting of Auto as opposed to On or Off, which controls *whether* the flash will fire, this setting of Auto controls *how* the flash will be fired—that is, through automatic exposure control, or manual setting of the flash output (which we'll discuss next). In many cases, such as with the Auto shooting mode and almost all of the SCN modes, this option is not available on the Flash Control submenu, because the camera sets Flash Mode to Auto without asking you. Also, when the shooting mode is set to Manual, the camera sets Flash Mode to Manual, again without consulting you. The only times this setting is available for you to set are when the Shooting mode is set to Av or Tv.

- **Flash Exposure Compensation.** This setting is available only when Flash Mode (see above) is set to Auto, meaning the camera will use its metering to determine the intensity of the flash exposure. The Flash Exposure Compensation setting is analogous to the standard exposure compensation setting. Although the camera will

Figure 8.12
The Flash mode setting on the Flash Control submenu can be set to either Auto or Manual, which determines whether or not the camera uses metering to determine the flash output.

initially determine the correct flash exposure, you have the option of dialing in positive or negative amounts of flash output, relative to that automatic setting. The adjustment is displayed numerically in 1/3 EV steps, up to 2 full steps positive or negative. When the Flash Mode is set to Manual, this option stays available, except that its name changes to Flash Output, discussed next.

■ **Flash Output.** As noted above, this setting is the counterpart to Flash Exposure Compensation, when Flash Mode is set to Manual (see Figure 8.13). In that case, you can dial in the amount of flash intensity, except that, because the flash exposure will be manual, you are actually determining the *absolute* amount of flash to be emitted, rather than the relative amount, as with Flash Exposure Compensation. When using the built-in flash, your choices for Flash Output are Minimum, Medium, or Maximum. If you use that setting, you are responsible for setting the camera so that the image is properly exposed; the camera will not be using any automatic exposure settings to determine the proper flash output.

■ **Shutter Sync.** You can choose 1st-curtain sync, which fires the flash as soon as the shutter is completely open (this is the default mode). Alternatively, you can select 2nd-curtain sync, which fires a preflash used to measure exposure as soon as the shutter release is pressed down all the way, but before the shutter opens, and then

Figure 8.13
When Flash Mode is set to Manual, the Flash Output setting is available for you to set at Minimum, Medium, or Maximum.

triggers a second flash at the end of the exposure, just before the shutter starts to close. This action allows photographing a blurred trail of light of moving objects with sharp flash exposures at the beginning and the end of the exposure, as I described earlier in this chapter. This setting is available in the M, Av, Tv, and P shooting modes, as well as in the Quick Shot shooting mode on the PowerShot G11.

- **Red-Eye Correction.** This setting is available in almost every shooting mode. With this option, the camera attempts to apply digital corrective measures to remove red areas near the eyes. You should note that, although all images you take will be processed somewhat by the camera for sharpness, noise, contrast, and the like, this option applies a form of processing that goes beyond those normal adjustments in that it can actually alter the content of the image, so you should be sure you want to take that risk before activating it. Remember that this option also can be applied to images after the fact, through the Playback menu.

- **Red-Eye Lamp.** This option, also, is available in the great majority of shooting modes. This feature is distinct from Red-Eye Correction; this one causes the camera to shine its bright lamp into the subject's eyes for an instant before the flash in an effort to cause his or her pupils to contract (assuming the subject is looking at the camera), thereby reducing the red-eye effect, as I explained in Chapter 4.

- **Safety FE.** This setting is available in the Av, Tv, and P shooting modes on the PowerShot G10, as well as the Quick Shot shooting mode on the G11. It is available only when Flash Mode is set to Auto, meaning the flash intensity is determined through the camera's auto-exposure system. This setting, which can be set either On or Off, acts as a safety net. If the camera senses that the image will be overexposed, if this option is activated, the camera adjusts the aperture or shutter speed to reduce the exposure so as to avoid blowing out the highlights. There is one other aspect of this setting that you should bear in mind. On the G11, it is possible to set the shutter speed as high as 1/2,000th second, even when using flash. However, if Safety FE is set to Off, then the highest shutter speed that can be used with flash is 1/500th second, the same maximum speed as on the G10.

- **Slow Synchro.** This setting is available for you to set in a few shooting modes, including Av and P. In several other modes, it is set to On and cannot be changed. When this option is turned on, the camera will set the shutter speed slower than it otherwise would, in order to allow time for the ambient light to expose the background, so the final image is not overwhelmed by the portion that is illuminated by the flash. This option is found on the Flash Control submenu on the PowerShot G10, but it is accessed through the Flash button on the G11. When Slow Synchro is available on the G11, it appears as one more option along with Auto, On, and Off on the Flash button's menu of options.

Using Built-In Flash with the Various Shooting Modes

We have now explored all of the options that are available for using the PowerShot G10/G11's built-in flash. As we have seen, although the little unit is not very powerful in terms of its flash intensity, it comes armed with an impressive set of control options that make it a very versatile and useful tool. Now, to make it clearer how these settings work in practice, I'm going to go through the various shooting modes briefly to point out just how the built-in flash acts in those modes, and what flash settings are available in each of them.

Auto Mode

When the PowerShot G10/G11 is set to the Auto shooting mode, the built-in flash will initially be set to Auto, and it will fire when needed to provide extra illumination in low-light situations, or when your subject matter is backlit and could benefit from some fill flash—with a few exceptions. You have the option of turning the flash off, which is good if you're in a location with a "no-flash zone." However, you cannot force the flash to be on; if you want flash, you have to rely on the camera's native intelligence to figure out if the flash will actually be fired. You can activate Red-Eye Correction and the Red-Eye Lamp. Other settings, such as Flash Exposure Compensation, are not available.

Program Mode

In P mode, just about all of the flash control options are available for you to set. However, you cannot set Flash Mode to Manual, and, therefore, you cannot control the absolute amount of flash (Flash Output). You can, however, adjust the relative amount of flash (Flash Exposure Compensation) and you can control the flash's other settings.

Manual, Aperture Priority, and Shutter Priority Modes

In M, Av, and Tv modes, virtually all of the flash control settings are available, except that you can't set the flash to Auto (the "Auto" meaning that the camera decides whether to fire the flash); if you want the flash to fire in either of these shooting modes, the flash has to be set to On. The other flash control settings are almost all available, although, on the G11, Slow Synchro is not available in M or Tv mode, and on the G10, Slow Synchro is always set to On in M and Tv modes. Flash Mode cannot be set to Auto (the "Auto" meaning the camera determines the amount of flash) in M mode.

SCN Modes and Special G11 Modes (Low Light and Quick Shot)

In the various SCN modes there are various flash control options, depending on the nature of the shooting scenario. As noted earlier, on the PowerShot G10, the flash is always turned off in Sports, Fireworks, and ISO 3200 modes, and cannot be turned on. In Aquarium mode, the flash can be turned on or off, but cannot be set to Auto. On the G11, in Sports and Fireworks modes the flash is always turned off. In Low Light mode on the G11, the flash can be set to either Auto or Off, but it cannot be set to On. In most of the SCN modes on both models, the flash is set to Auto, and the only flash control options available are Red-Eye Correction and Red-Eye Lamp. In Quick Shot mode on the G11, all flash control options are available except Flash Mode and Flash Output; the Flash Mode is set to Auto, so Flash Exposure Compensation is available rather than Flash Output.

If you happen to be shooting a sports or fireworks photo and do want to use flash for some reason, you will have to switch to another shooting mode. However, if you're using any one of the automatic modes (including Auto) and decide that you definitely *don't* want the flash to fire—in a museum with a "no flash" rule for example—you're in luck. With the PowerShot G10/G11 Canon has expressed its confidence in the ability of its users to make their own decisions about turning off the flash. So, unlike the situation with some other compact cameras, with the PowerShot G10/G11, you always have the option of turning the flash to its "Off" setting, ensuring that it will not fire, even if you enter the museum's simulation of the inside of King Tut's tomb and the door clanks shut behind you.

Using FE Lock

If you want to lock flash exposure for a subject that is not centered in the frame, you can use the FE Lock button (*) to lock in a specific flash exposure. First, you have to make sure the flash is set to On, not Auto. Then, depress and hold the shutter button halfway to lock in focus, center the viewfinder on the subject you want to correctly expose, and press the * button. The preflash fires and calculates exposure, displaying the * on the LCD screen to show that the exposure is locked. Then, recompose your photo and press the shutter down the rest of the way to take the photo. Of course, this procedure works only when the camera is using its automatic metering to determine the flash exposure. It will work at all times in P mode; when you're using Tv or Av mode, you need to make sure that Flash Mode is set to Auto. (It won't work in M mode, because the Flash Mode is always set to Manual in that shooting mode.)

Using External Electronic Flash

Canon offers a broad range of accessory electronic flash units that will work with the PowerShot G10/G11. They can be mounted to the flash accessory shoe, or used off-camera with a dedicated cord that plugs into the flash shoe to maintain full communications with the camera for all special features. They range from the Speedlite 580EX II, which can correctly expose subjects up to 24 feet away at f/11 and ISO 200, to the 270EX, which is good out to 9 feet at f/11 and ISO 200. (You'll get greater ranges at even higher ISO settings, of course.)

When you attach one of the compatible Canon Speedlites, you will notice some changes in the displays on the LCD screen and menus of the PowerShot G10/G11. First, once the external flash is attached, the built-in flash is disabled and cannot fire or be controlled, even if the external flash is turned off. (The exception is the Canon HF-DC1 High Power Flash, which is actually a *slave* unit triggered by other flashes, and needs no connection to the camera.) Second, once the non-slave external unit is attached and turned on, you will see an orange-red lightning bolt on the right side of the screen, indicating that an external flash is attached. You will never see any other flash icon, such as the icon for Auto or Off, because those settings would have no meaning once you have decided to use an external flash. Also, the Flash Control submenu will have different settings, depending on what flash unit you have attached. For example, you likely will have a greater range of Flash Exposure Compensation and Flash Output settings available than with the built-in flash, and there may be a setting for Hi-speed sync, along with 1st-curtain and 2nd-curtain sync.

Here are some details about the various external flash units that are compatible with the PowerShot G10/G11.

Canon HF-DC1 High-Power Flash

This is a tiny, pocket-sized portable slave flash that requires no connection to the G10/G11. It's triggered by the main flash's illumination (whether that main flash is the built-in flash or an external flash you've connected to the camera). The HF-DC1 mounts on a small, fold-down bracket that positions the flash at the side of the camera body by attaching to the camera's tripod socket. When the slave's sensor "sees" the camera's flash fire, it will also fire, in perfect synchronization with the main flash to increase the usable flash range (of the built-in flash) or to provide a kicker or fill light when used with another external flash.

The unit has two simple sliding controls on the back. One switch selects Auto or Manual operation, while the other switch adjusts the output level to any of three levels. In Auto there is a built-in delay, which keeps the slave flash from being triggered by the G10/G11's preflash. Instead, the slave waits and synchronizes with the main picture-taking flash.

Speedlite 220EX

This most basic Canon Speedlight offers automatic operation only, and none of the fancy features of its more expensive siblings. It is a lot beefier than the PowerShot G10/G11's built-in flash, making it a good choice as an auxiliary flash unit. It lacks a zoomable flash head to adjust coverage for different focal lengths, and offers fixed coverage equivalent to the field of view of a 28mm full-frame lens. Expect 250 to 1,700 flashes from a set of four AA batteries and recycle times of 0.1 to 4.5 seconds.

Speedlite 270EX

This newest Canon Speedlite (shown in Figure 8.14) is small enough at five ounces to fit in a pocket, and, instead of zooming, uses two fixed coverage levels for 28mm and 50mm focal lengths. It offers bounce-lighting capabilities, and uses two AA batteries, which provide enough power to recycle the unit in four seconds between flashes. Like its "big brothers," the 270X includes a built-in AF assist beam.

Figure 8.14
The Canon 270EX is small and makes a good add-on flash for the PowerShot G10/G11.

Speedlite 430EX II

This affordable electronic flash is nearly four times as powerful as the 270EX, and has zoom coverage from 24mm to 105mm. If you want to use this with your dSLR, too, it has a wide-angle pullout panel that covers the area of a 14mm lens on a full frame camera, and automatic conversion to the cropped frame area of some Canon digital cameras. The 430EX also communicates white balance information with your dSLR camera, and has its own AF assist beam. It, too, uses AA batteries, and offers recycle times of 0.1 to 3.7 seconds for 200 to 1,400 flashes, depending on subject distance.

Speedlite 580EX II

This flagship of the Canon accessory flash line is the most powerful unit the company offers, and probably is a bit of overkill for the PowerShot G10 or G11. It's slightly more than twice as powerful as the 430 EX II, and has a zoom flash head that covers the full frame of lenses from 24mm wide angle to 105mm telephoto. (There's a flip-down wide-angle diffuser that spreads the flash to cover a 14mm lens's field of view, too.) The unit offers full-swivel, 180 degrees in either direction, and has its own built-in AF assist beam. Powered by economical AA-size batteries, the unit recycles in 0.1 to 6 seconds, and can squeeze 100 to 700 flashes from a set of alkaline batteries. (See Figure 8.15.)

Figure 8.15
The Canon
Speedlite
580EX II is the
most powerful
shoe-mount
flash Canon
offers.

More Advanced Lighting Techniques

As you advance in your Canon PowerShot G10/G11 photography, you'll want to learn more sophisticated lighting techniques, using more than just straight-on flash, or using just a single flash unit. Entire books have been written on lighting techniques. I'm going to provide a quick introduction to some of the techniques you should be considering.

Diffusing and Softening the Light

Direct light can be harsh and glaring, especially if you're using the flash built into your camera, or an auxiliary flash mounted in the hot shoe and pointed directly at your subject. The first thing you should do is stop using direct light (unless you're looking for a stark, contrasty appearance as a creative effect). There are a number of simple things you can do with both continuous and flash illumination.

■ **Use window light.** Light coming in a window can be soft and flattering, and a good choice for human subjects. Move your subject close enough to the window that its light provides the primary source of illumination. You might want to turn off other lights in the room, particularly to avoid mixing daylight and incandescent light. (See Figure 8.16.)

Figure 8.16
Window light makes the perfect diffuse illumination for informal soft-focus portraits like this one.

■ **Use fill light.** Your PowerShot G10/G11's built-in flash makes a perfect fill-in light for the shadows, brightening inky depths with a kicker of illumination when it's switched on.

■ **Bounce the light.** As I noted, some external electronic flash units mounted on the PowerShot G10/G11 usually have a swivel that allows them to be pointed up at a ceiling for a bounce light effect. You can also bounce the light off a wall. You'll want the ceiling or wall to be white or have a neutral gray color to avoid a color cast.

■ **Use reflectors.** Another way to bounce the light is to use reflectors or umbrellas that you can position yourself to provide a greater degree of control over the quantity and direction of the bounced light. Good reflectors can be pieces of foamboard, Mylar, or a reflective disk held in place by a clamp and stand. Although some expensive umbrellas and reflectors are available, spending a lot isn't necessary. A simple piece of white foamboard does the job beautifully. Umbrellas have the advantage of being compact and foldable, while providing a soft, even kind of light. They're relatively cheap, too, with a good 40-inch umbrella available for as little as $20.

■ **Use diffusers.** Some other vendors offer clip-on diffusers like the one shown in Figure 8.17, that fit over your electronic flash head and provide a soft, flattering light. These add-ons are more portable than umbrellas and other reflectors, yet provide a nice diffuse lighting effect.

Figure 8.17
Some softboxes use Velcro strips to attach to third-party flash units (like the one shown) or any Canon medium-sized or larger external flash.

9

Downloading and Editing Your Images

Taking the picture is only half the work, and, in some cases, only half the fun. After you've captured some great images and have them safely stored on your Canon PowerShot G10/G11's memory card, you'll need to transfer them from your camera and memory card to your computer, where they can be organized, fine tuned in an image editor, and prepared for web display, printing, or some other final destination.

Fortunately, there are lots of software utilities and applications to help you do all these things. This chapter will introduce you to a few of them.

What's in the Box?

Your Canon PowerShot G10/G11 came with software programs on CD for both Windows PCs and Macs. Pop the CD into your computer and it will self-install a selection of these useful applications and utilities. Manuals for the key programs are included on CD, too, but here's a summary of what you get on the Canon Digital Solutions disk:

ZoomBrowser EX/ImageBrowser

ZoomBrowser EX is an image viewing and editing application for Windows PCs (the equivalent program for Macs is called ImageBrowser and performs the same functions). You can organize, sort, classify, and rename files, and convert JPEG files in batches. This utility is especially useful for printing index sheets of groups of images. It can also prepare images for e-mailing. It works with RAW Image Task for converting CR2 files to some other format, and it can be used to select images for merging using PhotoStitch.

When you connect your G10/G11 to your computer using a USB cable, ZoomBrowser first loads the CameraWindow DC utility, shown in Figure 9.1. There are three functions with this window. You can import images from the camera, choosing to preview the images to be transferred by date shot (as in Figure 9.2), by folder on the memory card, only the images that have not yet been transferred, or all the images on the memory card. Click on the images you'd like to transfer, then click the Import button in the lower-left corner of the window. The CameraWindow utility can also be used to make certain limited camera settings from your computer. You can select a start-up image, choose sounds, or select a theme, as shown in Figure 9.3.

Once you've transferred photos, you can do simple editing using the ZoomBrowser window that appears when you close CameraWindow. (See Figure 9.4.) The simple image-editing facilities of ZoomBrowser allow red-eye correction, brightness/contrast and color correction, manipulating sharpness, trimming photos, and a few other functions. For more complex editing, you can transfer images directly from this application to Digital Photo Professional, Photoshop, or another image editor.

Figure 9.1
ZoomBrowser EX's Camera-Window DC utility pops up when you connect the camera to your computer with a USB cable.

Figure 9.2
Select which files on the memory card to download from the camera to the computer.

Figure 9.3
You can change camera settings from your computer.

Figure 9.4 ZoomBrowser allows organizing your images and performing simple fixes.

PhotoStitch

This Windows/Mac utility allows you to take several JPEG images and combine them to create a panorama in a single new file. You can choose the images to be merged in ZoomBrowser and then transfer them to PhotoStitch, or operate the utility as a stand-alone module and select the images using the standard File > Open commands (see Figure 9.5).

Digital Photo Professional

While far from a Photoshop replacement, Digital Photo Professional is a useful image-editing program that helps you organize, trim, correct, and print images. You can make RAW adjustments, correct tonal curves, color tone, color saturation, sharpness, as well as brightness and contrast. Especially handy are the "recipes" that can be developed and saved so that a given set of corrections can be kept separate from the file itself, and, if desired, applied to other images (see Figure 9.6).

Figure 9.5
Panoramas are
easy to create
with
PhotoStitch.

Figure 9.6 Digital Photo Professional will never replace Photoshop, but it has some basic image-editing features.

Transferring Your Photos

While it's rewarding to capture some great images and have them ensconced in your camera, eventually you'll be transferring them to your laptop or PC, whether you're using a Windows or Macintosh machine. You have three options for image transfer: direct transfer over a USB cable, automated transfer using a card reader and transfer software such as ZoomBrowser EX/ImageBrowser or Adobe Photoshop Elements Photo Downloader, or manual transfer using drag and drop from a memory card inserted in a card reader.

Direct Transfer

There are some advantages to transferring photos directly from your G10/G11 to a computer. The destination computer doesn't need to have a card reader; all it requires is a USB port. So, if you have the USB cable that came with your camera, you can transfer photos to any computer that has the Canon utility software installed. However, direct transfer uses your G10/G11's internal battery power, while removing the card and transferring the photos with a card reader installed on the destination computer does not.

You can select which images are transferred to the computer, or transfer all the images, both RAW and JPEG, that are on the memory card. Just connect your camera to the computer using a USB cable, and either the Canon software will pop up or another file transfer program you may have installed, such as the Photoshop Elements Photo Downloader Utility will appear. Or, the file transfer program built into your computer's operating system may offer to do the job.

Elements' downloader includes a simple dialog box, like the one shown in Figure 9.7, and a more advanced set of choices. In the simple dialog box, you can choose the destination folder, whether to rename files (and a filename template if you do decide to

Figure 9.7

You can rename images as they are downloaded using Photoshop Elements' downloader.

rename them), and the choice of deleting the original photos from your memory card after they've been transferred, or leaving them on the card. I prefer the latter; it's best not to erase images until you're *positive* they've been transferred correctly and, in any case, reformatting the memory card rather than just deleting its old files is a better choice for starting over with a "clean" card.

The advanced dialog box lets you choose individual files to download, selecting from a thumbnail preview of the image on your camera. You can apply advanced options, such as automatic red-eye repair, or import the images into a suggested Elements "photo stack" (a group of like images organized for easier browsing). You can even add a copyright notice to the data embedded within your images.

Using a Card Reader and Software

You can also use a memory card reader and software to transfer photos and automate the process using the Canon utility, Photoshop Elements' Photo Downloader, or the downloading program supplied with some other third-party applications. This method is more frugal in its use of your G10/G11's battery and can be faster if you have a speedy USB 2.0 or FireWire card reader attached to an appropriate port.

The installed software automatically remains in memory as you work, and it recognizes when a memory card is inserted in your card reader; you don't have to launch it yourself. With Photoshop Elements Photo Downloader, you can click Get Photos to begin the transfer of all images immediately or choose Advanced Dialog to produce a dialog box like the one shown in Figure 9.8, and then select which images to download from

Figure 9.8

With Advanced view activated, Photoshop Elements' Photo Downloader allows you to select the photos you want to copy to your computer and apply some options such as new filenames or red-eye fixes automatically.

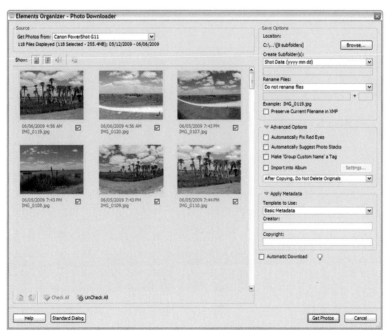

the memory card by marking them with a check. You can select the photos you want to transfer, plus options such as Automatically Fix Red Eyes. Start the download, and a confirmation dialog box like the one in Figure 9.9 shows the progress.

Figure 9.8
The Photo Downloader's confirmation dialog box shows the progress as images are transferred.

Dragging and Dropping

The final way to move photos from your memory card to your computer is the old-fashioned way: manually dragging and dropping the files from one window on your computer to another. The procedure works pretty much the same whether you're using a Mac or a PC.

1. Remove the memory card from the PowerShot G10/G11 and insert it in your memory card reader.

2. Using Windows Explorer, My Computer, or your Mac desktop, open the icon representing the memory card, which appears on your desktop as just another disk drive.

3. Open a second window representing the folder on your computer that you want to use as the destination for the files you are copying or moving.

4. Drag and drop the files from the memory card window to the folder on your computer. You can select individual files, press Ctrl/Command+A to select all the files, or Ctrl/Command+click to select multiple files.

Editing Your Photos

Image manipulation tasks fall into several categories. You might want to fine tune your images, retouch them, change color balance, composite several images together, and perform other tasks we know as image editing, with a program like Adobe Photoshop, Photoshop Elements, or Corel Photo Paint.

You might want to play with the settings in RAW files, too, as you import them from their CR2 state into an image editor. There are specialized tools expressly for tweaking RAW files, ranging from Canon's own Digital Photo Professional to Adobe Camera Raw, and PhaseOne's Capture One Pro (C1 Pro). A third type of manipulation is the specialized task of noise reduction, which can be performed within Photoshop, Adobe Camera Raw, or tools like Bibble Professional. There are also specialized tools just for noise reduction, such as Noise Ninja (also included with Bibble) and Neat Image.

Each of these utilities and applications deserves a chapter of its own, so I'm simply going to enumerate some of the most popular image-editing and RAW conversion programs here and tell you a little about what they do.

Image Editors

Image editors are general-purpose photo-editing applications that can do color correction, tonal modifications, retouching, combining of several images into one, and usually include tools for working with RAW files and reducing noise. So, you'll find programs like those listed here good for all-around image manipulation. The leading programs are as follows:

Adobe Photoshop/Photoshop Elements. Photoshop is the serious photographer's number one choice for image editing, and Elements is an excellent option for those who need most of Photoshop's power, but not all of its professional-level features. Both editors use the latest version of Adobe's Camera Raw plug-in, which makes it easy to adjust things like color space profiles, color depth (either 8 bits or 16 bits per color channel), image resolution, white balance, exposure, shadows, brightness, sharpness, luminance, and noise reduction. One plus with the Adobe products is that they are available in identical versions for both Windows and Macs.

Corel Photo Paint. This is the image-editing program that is included in the popular CorelDRAW Graphics suite. Although a Mac version was available in the past, this is primarily a Windows application today. It's a full-featured photo retouching and image-editing program with selection, retouching, and painting tools for manual image manipulations, and it also includes convenient automated commands for a few common tasks, such as red-eye removal. Photo Paint accepts Photoshop plug-ins to expand its assortment of filters and special effects.

Corel Paint Shop Pro. This is a general purpose Windows-only image editor that has gained a reputation as the "poor person's Photoshop" for providing a substantial portion of Photoshop's capabilities at a fraction of the cost. It includes a nifty set of wizard-like commands that automate common tasks, such as removing red eye and scratches, as well as filters and effects, which can be expanded with other Photoshop plug-ins.

Corel Painter. Here's another image-editing program from Corel for both Mac and Windows. This one's strength is in mimicking natural media, such as charcoal, pastels, and various kinds of paint. Painter includes a basic assortment of tools that you can use to edit existing images, but the program is really designed for artists to use in creating original illustrations. As a photographer, you might prefer another image editor, but if you like to paint on top of your photographic images, nothing else really does the job of Painter.

Corel PhotoImpact. Corel finally brought one of the last remaining non-Adobe image editors into its fold when it acquired PhotoImpact. This is a general purpose photo-editing program for Windows with a huge assortment of brushes for painting, retouching, and cloning, in addition to the usual selection, cropping, and fill tools. If you frequently find yourself performing the same image manipulations on a number of files, you'll appreciate PhotoImpact's batch operations. Using this feature, you can select multiple image files and then apply any one of a long list of filters, enhancements, or auto-process commands to all the selected files.

RAW Utilities

Your software choices for manipulating RAW files are broader than you might think. Camera vendors always supply a utility to read their cameras' own RAW files, but sometimes, particularly with those point-and-shoot cameras that can produce RAW files, the options are fairly limited.

The third-party solutions are usually available as standalone applications (often for both Windows and Macintosh platforms), as Photoshop-compatible plug-ins, or both. Because the RAW plug-ins displace Photoshop's own RAW converter, I tend to prefer to use most RAW utilities in standalone mode. That way, if I choose to open a file directly in Photoshop, it automatically opens using Photoshop's fast and easy-to-use Adobe Camera Raw (ACR) plug-in. If I have more time or need the capabilities of another converter, I can load that, open the file, and make my corrections there. Most are able to transfer the processed file directly to Photoshop even if you aren't using plug-in mode.

This section provides a quick overview of the range of RAW file handlers, so you can get a better idea of the kinds of information available with particular applications. I'm going to include both high-end and low-end RAW browsers so you can see just what is available.

Digital Photo Professional

Digital Photo Professional, introduced earlier in this chapter, is preferred by many for Canon digital cameras like the PowerShot G10/G11.

DPP offers much higher-speed processing of RAW images, rivaling third-party stand-alone and plug-in RAW converters in speed and features. It supports both Canon's original CRW format and the newer CR2 RAW format used by the G10/G11, along with JPEG and other file formats.

You can save settings that include multiple adjustments and apply them to other images, and use the clever comparison mode to compare your original and edited versions of an image either side by side or within a single split image. The utility allows easy adjustment of color channels, tone curves, exposure compensation, white balance, dynamic range, brightness, contrast, color saturation, ICC Profile embedding, and assignment of monitor profiles. A new feature is the ability to continue editing images while batches of previously adjusted RAW files are rendered and saved in the background.

IrfanView

At the low (free) end of the price scale is IrfanView, a Windows-only freeware program you can download at www.irfanview.com. It can read many common RAW photo formats. It's a quick way to view RAW files (just drag and drop to the IrfanView window) and make fast changes to the unprocessed file. You can crop, rotate, or correct your image, and do some cool things like swap the colors around (red for blue, blue for green, and so forth) to create false color pictures.

Phase One Capture One Pro (C1 Pro)

If there is a Cadillac of RAW converters for Nikon and Canon digital camera cameras, C1 Pro has to be it. This premium-priced program does everything, does it well, and does it quickly. If you can't justify the price tag of this professional-level software, there are "lite" versions for serious amateurs and cash-challenged professionals called Capture One digital camera and Capture One digital camera SE.

Aimed at photographers with high-volume needs (that would include school and portrait photographers, as well as busy commercial photographers), C1 Pro is available for both Windows and Mac OS X, and supports a broad range of Canon digital cameras. Phase One is a leading supplier of megabucks digital camera backs for medium and larger format cameras, so they really understand the needs of photographers.

The latest features include individual noise reduction controls for each image, automatic levels adjustment, a "quick develop" option that allows speedy conversion from RAW to TIFF or JPEG formats, dual-image side-by-side views for comparison purposes, and helpful grids and guides that can be superimposed over an image. Photographers concerned about copyright protection will appreciate the ability to add watermarks to the output images. See www.phaseone.com.

Bibble Pro

One of my personal favorites among third-party RAW converters is Bibble Pro, which just came out with a new version as I was writing this book. It supports one of the broadest ranges of RAW file formats available (which can be handy if you find yourself with the need to convert a file from a friend or colleague's non-Canon camera), including

NEF files from Nikon D1, D1x/h, D2H, D100; CRW files from the Canon C30/D60/ 10D/300D; CR2 files from the Canon PowerShot G10/G11 and other newer models; ORF files from the Olympus E10/E20/E1/C5050/C5060; DCR files from the Kodak 720x/760/14n; RAF files from the Fuji S2Pro; PEF files from Pentax ISTD; MRW files from the Minolta Maxxum; and TIF from Canon 1D/1DS.

The utility supports lots of different platforms, too. It's available for Windows, Mac OS X, and, believe it or not, Linux. Bibble works fast because it offers instantaneous previews and real-time feedback as changes are made. That's important when you have to convert many images in a short time. Bibble's batch-processing capabilities also let you convert large numbers of files using settings you specify without further intervention.

Its customizable interface lets you organize and edit images quickly and then output them in a variety of formats, including 16-bit TIFF and PNG. You can even create a web gallery from within Bibble. I often find myself disliking the generic filenames applied to digital images by cameras, so I really like Bibble's ability to rename batches of files using new names that you specify.

Bibble is fully color managed, which means it can support all the popular color spaces (Adobe sRGB and so forth) and use custom profiles generated by third-party color management software. There are two editions of Bibble, a Pro version and a Lite version. Because the Pro version is reasonably priced at $129, I don't really see the need to save $60 with the Lite edition, which lacks the top-line's options for tethered shooting, embedding IPTC-compatible captions in images, and can also be used as a Photoshop plug-in (if you prefer not to work with the application in its standalone mode). Bibble Pro now incorporates Noise Ninja technology, so you can get double-duty from this valuable application. See www.bibblelabs.com.

BreezeBrowser

BreezeBrowser was long the RAW converter of choice for Canon digital camera owners who run Windows and who were dissatisfied with Canon's lame antique File Viewer Utility (which has been gone from the scene for many years now). It works quickly and has lots of options for converting CRW and CR2 files to other formats. You can choose to show highlights that will be blown out in your finished photo as flashing areas (so they can be more easily identified and corrected), use histograms to correct tones, add color profiles, auto rotate images, and adjust all those raw image parameters, such as white balance, color space, saturation, contrast, sharpening, color tone, EV compensation, and other settings.

You can also control noise reduction (choosing from low, normal, or high reduction), evaluate your changes in the live preview, and then save the file as a compressed JPEG or as either an 8-bit or 16-bit TIFF file. BreezeBrowser can also create HTML web galleries directly from your selection of images. See www.breezesys.com.

Adobe Photoshop

The latest version of Photoshop includes a built-in RAW plug-in that is compatible with the proprietary formats of a growing number of digital cameras, both new and old. This plug-in also works with Photoshop Elements.

To open a RAW image in Photoshop, just follow these steps (Elements users can use much the same workflow, although fewer settings are available):

1. Transfer the RAW images from your camera to your computer's hard drive.

2. In Photoshop, choose Open from the File menu, or use Bridge.

3. Select a RAW image file. The Adobe Camera Raw plug-in will pop up, showing a preview of the image, like the one shown in Figure 9.10.

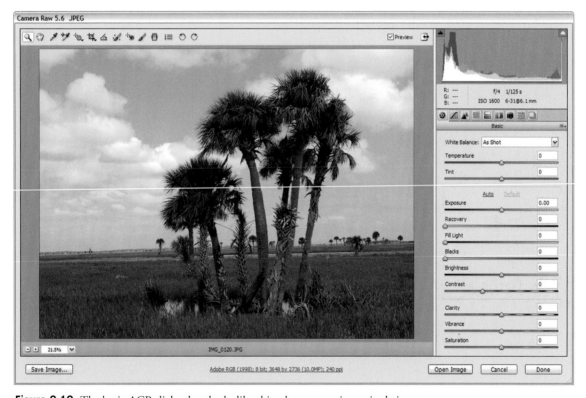

Figure 9.10 The basic ACR dialog box looks like this when processing a single image.

4. If you like, use one of the tools found in the toolbar at the top left of the dialog box. From left to right, they are:

- **Zoom.** Operates just like the Zoom tool in Photoshop.

- **Hand.** Use like the Hand tool in Photoshop.

- **White Balance.** Click an area in the image that should be neutral gray or white to set the white balance quickly.

- **Color Sampler.** Use to determine the RGB values of areas you click with this eyedropper.

- **Crop.** Pre-crops the image so that only the portion you specify is imported into Photoshop. This option saves time when you want to work on a section of a large image, and you don't need the entire file.

- **Straighten.** Drag in the preview image to define what should be a horizontal or vertical line, and ACR will realign the image to straighten it.

- **Retouch.** Used to heal or clone areas you define.

- **Red-Eye Removal.** Quickly zap red pupils in your human subjects.

- **ACR Preferences.** Produces a dialog box of Adobe Camera Raw preferences.

- **Rotate Counterclockwise.** Rotates counterclockwise in 90-degree increments with a click.

- **Rotate Clockwise.** Rotates clockwise in 90-degree increments with a click.

5. Using the Basic tab, you can have ACR show you red and blue highlights in the preview that indicate shadow areas that are clipped (too dark to show detail) and light areas that are blown out (too bright). Click the triangles in the upper-left corner of the histogram display (shadow clipping) and upper-right corner (highlight clipping) to toggle these indicators on or off.

6. Also in the Basic tab you can choose white balance, either from the drop-down list or by setting a color temperature and green/magenta color bias (tint) using the sliders.

7. Other sliders are available to control exposure, recovery, fill light, blacks, brightness, contrast, vibrance, and saturation. A check box can be marked to convert the image to grayscale.

8. Make other adjustments (described in more detail below).

9. ACR makes automatic adjustments for you. You can click Default and make the changes for yourself, or click the Auto link (located just above the Exposure slider) to reapply the automatic adjustments after you've made your own modifications.

10. If you've marked more than one image to be opened, the additional images appear in a "filmstrip" at the left side of the screen. You can click on each thumbnail in the filmstrip in turn and apply different settings to each.

11. Click Open Image/Open Image(s) into Photoshop using the settings you've made, or click Save Image at the bottom left to save the settings you've made without opening the file.

The Basic tab is displayed by default when the ACR dialog box opens, and it includes most of the sliders and controls you'll need to fine tune your image as you import it into Photoshop. These include:

- **White Balance.** Leave it As Shot or change to a value such as Daylight, Cloudy, Shade, Tungsten, Fluorescent, or Flash. If you like, you can set a custom white balance using the Temperature and Tint sliders.

- **Exposure.** This slider adjusts the overall brightness and darkness of the image.

- **Recovery.** Restores detail in the red, green, and blue color channels.

- **Fill Light.** Reconstructs detail in shadows.

- **Blacks.** Increases the number of tones represented as black in the final image, emphasizing tones in the shadow areas of the image.

- **Brightness.** This slider adjusts the brightness and darkness of an image.

- **Contrast.** Manipulates the contrast of the midtones of your image.

- **Convert to Grayscale.** Mark this box to convert the image to black-and-white.

- **Vibrance.** Prevents over-saturation when enriching the colors of an image.

- **Saturation.** Manipulates the richness of all colors equally, from zero saturation (gray/black, no color) at the −100 setting to double the usual saturation at the +100 setting.

Additional controls are available on the Tone Curve, Detail, HSL/Grayscale, Split Toning, Lens Corrections, Camera Calibration, and Presets tabs, shown in Figure 9.11. The Tone Curve tab can change the tonal values of your image. The Detail tab lets you adjust sharpness, luminance smoothing, and apply color noise reduction. The HSL/Grayscale tab offers controls for adjusting hue, saturation, and lightness and converting an image to black-and-white. Split Toning helps you colorize an image with sepia or cyanotype (blue) shades. The Lens Corrections tab has sliders to adjust for chromatic aberrations and vignetting. The Camera Calibration tab provides a way for calibrating the color corrections made in the Camera Raw plug-in. The Presets tab (not shown) is used to load settings you've stored for reuse.

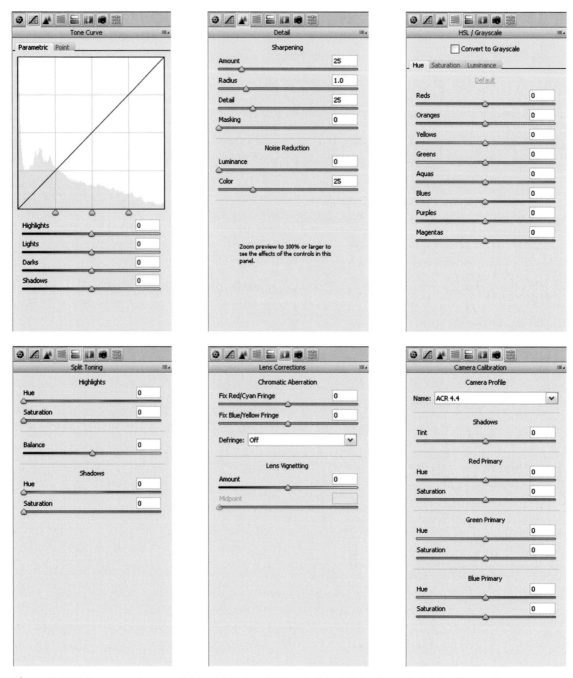

Figure 9.11 More controls are available within the additional tabbed dialog boxes in Adobe Camera Raw.

Glossary

Here are some terms you might encounter while reading this book or working with your Canon PowerShot G10 or G11.

additive primary colors The red, green, and blue hues that are used alone or in combinations to create all other colors that you capture with a digital camera, view on a computer monitor, or work with in an image-editing program, such as Photoshop.

ambient lighting Diffuse, non-directional lighting that doesn't appear to come from a specific source but, rather, bounces off walls, ceilings, and other objects in the scene when a picture is taken.

analog/digital converter The Canon DIGIC 4 electronics built into the G10/G11 that convert the analog information captured by the camera's sensor into digital bits that can be stored as an image bitmap.

angle of view The area of a scene that a lens can capture, determined by the focal length of the lens. Lenses with a shorter focal length have a wider angle of view than lenses with a longer focal length.

anti-alias A process that smoothes the look of rough edges in images (called *jaggies* or *staircasing*) by adding partially transparent pixels along the boundaries of diagonal lines that are merged into a smoother line by our eyes. *See also* jaggies.

Aperture Priority A camera setting, called Av (for Aperture Value), that allows you to specify the lens opening or f/stop that you want to use, with the camera selecting the required shutter speed automatically based on its light-meter reading. This setting is represented by the abbreviation Av on the G10/G11's mode dial. *See also* Shutter Priority.

artifact A type of noise in an image, or an unintentional image component produced in error by a digital camera during processing, usually caused by the JPEG compression process in digital cameras.

aspect ratio The proportions of an image as printed, displayed on a monitor, or captured by a digital camera.

autofocus   A camera setting that allows the Canon PowerShot G10/G11 to choose the correct focus distance for you, based on the contrast of an image (the image will be at maximum contrast when in sharp focus).

automatic exposure bracketing   Automatic exposure bracketing takes a series of pictures at different exposure increments to improve the chances of producing one picture that is perfectly exposed.

backlighting   A lighting effect produced when the main light source is located behind the subject. Backlighting can be used to create a silhouette effect, or to illuminate translucent objects. *See also* front lighting and sidelighting.

barrel distortion   A lens defect that causes straight lines at the top or side edges of an image to bow outward into a barrel shape. *See also* pincushion distortion.

blooming   An image distortion caused when a photosite in an image sensor has absorbed all the photons it can handle so that additional photons reaching that pixel overflow to affect surrounding pixels, producing unwanted brightness and overexposure around the edges of objects.

blur   To soften an image or part of an image by throwing it out of focus, or by allowing it to become soft due to subject or camera motion. Blur can also be applied in an image-editing program.

bokeh   A term derived from the Japanese word for blur, which describes the aesthetic qualities of the out-of-focus parts of an image. Some lenses produce "good" bokeh and others offer "bad" bokeh. Some lenses produce uniformly illuminated out-of-focus discs. Others produce a disc that has a bright edge and a dark center, producing a "doughnut" effect, which is the worst from a bokeh standpoint. Lenses that generate a bright center that fades to a darker edge are favored, because their bokeh allows the circle of confusion to blend more smoothly with the surroundings. The bokeh characteristics of a lens are most important when you're using selective focus (say, when shooting a portrait) to deemphasize the background, or when shallow depth-of-field is a given because you're working with a macro lens, a long telephoto, or a wide-open aperture. *See also* circle of confusion.

bounce lighting   Light bounced off a reflector, including ceiling and walls, to provide a soft, natural-looking light.

bracketing   Taking a series of photographs of the same subject at different settings, including exposure and white balance, to help ensure that one setting will be the correct one.

buffer   The digital camera's internal memory where an image is stored immediately after it is taken until it can be written to the camera's non-volatile (semi-permanent) memory or a memory card.

burst mode Known as continuous shooting modes in the PowerShot, burst shooting is the digital camera's equivalent of the film camera's motor drive, used to take multiple shots within a short period of time, with each shot stored in a memory buffer temporarily before writing it to the media.

calibration A process used to correct for the differences in the output of a printer or monitor when compared to the original image. Once you've calibrated your scanner, monitor, and/or your image editor, the images you see on the screen more closely represent what you'll get from your printer, even though calibration is never perfect.

Camera Raw A plug-in included with Photoshop and Photoshop Elements that can manipulate the unprocessed images captured by digital cameras, such as the Canon PowerShot G10/G11's .CR2 files. The latest versions of this module can also work with JPEG and TIFF images.

camera shake Movement of the camera, aggravated by slower shutter speeds, which produces a blurred image. You can minimize camera shake by using the PowerShot's image-stabilization feature.

center weighted meter A light-measuring device that emphasizes the area in the middle of the frame when calculating the correct exposure for an image. *See also* spot meter.

chromatic aberration An image defect, often seen as green or purple fringing around the edges of an object, caused by a lens failing to focus all colors of a light source at the same point. *See also* fringing.

circle of confusion A term applied to the fuzzy discs produced when a point of light is out of focus. The circle of confusion is not a fixed size. The viewing distance and amount of enlargement of the image determine whether we see a particular spot on the image as a point or as a disc. *See also* bokeh.

close-up lens A lens add-on accessory that allows you to take pictures at a distance that is less than the closest-focusing distance of the lens alone.

color correction Changing the relative amounts of color in an image to produce a desired effect, typically a more accurate representation of those colors. Color correction can fix faulty color balance in the original image, or compensate for the deficiencies of the inks used to reproduce the image.

compression Reducing the size of a file by encoding using fewer bits of information to represent the original. Some compression schemes, such as JPEG, operate by discarding some image information, while others, such as RAW, preserve all the detail in the original, discarding only redundant data.

contrast The range between the lightest and darkest tones in an image. A high-contrast image is one in which the shades fall at the extremes of the range between white and black. In a low-contrast image, the tones are closer together.

Creative Zone modes The PowerShot G10/G11's semi-automated and manual shooting modes, including, Program, Aperture Priority, Shutter Priority, and Manual, that allow you to select shutter speed and/or aperture yourself, with the camera calculating the proper exposure based on those parameters.

dedicated flash An electronic flash unit, such as the Canon 220EX Speedlight, designed to work with the automatic exposure features of a specific camera.

depth-of-field A distance range in a photograph in which all included portions of an image are at least acceptably sharp. With the Canon PowerShot G10/G11, you can see the available depth-of-field at the taking aperture by pressing the Depth-of-Field Preview button, or estimate the range by viewing the depth-of-field scale found on many lenses.

diaphragm An adjustable component, similar to the iris in the human eye, that can open and close to provide specific-sized lens openings, or f/stops, and thus control the amount of light reaching the sensor or film.

diffuse lighting Soft, low-contrast lighting.

digital processing chip A solid-state device found in digital cameras, such as the DIGIC 4 chip in the PowerShot G10/G11, that's in charge of applying the image algorithms to the raw picture data prior to storage on the memory card.

diopter A value used to represent the magnification power of a lens, calculated as the reciprocal of a lens's focal length (in meters). Diopters are most often used to represent the optical correction used in a viewfinder to adjust for limitations of the photographer's eyesight, and to describe the magnification of a close-up lens attachment.

Evaluative metering One system of exposure calculation used by the PowerShot G10/G11 that looks at many different segments of an image to determine the brightest and darkest portions.

exchangeable image file format (Exif) Developed to standardize the exchange of image data between hardware devices and software. A variation on JPEG, Exif is used by most digital cameras, and includes information such as the date and time a photo was taken, the camera settings, resolution, amount of compression, and other data.

Exif *See* exchangeable image file format (Exif).

exposure The amount of light allowed to reach the film or sensor, determined by the intensity of the light, the amount admitted by the iris of the lens, the length of time determined by the shutter speed, and the ISO sensitivity setting for the sensor.

exposure values (EV) EV settings are a way of adding or decreasing exposure without the need to reference f/stops or shutter speeds. For example, if you tell your camera to add +1EV, it will provide twice as much exposure by using a larger f/stop, slower shutter speed, or both.

fill lighting In photography, lighting is used to illuminate shadows. Reflectors or additional incandescent lighting or electronic flash can be used to brighten shadows. One common technique for outdoors is to use the camera's flash as a fill.

filter In photography, a device that fits over the lens, changing the light in some way. In image editing, a feature that changes the pixels in an image to produce blurring, sharpening, and other special effects. Photoshop includes several interesting filter effects, including Lens Blur and Photo Filters.

focal length The distance between the film and the optical center of the lens when the lens is focused on infinity, usually measured in millimeters.

format To erase a memory card and prepare it to accept files.

fringing A chromatic aberration that produces fringes of color around the edges of subjects, caused by a lens's inability to focus the various wavelengths of light onto the same spot. Purple fringing is especially troublesome with backlit images.

front lighting Illumination that comes from the direction of the camera. *See also* backlighting and sidelighting.

f/stop The relative size of the lens aperture, which helps determine both exposure and depth-of-field. The larger the f/stop number, the smaller the f/stop itself.

graduated filter A lens attachment with variable density or color from one edge to another. A graduated neutral density filter, for example, can be oriented so the neutral density portion is concentrated at the top of the lens's view with the less dense or clear portion at the bottom, thus reducing the amount of light from a very bright sky while not interfering with the exposure of the landscape in the foreground. Graduated filters can also be split into several color sections to provide a color gradient between portions of the image.

gray card A piece of cardboard or other material with a standardized 18-percent reflectance. Gray cards can be used as a reference for determining correct exposure or for setting white balance.

HDMI (High Definition Multimedia Interface) An interface for transmitting audio and video information between a source, such as a digital camera or television tuner, to an output device, such as a high definition television (HDTV) monitor.

high contrast A wide range of density in a print, negative, or other image.

highlights The brightest parts of an image containing detail.

histogram A kind of chart showing the relationship of tones in an image using a series of 256 vertical bars, one for each brightness level. A histogram chart, such as the one the Canon PowerShot G10/G11 can display, typically looks like a curve with one or more slopes and peaks, depending on how many highlight, midtone, and shadow tones are present in the image.

hot shoe A mount on top of a camera used to hold an electronic flash, while providing an electrical connection between the flash and the camera.

hyperfocal distance A point of focus where everything from half that distance to infinity appears to be acceptably sharp. For example, if your lens has a hyperfocal distance of four feet, everything from two feet to infinity would be sharp. The hyperfocal distance varies by the lens and the aperture in use. If you know you'll be making a grab shot without warning, sometimes it is useful to turn off your camera's automatic focus, and set the lens to infinity, or, better yet, the hyperfocal distance. Then, you can snap off a quick picture without having to wait for the lag that occurs with most digital cameras as their autofocus locks in.

image rotation A feature that senses whether a picture was taken in horizontal or vertical orientation. That information is embedded in the picture file so that the camera and compatible software applications can automatically display the image in the correct orientation.

image stabilization A technology that compensates for camera shake, usually by adjusting the position of the camera sensor (with some vendors) or, in the case of Canon's PowerShot G10/G11 cameras, with lens elements that shift in response to movements of the camera.

incident light Light measured as it falls on a surface, as opposed to light reflected from that surface.

International Organization for Standardization (ISO) A governing body that provides standards used to represent film speed, or the equivalent sensitivity of a digital camera's sensor. Digital camera sensitivity is expressed in ISO settings.

interpolation A technique digital cameras, scanners, and image editors use to create new pixels required whenever you resize or change the resolution of an image based on the values of surrounding pixels. Devices such as scanners and digital cameras can use interpolation to create pixels in addition to those actually captured, thereby increasing the apparent resolution or color information in an image.

ISO *See* International Organization for Standardization (ISO).

jaggies Staircasing effect of lines, most easily seen at large magnifications, that are not perfectly horizontal or vertical, caused by pixels that are too large to represent the line accurately. *See also* anti-alias.

JPEG Short for Joint Photographic Experts Group. A file "lossy" format that supports 24-bit color and reduces file sizes by selectively discarding image data. Digital cameras generally use JPEG compression to pack more images onto memory cards. You can select how much compression is used (and, therefore, how much information is thrown away) by selecting from among the Standard, Fine, Super Fine, or other quality settings offered by your camera. *See also* RAW.

Kelvin (K) A unit of measure based on the absolute temperature scale in which absolute zero is zero; it's used to describe the color of continuous-spectrum light sources and applied when setting white balance. For example, daylight has a color temperature of about 5,500K, and a tungsten lamp has a temperature of about 3,400K.

lag time The interval between when the shutter is pressed and when the picture is actually taken. During that span, the camera may be automatically focusing and calculating exposure. With digital cameras like the Canon PowerShot G10/G11, lag time is generally very short.

latitude The range of camera exposure that produces acceptable images with a particular digital sensor or film.

lens flare A feature of conventional photography that is both a bane and a creative outlet. It is an effect produced by the reflection of light internally among elements of an optical lens. Bright light sources within or just outside the field of view cause lens flare. Flare can be reduced by the use of coatings on the lens elements or with the use of lens hoods. Photographers sometimes use the effect as a creative technique, and Photoshop includes a filter that lets you add lens flare at your whim.

lighting ratio The proportional relationship between the amount of light falling on the subject from the main light and other lights, expressed in a ratio, such as 3:1.

lossy compression An image-compression scheme, such as JPEG, that creates smaller files by discarding image information, which can affect image quality.

maximum burst The number of frames that can be exposed at the current settings until the buffer fills.

midtones Parts of an image with tones of an intermediate value, usually in the 25 to 75 percent brightness range. Many image-editing features allow you to manipulate midtones independently from the highlights and shadows.

neutral color A color in which red, green, and blue are present in equal amounts, producing a gray.

neutral density filter A gray camera filter that reduces the amount of light entering the camera without affecting the colors. The PowerShot G10/G11 has a feature that acts as a neutral density filter built into the camera.

noise In an image, pixels with randomly distributed color values. Noise in digital photographs tends to be the product of low-light conditions and long exposures, particularly when you've set your camera to an ISO rating higher than about ISO 800.

noise reduction A technology used to cut down on the amount of random information in a digital picture, usually caused by long exposures at increased sensitivity ratings. In the Canon PowerShot G10/G11, noise reduction is automatically applied for long exposures. Noise reduction can be switched off if you'd rather not use it.

overexposure   A condition in which too much light reaches the film or sensor, producing a dense negative or a very bright/light print, slide, or digital image.

pincushion distortion   A type of lens distortion in which lines at the top and side edges of an image are bent inward, producing an effect that looks like a pincushion. *See also* barrel distortion.

polarizing filter   A filter that forces light, which normally vibrates in all directions, to vibrate only in a single plane, reducing or removing the specular reflections from the surface of objects. Such filters tend to increase the contrast between colors and make blue skies more dramatic, most strongly when the sun is located at a 90-degree angle from the direction the camera is pointed.

RAW   An image file format, such as the CR2 format in the Canon PowerShot G11, which includes all the unprocessed information captured by the camera after conversion to digital form. RAW files are very large compared to JPEG files and must be processed by a special program such as Canon Digital Photo Pro or Adobe's Camera Raw filter after being downloaded from the camera.

saturation   The purity of color; the amount by which a pure color is diluted with white or gray.

selective focus   Choosing a lens opening that produces a shallow depth-of-field. Usually this is used to isolate a subject in portraits, close-ups, and other types of images, by causing most other elements in the scene to be blurred.

self-timer   A mechanism that delays the opening of the shutter for some seconds after the release has been operated.

sensitivity   A measure of the degree of response of a film or sensor to light, measured using the ISO setting.

shadow   The darkest part of an image, represented on a digital image by pixels with low numeric values.

sharpening   Increasing the apparent sharpness of an image by boosting the contrast between adjacent pixels that form an edge, whether done in the camera or in image-editing software.

shutter   In a conventional film camera, the shutter is a mechanism consisting of blades, a curtain, a plate, or some other movable cover that controls the time during which light reaches the film. Digital cameras may use actual mechanical shutters for the slower shutter speeds (less than 1/200th second) and an electronic shutter for higher speeds.

Shutter Priority   An exposure mode, represented by the letters Tv (Time Value) on the G10/G11's mode dial, in which you set the shutter speed and the camera determines the appropriate f/stop. *See also* Aperture Priority.

sidelighting Applying illumination from the left or right sides of the camera. *See also* backlighting and front lighting.

slave unit An accessory flash unit that supplements the main flash, usually triggered electronically when the slave senses the light output by the main unit, through radio waves, or through a pre-burst emitted by the camera's main flash unit.

slow syncro An electronic flash synchronizing method that uses a slow shutter speed so that ambient light is recorded by the camera in addition to the electronic flash illumination. This allows the background to receive more exposure for a more realistic effect.

specular highlight Bright spots in an image caused by reflection of light sources, often from shiny surfaces.

spot meter An exposure system that concentrates on a small area in the image. *See also* center weighted meter.

time exposure A picture taken by leaving the shutter open for a long period, usually more than one second. The camera is generally locked down with a tripod to prevent blur during the long exposure.

tungsten light Light from ordinary room lamps and ceiling fixtures, as opposed to fluorescent illumination.

underexposure A condition in which too little light reaches the film or sensor, producing a thin negative, a dark slide, a muddy looking print, or a dark digital image.

vignetting Dark corners of an image, often produced by using a lens hood that is too small for the field of view, a lens that does not completely fill the image frame, or generated artificially using image-editing techniques.

white balance The adjustment of a digital camera to the color temperature of the light source. Interior illumination is relatively red; outdoor light is relatively blue. Digital cameras like the PowerShot G10/G11 set correct white balance automatically or let you do it through menus. Image editors can often do some color correction of images that were exposed using the wrong white balance setting, especially when working with RAW files that contain the information originally captured by the camera before white balance was applied.

Index